WEST WINDS

WEST WINDS

Recipes, history and tales from Jamaica

Dedicated to Sandi Phillips

Riaz Phillips

er Sim Presents **THE PREMIER**

Of

s **LUNCH TIME**

Friday, MARCH 23, 2018
MENU
FRIED & BBQ CHICKEN
ESCOVEITCHED FISH
CURRIED GOAT
SERVED WITH RICE & PEAS or WHITE RICE
SIDES: FRIED PLANTAIN
PASTA & FESTIVAL

CHICKEN $500.⁰⁰ $700.⁰⁰   CURRIED GOAT $700.⁰⁰

Digi (876) 320

Introduction

My grandmother Mavis always cooked. I can still hear the sound of her flickering gas hob boiling a pan of water in her Hackney estate flat in East London. From among the supermarket shopping bags in her trolley always emerged more bags: brown paper ones, bright blue, or red and white-striped plastic bags in which plantain, Scotch bonnets, green bananas and yams were nestled. As a child I didn't give this a second thought. It wasn't Jamaican food, it wasn't Caribbean food or anything foreign, it was just food, and I don't remember any sort of culinary life before it.

If curry goat, stew or soup weren't on the day's menu, whatever the centrepiece of the meal, be it chicken, beef or even fish fingers, island produce, grounded in my grandmother's Jamaican-born upbringing, were always present. For me, it never really warranted any thought at the time. If I went to my friends' houses on the estate, I just assumed they weren't eating what I usually ate on that day: the West African stews, Turkish spreads and South Asian curries of the East London estate were similar enough in sensibility that I ate them with no problem, thinking they were most probably regional variations of what my family cooked.

It wasn't until I went to school in Highgate, North London, that I began to realize the food I had grown up with was markedly different, alien even, to that of my schoolmates. I may have let it get to me, but I found solace in one of the few other kids at the school who had Caribbean parents, and whose packed lunches also consisted of leftover curry as well as sandwiches made with hardo bread. It was our secret club and in-joke, and I was happy with that. Even then, I still didn't think our food was THAT alien.

As homely Caribbean food became more of a rarity over the years, family functions were pencil marked on the calendar and I looked forward to the food with eager anticipation on the way to whatever the event was – wedding,

christening or funeral. As was custom at a buffet, you had to tensely wait in turn for your table to be motioned to, or if the reception was at someone's house you had to wait for the kids to be allowed their turn. Pepper-covered snapper fish, mac 'n' cheese, curries, plantain, jerk chicken were the hallowed ground of home-cooked meals, all a firework display of flavour – school dinners or fast food just couldn't compete.

As I progressed through school, college and university outside of London, then corporate life, it became harder to see my grandmother. In the latter years of her life one of her legs became nearly paralyzed with disease and yet she still journeyed, stick in hand, taking the number 30 bus from Homerton to Dalston to go to Ridley Road Market to buy her provisions. It was only after she passed away that I realized I had never actually asked her why. Why did she always go out of her way to buy this food? Why did she always eat it, and make sure we did too?

Perusing bookstores as I often do, even with no intent on buying, I noticed anything to do with Caribbean food and culture was sparse. Asking around my university friends, who ironically had started moving to places like Hackney, Peckham and Brixton, they always acknowledged the local Caribbean presence in the form of takeaways, but their engagement was pretty much limited to the yearly Notting Hill Carnival. Even before the famed Windrush Generation, a Caribbean populace had lived on these isles so why was an awareness of the food and culture so low among the public? This was yet another question that stumped me.

I started having chit-chats with some of my local Caribbean takeaway owners. Louis at Smokey Jerkey and Richard of Cummin Up, both in New Cross, and Bill of JB's Soul Food in Peckham. This two-mile patch is one of the holy grails of Afro-Caribbean food in London. Posing such questions to these people I realized I was engaged in a therapy of sorts, trying to gather answers to the questions that I had never asked my grandmother. I needed to record this history and I believed something different from the usual cookbook would be a great way to do it, while also demystifying Caribbean food and culture to those who are unfamiliar with it. This was the impetus behind my first book *Belly Full: Caribbean Food in the UK.*

What I found time and time again when researching that book was that these restaurants and takeaways weren't just businesses, they were entities deeply rooted in their heritage. Food and the passing down of knowledge were so pivotal to these people's lives, the majority of whom were born and raised in the Caribbean. These owners, like my grandparents, came or rather were invited to the UK to serve the mother country and help it rebuild after the world wars. On arrival their identity was tested time and time again, be it from their new fellow citizens, the police, and even politicians. Demonized, ostracized and criminalized, they found solace in two things: music and food. The idea of even remotely adapting the recipes from home arguably meant compromising their identity and as such it was rarely done.

Meat stews and curries, still with their bones, soups peppered with chillies, and miscellaneous beige starchy foods, much denser than potatoes, were all seemingly hard to stomach for the nation housing this new group of diaspora. There was no sustained campaign to adapt the food to make it more palatable to the general populace and this hasn't really changed. As such, unlike contrived versions of Chinese and Indian food that boomed in the 1980s and 90s in the UK, Caribbean food has largely remained a mystery.

This was a revelation to me and what's more, something to contemplate. I knew the names of certain ingredients and I had come to understand why it was so important for people to carry on cooking with these foods, but I didn't know anything about their origins. Born in East London, these foods and the stories behind them told at family functions, were the limit of my connection with Jamaica and the wider Caribbean. Thinking about it, below the surface, I knew just as much, or rather as little, about the region that my family hailed from as anyone else.

Spending most of my life having to face the question, "Where are you from?" left me in an identity limbo. After years of being part of a family that celebrated Jamaican culture, but never actually actively encouraged any of us to explore the country in more depth, the advent of social media hooked me into the idea of going. Kingston, Georgetown, Port of Spain were places I'd heard about my whole life but had no clue what lay there, save from a few holidays as a kid to beach resorts with the odd

excursion up the hills. About a year and a half of conversations later while writing *Belly Full* and a UK winter snowstorm on the horizon, clinched it.

After I arrived, it took me about a week or so to acclimatize to Jamaica, both physically and mentally. For the first time in my life my skin colour wasn't a differentiator. Here was a whole island of people who looked and sounded like my family. With a quarter of a century of Caribbean upbringing, I understood most of the patois lingo being bandied about and, more importantly, the food menus were easy to navigate. I was eager to immerse myself into the country, although a series of events made me realize I was more disconnected from my Jamaican roots than I'd imagined.

A driver who'd been pre-arranged to pick me up from the desolate peak of the Blue Mountains and take me back to Papine in the western edges of Kingston, stopped in the middle of nowhere, opened his trunk, grabbed two large bottles, hopped over to a small gap in the greenery and to my surprise started filling them with fresh spring water. Intrigued, I followed, "Is that allowed?" I asked. "Is it safe to drink?" Both daft questions that tickled the driver and firmly put me in the box labelled "tourist".

In the hills of Ocho Rios in northern Jamaica, known as Great Pond, I spent a few nights sleeping on the patio at Redemption Ground – a Rastafari religious compound. Wandering around I noticed spiked leaves growing from the ground and queried, "Is that aloe vera?" The elder responded puzzled, "No, it's pineapple!" before waltzing off. I remember this moment so vividly. I felt like a child again. I had always assumed pineapples grew on trees, then it occurred to me, even though I'd been eating them forever, I had never actually considered how they grow.

The third incident was when one of the Rasta elders preparing a soup in their outdoor kitchen realized he was short of coconut water. Motioning to one of the kids nearby he requested, "Go get some coconuts." Expecting him to head to the local market or shop, he grabbed a ladder instead and delegated the task to his younger brother. Offering support at the base of the ladder, his brother, on reaching the top, clutched onto the tree and shimmied even higher until shrouded in palm leaves. Several thuds on the ground later, we had coconuts. Okay, this wasn't entirely a shock, however, it brought back memories of the Caribbean elders I had interviewed back in the UK for *Belly Full,* and now I was able to understand why my grandparents and their generation had such a vivid connection to this food. It was because it was more than food on a market stall or in a supermarket, it was food you could reach out from your kitchen window and touch, food so plentiful and abundant.

Everywhere I went people explained their food and recipes to me, whether I asked them to or not. People invited me into their houses and kitchens to watch them cook. Even though I had my family growing up in the UK, I had never felt this sense of community before, and I now understood why it was so important to my grandmother. Instead of papayas, soursop and jackfruit, I grew up inundated with commercials for French fries, turkey drumsticks and pizza. Furthermore, possibly due to single-child, male privilege, I was never encouraged to learn to cook in the same way my female cousins were. Where I may have literally had a whole village and community to impart their culinary wisdom, I grew up in a massive vacuum. Now I was playing catch-up.

Apart from a small notebook I carried with me, I hardly took any notes on my various Caribbean excursions. I rarely travel with my laptop but fortunately, or unfortunately for whoever tags along with me, I take thousands of photos and record hundreds of hours of video. Most of the previously told stories are chronicled in some form on one of my various blogs. I just can't help whipping the camera out – I want to share what I'm seeing and feeling in that moment with others. This is fortunate as there are no recipes in the Caribbean in the traditional Western format sense – rather there are folk tales, short stories, songs and anecdotes.

THE RECIPES

The thing about Jamaican food, like other types of migrant food, is that while most people have a ridiculously strong opinion on what tastes good, if you ask why or specifically how to make it, you are left with incredibly vague answers. How does, "It needs more fire!" translate into just add more Scotch bonnet peppers; and how does the perfect amount of black char on a jerked chicken translate into minutes and degrees Celsius. Answers are usually just "add a dash of this, a lickle bit of that".

This can make recreating recipes tricky as everyone's own relationship with the food and certain meals is so incredibly nostalgic that any derivation is almost taken as an offence. That said, when I asked my mother for the recipes for a select dozen meals that she has made hundreds of times before she was stumped, remarking that she'd never really thought of them in recipe form.

In this book's recipes, you'll notice that it's as much about the shopping and prepping as the cooking. Time is spent perusing kaleidoscopic produce, peeling, chopping, dicing and seasoning simple ingredients, while actual cooking arguably plays a smaller role. Added to this, many of the recipes in this book require no cooking at all. Ingredients are simply enjoyed raw with a blender being the only necessity, and warm sun being a bonus for sun-drying. In others, flavour comes through the process of fermentation or preservation, both of which have a storied history on the island due to both its heat and geography.

INTRODUCTION

Travelling across Jamaica, I soon learned that the food of my heritage wasn't as alien as the distance from the UK may suggest. For example, the British Empire's influence on the consumption and farming of wheat means that many baked goods have similarities with English ones, such as the Jamaican patty and the Cornish pasty. Additionally, supposedly new "superfoods", such as moringa and spirulina, promoted as novel discoveries in the UK, Europe and the US, have been the cornerstone of diets in Jamaica and across the Caribbean islands for aeons.

Similarly, abstinence from animal by-products appears on record in the 1930s with Jamaica's Rastafari community, while vegetarianism brought to the Caribbean by indentured Indian workers originated many years before that. Of all the food trends that have gained momentum in recent years, veganism may be the most prevalent, although plant-based dishes from Jamaica are little known outside the region.

The Rastas, who shunned western tableware and plastic containers in favour of their own naturally made calabash bowls and flasks, showed early signs of environmental awareness and zero-waste ideals, which seems a natural progression from their enslaved ancestors who could ill-afford to waste anything. Any notion of nose-to-tail dining being a new trend would be laughable to my grandmother and her predecessors, who've eaten curried tripe, stewed liver and chicken foot for centuries.

In the same way, no part of a fish ever went to waste. I have a few aunties who love nothing more than to snack on a fish head and bones. These are also used to make broths for fish tea and rich gravies to accompany the wide range of fish and seafood dishes enjoyed across the island, which utilize its plentiful aquatic resources. Where fish wasn't available, including in the hills and mountains, equally amazing meals were created with shellfish from the rivers, and many of these are still enjoyed today.

Uniting these ingredients in one big magical pot are soups. Encompassing elements from nearly every chapter of this book, be it raw, vegan, seafood or nose-to-tail eating, soups are the great unifier of food in Jamaica. Rightfully so, they warrant their own chapter. In each chapter, the ingredients and recipe techniques highlight a connection with the water and land.

The recipes in this book can't claim to be completely authentic Jamaican or Caribbean. As mentioned, one Jamaican family's style of cooking can be vastly different to another's, and so who can lay claim to authenticity is a loaded question. I've had numerous experiences that made me question what Jamaican food even is! When delving into the history of certain foods, I found it ironic that non-native foods, like ackee from West Africa and salted fish from Europe, could be seen as more Jamaican than a meal cooked in and by Jamaicans using ingredients indigenous to the island. If it is the case that it's simply Jamaican food because a group of Jamaicans declared it so and then cooked it over generations, then that opens the floodgates for all manner of foods to be termed as Jamaican. Naturally, the same holds true for foods from all reaches of the Caribbean.

Regardless, I hope to dispel the notion that the food eaten in the Caribbean is some faraway food that is unattainable in homes in the UK, Europe, North America and beyond. Be it Birmingham, Brooklyn, Brampton or Berlin, there are few alien or mysterious ingredients that you can't find at your local market, supermarket "world food" section, butchers or health food shop, so what better time to illustrate the true embodiment of Caribbean, and more specifically Jamaican, food; not fanciful cocktails, elaborately plated fusion dishes nor the generic dishes that are wheeled out and hash-tagged at the Notting Hill Carnival each year, but the true essence of the cooking.

The recipes are important but so are the connection and tales behind them, and how they improve our understanding of our ancestors and heritage. West African cultures have undoubtedly shaped and formed belief systems and norms in Jamaica and the wider Caribbean, influencing language, music, dress, dancing, folklore, family, medicine, magic, religion and, of course, diet. Unfortunately, most of the written records we rely on are from the viewpoint of colonial bureaucrats, travellers and the planters themselves, so the perspective of those souls who were forced across the Atlantic are scant. Given this, direct notation of recipes and culinary knowledge from the source are lacking, and tracing direct genealogy of certain foods and recipes proves difficult. Bearing this in mind, nobody is going to worry if you neglect a few of the herbs and spices, or up the amount of ginger. At worst you may get a cut-eye or tooth-kissed by a veteran Caribbean food connoisseur! The specificity of listed ingredients is simply for the sake of being specific. Use them as a benchmark and feel free to freestyle (this becomes much easier if you have stocked up on Pantry items, see overleaf). This explains why one aunty's mac 'n' cheese often tastes different to the other's, however, don't ever make the mistake of vocalizing which one you prefer. Use the recipes here as a starting point and follow your taste buds because, as they say, a hummed tune can still effectively convey a song without you knowing the exact lyrics.

THE BOOK

Throughout this book you will read about global influences on Caribbean cooking, and whether you are from Latin America, West Africa, Europe or Asia you'll likely experience a shared heritage with much of the food. Hopefully, this will help to destroy the myth that only Caribbean people can cook Caribbean food. Living in Jamaica and seeing first-hand how preparation and cooking is weaved into daily life illustrated just how simple it is – with a bit of patience anyone can do it.

This book isn't about providing a checklist or anthology of Jamaican cuisine. Additionally, it would be incredibly hard to whittle down the food of any Caribbean island into an all-pleasing single archive. Instead, the recipes and their stories throughout are the narrators of time – past, present and future. I want to illuminate a legacy of an intellectual and innovative food culture among the islands that has been relegated as simply "exotic" or "tropical" carnival food. It's important to illustrate the Jamaica outside the white-sanded confines of internationally owned beach resorts.

So, what exactly is the difference between Jamaican food and Caribbean food? While I don't pretend to have an all-encompassing academic answer, at its core Jamaican food,

as the recipes illustrate, is an extravagant creolization of human pathways, both chosen and forced, from all corners of the world.

What many don't realize about the individual Caribbean islands is how much the ethnic diversity and types of international influence differ. More so, given the relatively small size of each island, the intensity of the diverse ethnic makeup may be unrivalled anywhere else in the world, which makes for wildly exciting cuisines. This explains why foods from Jamaica shouldn't be shoehorned with those from, say, Martinique with its French influence, or the Spanish islands like Cuba, or the more heavily Indian-influenced domains of Trinidad and Tobago, Guyana, and Suriname, for example. To me, saying you're going to eat "Caribbean" food sounds as non-descript as saying you are going to eat "Asian" food.

What we've come to know as "Caribbean" food in diasporas like the UK and US is a new layer of creolization, one brought about by the veterans of the worlds wars and Windrush Generation that ferried not only Jamaicans, but Trinidadians, Antiguans, St. Lucians, Bermudans and so forth. The likes of Samuel Selvon's novel *The Lonely Londoners,* or Andrea

Levy's *Small Island;* poems by Linton Kwesi Johnson, such as *It Dread Inna Inglan;* and films like Horace Ové's *Pressure,* all eloquently depict the harsh reality of the new lives of this cohort. As such, ostracized people, from islands that are actually located thousands of miles apart, formed communities for solace, after all they were seen as a monolith by Europeans – basically "Caribbean". As Jamaica was the leading source of this human movement, naturally the cuisine of the island came to dominate what was seen as the region's fare, and accounts for why foods like roti, which are more popular in places like Trinidad and Tobago and Guyana than in Jamaica, are sold in many Jamaican-owned Caribbean eateries in the UK.

My personal journey into the food and culture of Jamaica has helped me answer many questions I never thought to ask my Jamaican grandma Mavis, while we sat in her Hackney council flat eating digestives and watching *The Weakest Link* on a TV from the 70s. Asking the why's, and the how's about the food I ate growing up unravelled a food culture so deep and fantastic it's a shame that it has been reduced or is non-existent in some places. I hope this book helps to champion the culture and illuminate the food beyond stereotypical, long-standing tropical tropes. I want this book to appeal to those of the diaspora hoping to reconnect with the food and culture of their heritage in the same way I have done. Those separated from the poetic beat of patois lingo recanting everlasting tales, tips and recipes. Through this book I hope to capture a modicum of the spirit of the towns and villages that many of us diaspora are separated from, and subsequent generations will become further distanced. Places where the transferral of ancestral knowledge is an everyday norm.

Equally, I believe there are scores of people with no lineage to the Caribbean, who either have an affinity to the region or are engaged in a wider culinary interest in learning about under-represented culinary styles, and this certainly is one of them.

With a life steeped in Caribbean food and culture and since becoming a citizen of Jamaica, I feel I'm in a good position to distil a fragment of the spirit of the food of the island. Despite its minute population, their music took over the world and I believe their food can too. When up in the Blue Mountains looking over Kingston you can see the effect of the breeze from a distance. It picks up leaves and carries them for miles and miles before dropping them. I hope this book is like a gust of wind that does the same with these stories and recipes.

Pantry

My shopping list of items is for anyone cooking Caribbean-inspired food with regularity, and ideally you shouldn't be without these staples. You'll find these ingredients peppered throughout the following recipes; many will be familiar, while others may be new to you. Outside diaspora regions, such as London and Manchester, Caribbean food shops may be a rarity but fortunately the shared heritage with West African and Southeast Asian cultures means that you should be able to find essential ingredients in those grocery stores, too, along with general supermarkets and markets.

APPLE CIDER VINEGAR

This vinegar is used throughout the recipes for everything from preserving foods to adding a touch of acidity to dressings and cooked dishes.

ALL-PURPOSE SEASONING

This classic Caribbean spice blend is easy to source at any diaspora grocery shop or larger supermarket. I have also included my own recipe (see p239), a typical blend of paprika, pimento, nutmeg, cumin and cayenne. Do not confuse all-purpose seasoning with allspice, which is a spice staple in Caribbean cooking (see Pimento Seeds, right).

BASMATI RICE

In my family, it's always basmati, followed by regular long-grain – the bigger the bag the better.

BROWN SUGAR

Although light soft brown sugar is called for in this book, this is mostly down to preference – do use demerara or dark brown sugar instead, if you like.

BROWNING

This condiment gives a deep colour and a rich caramel flavour to gravies and stews; dark soy sauce or Worcestershire sauce make good alternatives.

COCONUT

I use coconut in various guises – oil, milk, water, shredded, desiccated and cream – in the recipes, so you could say it is a mainstay ingredient. There is also my own recipe for coconut water, milk, flour and desiccated (see p90). If buying canned coconut milk, I've found those from Thailand to be especially creamy.

CITRUS FRUIT

Orange, lemon and lime all come in handy, from adding an acidic blast of flavour and helping preservation to use as a cleaning aid when preparing meat and fish, and also as a garnish.

CURRY POWDER

Try to use a Jamaican curry powder, which includes spices such as pimento seeds, fenugreek and star anise, otherwise a good-quality mild or hot curry blend are worthy alternatives.

FLOUR

Since I like to add some form of dumpling or fritter to most of my meals, a bag of wholemeal or plain (all-purpose) flour is a necessity in my kitchen. I also like to use coconut flour (see p91) and cornmeal as well as cornflour (corn starch) as a thickener.

GARLIC, GINGER & ONION

This trinity of ingredients is found in some form and combination in nearly every savoury recipe in this book, and so I always have a small bag of each in the kitchen. I also like to keep the powdered version of each in the store cupboard.

HERBS

Most herbs I use, such as coriander (cilantro) and basil, can be bought in dried form, although for some dishes fresh is definitely best. When it comes to thyme, fresh on the stalk is recommended and features in many recipes in this book.

JERK SEASONING

I have included a recipe for my own jerk spice paste (see p238), but you can usually find a ready-made paste or a dry jerk spice rub in food shops. Although the mix of herbs, spices and flavourings can vary, common ingredients include pimento seeds, garlic, Scotch bonnet, cinnamon, nutmeg, brown sugar, ginger and thyme.

BELL PEPPERS

In the book, I often leave it up to you to choose which colour of pepper to use, whether it's red, orange, yellow or green – or even a mixture. Feel free to use whichever colour of pepper you have to hand - it won't be detrimental to the taste of the final dish.

PIMENTO SEEDS (ALLSPICE BERRIES)

These dried berries are used in many of the recipes and I use them whole, crushed or ground. When ground, the seeds are known as allspice.

PLANTAIN

Life itself... for me, plantain, golden in colour, is a regular buy. My dearest condolences if you have to pay more than the usual £1.50 for 3! Please note that green plantains are not the same as green bananas. If you forget to eat your plantain immediately and they ripen and the skins turn pitch black, don't throw them away as they can still be used in a variety of recipes, such as cakes, fritters and smoothies.

PULSES

Unless I am really p for time I'll cook with dried lentils, kidney beans and chickpeas, which I keep in jars and soak before use. When time is short, I'll resort to canned beans.

SCOTCH BONNET PEPPERS

These are now thankfully widely available, but if you have difficulty finding them it's a good idea to buy in bulk and freeze until ready to use. Jalapeño or habanero chillies are good alternatives, but only as a last resort as they have a different, slightly bitter flavour.

SPICES

I've mentioned must-have spice blends, like all-purpose and jerk seasoning, but I also like to keep a stock of single spices, both ground and whole. These include black pepper, cloves, cinnamon, coriander, cumin, pimento/allspice (see above), nutmeg, paprika and turmeric.

SPRING ONIONS (SCALLIONS)

Always keep a bunch handy to add flavour and texture to marinades, spice pastes, curries and stews. The green part makes a good garnish, too.

VEGAN

"The abstinence from meat is rooted in a religious reverence for all of God's creatures."

The spiritual meditation of a Rastafari Nyabinghi ceremony can't be adequately summed up in words or visuals. The ascending journey from the city, such as Kingston, up the meandering country hills and rocky footpaths to one of the many settlement communes that breach the Jamaican clouds is a cause for introspection in itself. Up far above sea level, the unrelenting heat of the Jamaican streets turns into fresh, nippy mountain air. Here, every Saturday as the sun sets, beaconing calls emerge and people of all ages, from one to one hundred, gather in the focal place of worship known as the tabernacle.

With waist-length dreadlocks flowing, the fellows are usually clad in the pan-African colour palette of red, gold and green. However, on this spring day everyone, including myself, is dressed head-to-toe in white as it is Grounation Day. This day celebrates the anniversary of the former Emperor of Ethiopia Haile Selassie's arrival in Jamaica in 1966, and who was greeted by a welcoming committee of 100,000 Rastafari disciples. Selassie was, and still is, heralded by many of the Rastafari as the incarnate of Christ and as such is venerated in art, words and music across the island.

As the Nyabinghi session begins, Selassie's name becomes a constant feature of the chants. The drums increase in pace and bass, the rhythmic chants grow louder, and the generation-stretching congregation begin to leap and dance. The spiritual passion of the dance nearly mirrors the movement of the flames of the fire that burns at the hub of the tabernacle. The pimento-coloured smoke from the firepit merges with the fumes of marijuana, filling the air. Darkness sets in, the stars shine as bright as the sun, and many hours pass just gazing above. As the sun rises and a new day begins, I remember that I haven't eaten for nearly half a day.

Building on a legacy of plantation sustenance in the overwhelming island heat, the Rastafari have perfected the utilization of root vegetables, plants, fruit, herbs and spices in a meal or "cook-up", which can sustain a small village for days. As dawn turns fully into day, a rainbow-esque array of produce is summoned and the day's meals are prepared. Deeply rooted in the Rasta system of beliefs is the disconnect from "Babylon" or the establishment, highlighting a deep-held distrust of the state, legal system and commerce. Consequently, most Rasta communes I visited have their own river irrigated farms, and the vast majority of everything cooked is sourced from walking distance.

The abstinence from meat is rooted in a religious reverence for all of God's creatures, termed "livity" and adapted from the Christian Old Testament scriptures in the Bible. The spectrum of this spans from raw veganism to pescatarianism.

This chapter doesn't aim to dictate a meat-free lifestyle. Everyone is different and I believe it's up to each individual to find what works for them within a range of ethical consumption. The underlying ethos, however, is a respect for the order of life and sustainability of the earth. Before the word vegan became mainstream in food cultures across the world, the Rastafari equivalent "Ital" (derived from the word vitality) is a way of eating and living that has been cultivated in this corner of the world for nearly a century.

The red, gold and green tricolour permeates much of Jamaica now and the music of Rastafari envoys, like Bob Marley, has had a generational transcendence across the world. Given this, the deluge of commercialized wares from key rings and towels to necklaces, has diluted the culture to dreadlocks and weed, overshadowering the fact that Rasta culture is still very much on the fringe, including their food.

For such a dominant culture, Rasta devotees appear to be relatively few in number. One study suggests that less than 1 per cent of Jamaicans describe themselves as such. Perhaps it's surprising to find then that the average non-Jamaican assumes that the way of the Rasta is the national religion of Jamaica. This couldn't be further from the truth. Rastafari in Jamaica have historically been total outcasts of society and were victim to decades of persecution by the Jamaican state and police. Many were regarded as "*useless, lazy, half-insane, ganja-smoking illiterates who were of no value to society*". (E.B. Edmonds, *Rastafari: From Outcasts to Culture Bearers*.) Dreadlocks were a complete no-no and families would go into mourning if their sons started wearing them.

Given this, the many tenets of what the Rasta have preached since their inception, be it forms of vegetarianism, organic produce, notions of farm-to-table eating, via growing your own food and herbs and, of course, marijuana consumption, have all become mainstream overseas.

It must be noted, too, that an abstinence of meat for many in Jamaica, including Rastafari, Christian and sectarian alike, is very much borne out of generational poverty among anything else. As seen in the Nose-to-Tail chapter (see pp124–51), meat consumption was a rarity. A 1774 English study of Jamaica mentioned in E. Long's *The History of Jamaica* noted on the native diet, "*They make their principle daily meal consist chiefly of vegetables in their pepper-pots; eat plantains, yams, and cocoes, instead of bread; and are fond of salads, fruits and sugared preparations.*"

For a culture that was once so connected to the land and its harvest, the eating of meat has since become overwhelmingly ingrained in Caribbean culture. Veganism and vegetarianism have now become a contentious

"The almost endless combinations of fresh produce fused with even the simplest of seasoning and spice yield so much flavour and magic."

"lifestyle" that is fraught with pain points for beginners. Ironically, given their history, many people of Afro-Caribbean upbringing can attest to the comedy of discussing the idea of living without consuming meat and fish to family members. In an imaginary world with no travel costs or emissions, for anyone attempting to convince a loved one of such a dietary shift a sure-fire solution would be to whisk them away to spend time, even a day, with the Rastafari. (More realistically, an attempt to seek out a local Ital eatery in your city will do!)

Each season in Jamaica provides its own beautiful array of produce from mangoes, ackee, callaloo, breadfruit and yams to June plums, star apples, avocado pears, custard apples and sugar cane: the full list could fill a book in itself. The almost endless combinations of fresh produce fused with even the simplest of seasoning and spice yield so much flavour and magic they can make the most ardent of carnivores forget about meat. I am one of those people – after consuming meat on my first day of a living stint in Jamaica, my desire for it completely waned and I felt much more of a pep in my step after a wholesome Ital meal, even amid the creeping fatigue caused by the relenting island heat.

When creating the meals in this chapter, I was stunned by how much flavour and texture can be compounded into such seemingly effortless dishes, which incidentally also kept me full for much of the day. Often, when testing these recipes, I found myself eating a dish as a meal in itself, despite the joy that can be had when different dishes are pick-and-mixed together in a rainbow-coloured feast.

While the words of the Bible are sacred and dissected to a tee in Rasta culture, there is no such manual for the recipes they cook. They seemingly emerge from a freestyle of whatever taste or texture they feel that day – salad, soup, curry, etc. – and whatever is in season, ripe and fresh. This is noticeable across Jamaica at the various Ital outposts, with their daily changing menus always providing some intrigue for the meal ahead. The same can be said of the Jamaican cookshops run by Christian Seventh-day Adventists, who also strongly lean on the foods of the Rastafari.

Some people have attempted to hone the culinary fare of the Rastafari to a rigid set of laws, but it seems that there are no real rules and, like all matters, this is heatedly debated in the tabernacle. What does exist, however, is a ranging base of omissions, such as processed salt and refined sugar, and then a philosophy that pervades much of Caribbean cooking, namely a broad roster of herbs and spices, like thyme and pimento, combined with blended, chopped, sliced and grated fresh produce – the majority of which you'll thankfully find are now largely available in a great many places across the UK, Europe and the US.

Ackee & hearts of palm

It's not easy to describe ackee to someone who's never heard of, or seen it, before. Yes, it's a fruit but so are tomatoes, okra and aubergines (eggplant), so that's of no use. The alternative "it's sort of like scrambled eggs" kind of gives the right impression, but if you like your scrambled eggs well done, like me, it definitely doesn't. The often-used "it tastes like chicken" doesn't cut it either. There's just no comparison. The sun-washed yellow skin of the ackee also does well to belie its wickedly inherent poisonous trait that can be fatal if eaten before fully ripened. The only way to be initiated into the ackee fraternity is to try it.

The first pit stop would naturally be Ackee & Saltfish (see p158), the pride and joy of modern Jamaica. Although non-aquatic alternatives to saltfish, from cabbage and mushrooms to jackfruit, are becoming more common, especially since traditional dried salted cod is now seen as a luxury of sorts. The best alternative I've found is certainly hearts of palm (or palmetto), harvested from the core of palm trees and commonly found canned in US, UK and European supermarkets. When sliced and steamed, the slightly saline, similarly translucent and pliable vegetable makes a more than adequate substitute. This makes a great brunch.

——

Heat the oil in a medium-large saucepan, add the vinegar, onion, red and green bell peppers and garlic and sauté for 3–4 minutes, until softened.

Add the hearts of palm, white part of the spring onion and half the tomatoes, stir, then add the Scotch bonnet or paprika, thyme and all-purpose seasoning and cook for 1 minute, stirring. Using the back of a fork, gently mash the hearts of palm, then add the coconut milk or cream. Turn the heat down to medium-low, cover with the lid and simmer for 3–4 minutes.

Remove the lid, gently mash the hearts of palm again until they resemble flakes of fish. Turn the heat up a notch, add the ackee and gently fold (too much force and the ackee will break up) into the other ingredients. Cook for 3 minutes until heated through. Season with salt and pepper to taste.

Top with the remaining tomatoes, the green part of the spring onion, dill or parsley and extra black pepper before serving.

SERVES 4

2 tbsp cooking oil of choice
1 tbsp apple cider vinegar
½ onion, chopped
1 bell pepper, (½ red and
    ½ green), deseeded and cut
    into 1cm (½in) dice
2 garlic cloves, minced
410g (14oz) can hearts of palm,
    drained and cut into 1cm (½in)
    thick rounds
1 spring onion (scallion), white
    and green parts separated,
    finely chopped
8 cherry tomatoes, quartered
1 Scotch bonnet pepper, finely
    chopped, or 1 tsp paprika
3 sprigs of thyme
1 tsp All-purpose Seasoning
    (see p239)
2 tbsp coconut milk
    or coconut cream
540g (19oz) can ackee, drained
sea salt and freshly ground
    black pepper
1 tbsp chopped dill or parsley,
    to garnish

Creamed coconut ackee

The ackee fruit, and the tree that bears it, is a relative newcomer to Jamaica compared with other favourite island produce. A 1778 description of the fruit in a record of "Exotic Plants Cultivated in the Botanic Garden owned by slave owner, Hinton East, in the Liguanea area of Kingston" reads, *"This plant was brought here in a Slave Ship from the Coast of Africa, and now grows very luxuriant."* So luxuriant that some two centuries later ackee grows in such abundance that school kids and workers indifferently kick the fallen fruits out of the way on their daily commutes.

Even with its West African heritage, ackee has never found the same prominence there as it has in Jamaica, where it seems near impossible that anyone could exist without knowing it. For the Jamaican diaspora in places like the US and England, the purchase of a can of ackee is such an occasion it's almost sacrilegious not to pair it with saltfish, or suitable alternative, and an array of sautéed vegetables and spices.

The house where I stay near Half Way Tree in Kingston, coincidentally just a mile or so from where the botanic garden would have been, has an ackee tree. There's also no shortage of higglers selling ackee from here to Coronation Market, meaning there is no such pressure to bolster or bulk the dish with any headlining partner, which can admittedly overpower sometimes. This dish reflects that simplicity, a simple boost from the subtly sweet coconut milk produces something between a curry, stew or rundown that allows the fruit to be the star of the show.

Heat the oil in a medium-large sauté pan over a medium heat. Add the onion and sauté for 1 minute before adding the garlic, thyme and spring onions, saving some of the green part for later, stir and sauté for 3 minutes.

Next, stir in the Scotch bonnet and green pepper followed by the coconut milk and salt or all-purpose seasoning. Add the paprika and allspice, if using. Finally, stir in the brown sugar until combined. Turn the heat up to medium-high and when the coconut milk starts to bubble, turn the heat down to low.

SERVES 4

2 tbsp coconut or vegetable oil
1 onion, finely diced
3 garlic cloves, minced
4–5 sprigs of thyme
2 spring onions (scallions), white and green parts separated, finely chopped
½ Scotch bonnet pepper, deseeded, sliced or left whole
½ green bell pepper, deseeded and finely diced
200ml (¾ cup) coconut milk
¼–½ tsp sea salt or All-Purpose Seasoning (see p239)
½ tsp paprika (optional)
½ tsp ground allspice (optional)
½ tsp light soft brown sugar
540g (19oz) can ackee, drained and gently rinsed
2 tsp desiccated coconut
freshly ground black pepper

Add the ackee and gently stir to combine, or use a spoon to ladle the coconut milk over the ackee. Cover with the lid and simmer for 3 minutes, until heated through. Turn the heat off, sprinkle over the desiccated coconut and leave to cool slightly. Spoon into a serving dish and garnish with the saved green part of the spring onion and a little black pepper.

Jackfruit stew

Whenever I return to Jamaica, I always have a set fruit shopping list that must be checked off before absolutely anything else occurs, and top of my list is a bag of jackfruit pods. These golden pockets of fruit manage to be both sweet and slightly saline, as well as chewy and crunchy at the same time.

Key, of course, is not to buy a bag that's been sitting in the sun for hours, but rather one full of pods plucked straight out of the luminous, yellowy-green, beehive-shaped jackfruit. Firstly, a machete is taken to the middle of the jackfruit, slicing through it effortlessly and its natural white discharge is mopped away with a rag. In the markets, many opt for a whole segment, but for walkers-on-the-go a bag of pods prised away from the body with the seeds still inside is a must-have, understood with just a nod and a point.

Removing these seeds is where the fun begins. I've never actually seen anyone use their hands to do so: instead, people manoeuvre their tongue and front teeth meticulously shredding the flesh to dislodge the seed. After this, the flesh is firmly held in one part of the mouth, while the seed is spat into the bag, one pod at a time.

I didn't have much culinary knowledge of what do with jackfruit until a local Rasta, named Marlon, of the Lion House beside the Fern Gully, told me not to throw my remains away, but to keep the seeds for a roast, or soak the flesh and use it to bolster a curry or stew. Another acquaintance, Delroy Dixon, who runs the fabulous Rhythm Kitchen Caribbean restaurant in London, then shared with me a recipe for jackfruit curry, of which this is an adaptation. Outside of the islands, fresh jackfruit can be hard to come by, but fortunately it's now readily available canned in brine in Asian and Afro-Caribbean supermarkets, and some major supermarkets.

———

Soak the jackfruit for 8 hours, or overnight, in warm water, changing the soaking water at least a couple of times. If you do not have time to soak the jackfruit overnight then 1–2 hours will do.

Preheat the oven to 220°C (200°C fan/425°F/Gas 7) and line a baking tray with baking paper.

Heat half the coconut oil in a large saucepan or Dutch pot over a medium heat. Add 1 teaspoon of the all-purpose seasoning, the ginger and 2 tablespoons of

SERVES 4

500g (1lb 2oz) can young green
    jackfruit in brine, rinsed
2 tbsp coconut oil
2 tsp All-purpose Seasoning
    (see p239)
2.5cm (1in) piece of fresh root
    ginger, peeled and minced,
    or 1 tsp ground ginger
5 tbsp medium massala curry
    paste or 2 tbsp curry powder
400ml (13.5fl oz) can coconut milk
pinch of light soft brown sugar
    (optional)
1½ bell peppers (mix of colours),
    deseeded and sliced or chopped
½ small onion, finely chopped
5 spring onions (scallions),
    thinly sliced
1 Scotch bonnet pepper, whole
sea salt and freshly ground
    black pepper
parsley or coriander (cilantro),
    to garnish

the paste or 1 tablespoon of the curry powder. Stir for 1–2 minutes to combine. Turn the heat down a little, then add half the coconut milk and stir to combine.

Drain the jackfruit, add to pan or pot, stir until coated, and cook for 20–25 minutes, adding a splash of water if it looks dry. Add the sugar, if using, and season with salt and pepper to taste. Using a fork or potato masher, shred or mash the jackfruit until it resembles strands of meat that look similar to pulled pork.

Spread the jackfruit out on the lined baking tray and cook in the oven for 10 minutes, until starting to colour.

Meanwhile, heat the remaining oil in the pan or pot over a medium heat, add the rest of the all-purpose seasoning, paste or curry powder and cook, stirring, for 1–2 minutes to combine. Add the rest of the coconut milk and combine until smooth. Add the baked jackfruit, bell peppers, onion, spring onions and Scotch bonnet and cook for 10–15 minutes, until tender. Scatter over the parsley or coriander before serving with rice.

Pakassa

The genesis of the famed Caribbean dish, rundown, is up for contention, as you'll read in the fish-based version (see p162). Some suspect that rundown comes from Jamaica's Indian descendants, who knew the dish as *pakassa,* which sometimes featured fishes' or pigs' tails but was often an inherently vegan dish. Those from Guyana may also recognize it as *metemgee* (or *mettagee*).

No words can obviously describe the harrowing experience of those taken to the Caribbean, but the fact that the enslaved were forbidden to read and write creates an everlasting trauma for future generations as we can seldom refer to a history written by them for answers, including a written record of recipes.

Yet, what we do know about rundown is that the dish features coconut milk or cream and is cooked for long enough to evaporate the water content, leaving behind a tart oil sauce that is fused with herbs, spices and hot peppers. The addition of slow-cooked, sweet starchy vegetables has kept rundown in the minds of Jamaicans displaced around the world for centuries.

The difference between this dish and a general vegetarian or Ital rundown is the initial use of water to boil the hard food, like yams and boiled dumplings (or *duff* as people call them in the Eastern Caribbean reaches). After this stage, the coconut element is introduced and boiled off. Like island life, this dish moves slow in every sense of the word. Thick, starchy chunks, oozing coconut residue and errant flour from the dumplings, mean this dish should not be made in a hurry, nor eaten in a hurry!

———

Place all the hard food ingredients in a bowl, then cover with water and set aside for 10 minutes.

Place all the seasoning ingredients in a separate small bowl and set aside. Now is a good time to make the spinners or boiled dumplings and set aside.

Heat the butter or oil in a large saucepan or Dutch pot over a medium heat. Add the onion and cook for 2 minutes, stirring, before adding the thyme, spring onions, garlic and ginger. Continue to cook for 2 minutes, stirring. Next, stir in the seasoning ingredients and cook for 1 minute.

Drain the hard food, add to the pan or pot with the hot stock and 400ml (1¾ cups) of the coconut milk. Stir to mix, then add the tomatoes and Scotch bonnet.

SERVES 4

1 recipe quantity Spinners or Boiled Dumplings (see p57)
2 tbsp vegan butter, or cooking oil of choice
1 onion, finely diced
4–5 sprigs of thyme, or ½ tsp dried
2–3 spring onions (scallions), finely sliced
2–3 garlic cloves, minced
2.5cm (1in) piece of fresh root ginger, peeled and minced
400ml (1¾ cup) hot vegetable stock
400–500ml (13.5–17fl oz) coconut milk
100g (3½oz) cherry tomatoes, quartered
1 Scotch bonnet pepper, whole
½ plantain, peeled, sliced lengthways, then halved
6–8 okra, topped and tailed, halved lengthways, plus extra, sliced, to garnish
¼ red bell pepper, deseeded and finely diced, to garnish (optional)

FOR THE SEASONING:

1 tsp freshly ground black pepper
¾ tsp garam masala (optional)
½ tsp All-purpose Seasoning (see p239), or extra sea salt
½ tsp annatto powder (optional)
6 pimento seeds (allspice berries), crushed, or ½ tsp ground allspice
½ tsp sea salt

FOR THE HARD FOOD:

400g (14oz) white or yellow yam, peeled and cut into bite-sized chunks
300g (10oz) sweet potato, peeled and cut into bite-sized chunks
2 cocoyams (taro), about 140g (5oz) each, peeled and cut into bite-sized chunks
200g (7oz) pumpkin, cut into bite-sized chunks (optional)
1 green banana, peeled and sliced into 2cm (¾in) rounds

Turn the heat up to high and bring to the boil. When it starts to bubble, turn the heat down to medium-high, part-cover with the lid, and simmer for 15 minutes. After this, remove the lid, taste and adjust the seasoning if needed. Cook for another 10 minutes, uncovered. If the pot is bubbling too ferociously, turn the heat down a notch and stir to ensure it doesn't stick to the bottom.

Turn the heat down to medium-low, add the plantain, stir and cook for 5 minutes. By this time the liquid should have turned a thick, custard-like consistency. If it is too thick, add the extra coconut milk or water to the pan.

Add the okra and spinners or dumplings, leaving some space between each one. Cover with the lid and cook for 5–8 minutes, until the vegetables are tender. Turn off the heat and leave to rest for 10 minutes. Garnish with the red bell pepper and extra okra, then serve with breadfruit (see p58), if you like.

Curry vegetables

For a long time, one of my favourite Trini spots in London, Roti Joupa, was tagged as an Indian restaurant online. Due to the large number of Indian subcontinent dishes on the menu, from *bodhi* and *choka* to *channa*, the error may be forgiven, though it highlights a lack of knowledge of the Indian presence in the Caribbean.

With the abolition of slavery, colonial forces sought indentured workers from the colonies to fill the void, and the majority were from India and the south of China. Their presence was evident across all the British-ruled Caribbean islands, including Jamaica, and the aftermath of this cultural influence over the years is still seen on menus in the Caribbean and the diaspora. In Jamaica, various foods from India are still enjoyed but most are commonly referred to by their English names, including the word curry, a supposed anglicized version of the Tamil word *kari*, meaning sauce.

I remember a past roommate, not from the Caribbean, being shocked that I would even consider eating savoury foods like rice and curry for breakfast, although there does seem to be historical grounding for my preference. Records for Indian indentured workers states that the first meal of the day on plantations was *"black tea, roti with fried or curried vegetables or chokha (roasted aubergine)."* Curry in all forms is widely enjoyed in Jamaica, whether it's goat or chicken, however, vegans and carnivores alike can enjoy this simple version loaded with spiced vegetable goodness.

———

Heat 2 tablespoons of the oil in a medium-large saucepan or Dutch pot over a medium heat. Add the onion and sauté for 5 minutes, until softened. Stir in the ginger, garlic and spring onions and add a splash of water if the onion starts to stick to the base of the pan or pot. Add the thyme, coriander, turmeric and cumin and cook, stirring, for 2 minutes until combined.

Stir in the potatoes, carrot, tomatoes and chickpeas, then add the coconut milk and 200ml (¾ cup) water. At this point, you can dictate the consistency of your curry by adding more water, if you like – personally I prefer the vegetables to sit 1cm (½in) or so above the liquid.

Turn the heat to high and bring to the boil, let it bubble for 30 seconds, then turn it down to low. Add the Scotch bonnet or jalapeño and pimento or allspice,

SERVES 4–6

3 tbsp oil, such as avocado, rapeseed or coconut
1 onion, chopped
2.5cm (1in) piece of fresh root ginger, peeled and chopped
4 garlic cloves, chopped
2 spring onions (scallions), chopped
1 tsp dried thyme
1 tsp ground coriander
1½ tsp ground turmeric
1 tsp ground cumin
3 large white potatoes, peeled and cut into chunks
1 large carrot, thinly sliced into rounds
8–10 cherry tomatoes, or 2–3 medium tomatoes, chopped
400g (14oz) can chickpeas, drained
400ml (13.5fl oz) can coconut milk
1 Scotch bonnet pepper or jalapeño chilli, whole
6 pimento seeds (allspice berries), crushed, or ½ tsp ground allspice
1 large aubergine (eggplant), cut lengthways into 5mm (¼in) thick slices
1 tsp sea salt
1 tsp freshly ground black pepper
2 bell peppers (colour of choice), deseeded and thinly sliced
200g (7oz) frozen peas
1 lime, cut into wedges

cover and simmer for 25 minutes, stirring occasionally.
Meanwhile, preheat the oven to 200°C (180°C fan/
400°F/Gas 6) and line a baking tray with baking paper.

Put the aubergine in a bowl with the salt, pepper
and the remaining oil. Massage the seasoned oil into the
aubergine, then arrange on the lined baking tray and
cook for 25 minutes, turning once, until tender.

Add the bell peppers and roasted aubergine to the
curry and cook for another 5 minutes over a low heat,
adding a splash more water if needed. Add the peas
and cook for another 5 minutes, until tender. Decant
the curry into a large serving bowl. Add more salt
and pepper to taste. Serve with rice and flatbreads,
and wedges of lime for squeezing over.

Sweet potato, chickpea & coconut curry

Curried chickpeas, also known as *channa*, are hard to come by in Jamaica (and consequently diaspora restaurants) due to the smaller Indian community. Whereas at respective Guyanese and Trini outposts, which have a larger Indian populace, the dish is as common as water. Of all the various curry dishes that I could eat every day without much distress, *channa* is definitely one. Rather than directly replicate it, this dish organizes a meeting somewhere in the metaphorical middle of the Caribbean seas and fuses *channa* with a Jamaican vegetable curry. Here, the softened chickpeas are swamped in a silky coconut curry sauce, with the heat dialed up thanks to the fresh ginger and a whole Scotch bonnet. This dish can be altered to suit personal taste, and I often enjoy a "butter" version made with butternut squash in place of the sweet potato, and butter beans (lima beans) instead of chickpeas, which results in a slightly less sweet dish but an equally abundant one.

SERVES 4–6

75ml (⅓ cup) rapeseed
   or vegetable oil
½ large onion, finely chopped
3 garlic cloves, minced
2.5cm (1in) piece of fresh root
   ginger, peeled and minced
2 spring onions (scallions), white
   and green parts separated,
   thinly sliced
1½ tbsp curry powder
1 tbsp ground cumin
400g (14oz) can chickpeas,
   drained
400ml (13.5fl oz) can coconut milk
1 tbsp All-purpose Seasoning
   (see p239)
½ tsp ground cinnamon
250g (9oz) sweet potato, peeled
   and cut into 2.5cm (1in) pieces
1 large carrot, sliced
1½ bell peppers (mix of colours),
   deseeded and cut into
   1cm (½in) dice
2 large tomatoes, or 8 cherry
   tomatoes, halved
4 sprigs of thyme
1 tsp sea salt
1 tsp freshly ground black pepper
1 tbsp maple syrup or light soft
   brown sugar (optional)
1 tbsp desiccated coconut
1 Scotch bonnet pepper, whole

FOR THE OKRA:

2 tbsp coconut oil
pinch of dried chilli flakes
5–6 okra, topped and tailed,
   halved lengthways

Heat the oil in a large saucepan or Dutch pot over a medium heat. Add the onion and sauté for 2 minutes before adding the garlic, ginger and the white part of the spring onions, then cook for another 2 minutes.

Add the curry powder, cumin and 1 tablespoon water and stir for 1 minute to combine. Stir in the chickpeas until coated in the seasonings. Pour in the coconut milk, then stir in the all-purpose seasoning and cinnamon, and keep stirring for 30 seconds to 1 minute.

Next, stir in the sweet potato, carrot, bell peppers, tomatoes and thyme. Add the salt, black pepper, maple syrup or sugar and desiccated coconut, if using, then stir to combine. Add the Scotch bonnet, turn the heat down to low, cover with the lid and simmer for 15 minutes, then stir. Cover again and simmer for a further 10–15 minutes, until the sweet potato is tender.

Meanwhile, cook the okra. Heat the coconut oil in a frying pan over a medium heat and add the chilli flakes. Add the okra and fry until they start to brown slightly. Remove with a spatula and drain on kitchen paper before adding them to the pan of coconut chickpeas or serving them separately. Add any oil left in the frying pan, too.

Garnish the sweet potato and coconut chickpeas the green part of the spring onions.

"Corned beef"

Corned beef is one of those foods so ingrained in Jamaican society, you'd think it was from there. However, the staunch red metallic cans perfectly stuffed with mystery meat are a back-of-the-cupboard dweller in homes from the Philippines and Brazil to Israel, as they are in the Caribbean.

The legacy of this inexpensive protein goes back to the era of slavery when colonial settlers are said to have imported it. It was also produced in local pens and became a staple of the enslaved diet when they could purchase small amounts with money earned. As mentioned by J.B. Moreton in *West India Customs and Manners*, enslaved pregnant women were each given *"about a pound of salt beef… to comfort them"* before being sent back to the fields to work shortly after giving birth with the *"pickannies"* (children) on their backs. In contrast, plantation overseers from Europe were said to be furnished with all manner of complementary rations, including salted beef in abundance.

Over the centuries and years, when Irish and English canned "Bully Beef" imports drove the price down, the popularity of corned beef boomed. After independence a great deal of Jamaicans remained financially constrained, both on the island and in the diaspora, so cheap Bully Beef continued to be popular; it has since become almost a tradition passed down from generation to generation as a form of sustenance.

Growing up and finding out corned beef was for tea, wasn't the most exciting news. For me, the trick was to surround the corned beef with enough Hardo Bread (see p208) or white rice, steamed cabbage and dollops of ketchup to mask the taste. Naturally, as I've got older, I have never found reason to forego almost any other meal in the world to use corned beef, however, when a friend made this somewhat tastier vegan version for me using soya-based mince, it instantly conjured up a nostalgia that only the multi-sensory aspect of food can. This is the recipe that recreates a childhood tea.

SERVES 4

200g (7oz) dried soya mince (plant-based ground mince)
3 tbsp coconut oil
2 onions, finely chopped
1 rib of celery, finely chopped
1 tsp sea salt
3 garlic cloves, minced
250g (9oz) mushrooms, finely diced
100g (3½oz) tomato purée (tomato paste)
1 tbsp nutritional yeast flakes (optional)
1 tsp dried thyme
2 tsp All-purpose Seasoning (see p239)
1 tsp garlic powder (optional)
250–400g (9–14oz) canned chopped tomatoes
1 potato, peeled and diced
75ml (⅓ cup) soy sauce
freshly ground black pepper

———

Put the mince in a large bowl, pour over enough hot water to cover and leave to rehydrate for 5 minutes. Drain, then squeeze the mince, a handful at a time, to remove any excess water. Set aside until needed.

Heat the oil in a large saucepan over a medium heat. Add the onions and celery and sauté for 2 minutes, adding the salt while you stir. Stir in the garlic, then the mushrooms and cook for 2 minutes.

Add the tomato purée and cook for a few minutes, stirring, before adding the mince. Continue to cook until the mince takes on a reddish-brown hue. Add the nutritional yeast flakes, if using, the thyme, all-purpose seasoning and garlic powder.

Stir the mixture ensuring everything is combined, then add the tomatoes and a splash of water if the sauce looks dry. Add the potato and cook for 3 minutes, stirring. Stir in the soy sauce, then cover the pan with the lid, turn the heat down and simmer for 10 minutes, stirring occasionally, until the potato is tender. Season with pepper.

Serve with rice, Steamed Vegetables (see p52), Fried Plantain (see p61) and Scotch Bonnet Ketchup (see p243), if you like.

Peppered tofu

While tofu was made, cooked and publicly served by those of Chinese descent for many years it became more mainstream in Jamaica in the mid-1980s. Yet, for as long as tofu, and soya, has been available in Jamaica, its presence has been the cause of much culinary contention.

Even though soya is inherently meat free, the overtly processed nature of it means many Rastas shy away from eating it, though they may still sell it at their eateries in the form of veggie chunks and tofu. One of the dishes that has popped up at many of the Ital shacks and restaurants is this sticky, sweet and sour vegan version of Peppered Steak (see p138), which is influenced by the country's Chinese heritage. Strips of beef steak are reimagined in the form of tofu, residing in a thickened sweet soy sauce blend that you'll be hard-pressed not to enjoy every last scraping of.

———

SERVES 4

400g (14oz) firm tofu, drained well, patted dry and cut into 2.5cm (1in) wide slices (they can be different lengths for visual appeal)
5 tbsp light soy sauce
4 tbsp cornflour (corn starch)
2 tbsp black soy sauce, tomato ketchup or Scotch Bonnet Ketchup (see page 243)
1 tsp browning (optional)
5 tsp apple cider vinegar
3 tbsp maple syrup or light soft brown sugar
4 tbsp rapeseed oil
½ onion, thinly sliced
2 spring onions (scallions), white and green parts separated, thinly sliced
3 sprigs of thyme
½ Scotch bonnet pepper, deseeded and thinly sliced
3–4 garlic cloves, minced
2.5cm (1in) piece of fresh root ginger, peeled and minced
½ carrot, cut into julienne
1 red bell pepper, deseeded and sliced
½ tomato, chopped (optional)

Put the tofu in a shallow bowl and add the soy sauce. Gently turn the tofu until coated, taking care not to break up the slices. Add 3 tablespoons of the cornflour, then turn to coat all sides of the tofu and set aside.

In a bowl, combine the black soy sauce or ketchup, browning, if using, vinegar, maple syrup or sugar and 90ml (⅓ cup) water, then set aside. In a separate bowl, mix 3 tablespoons water with the remaining cornflour.

Heat 3 tablespoons of the oil in a large wok or frying pan over a medium heat. Fry the tofu, in batches, for a few minutes on each side until golden brown. Drain on kitchen paper while you cook the rest of the tofu, adding more oil when needed. Drain and set aside.

Wipe the wok or pan clean, heat the remaining oil over a medium-high heat. Add the onion, spring onions, saving some of the green part to garnish, thyme and Scotch bonnet. Stir-fry for 3–5 minutes before adding the garlic and ginger, then cook for another 2 minutes.

Add the black soy sauce mixture and stir to combine. Next, add the cornflour-water and cook, stirring, for 1–2 minutes, until the sauce starts to thicken.

Add the carrot, bell pepper and tomato, if using, and 3 tablespoons water and stir until combined. Cover with the lid and cook for 2 minutes. Add the tofu and heat through, adding an extra 2–3 tablespoons water if needed. Cover and heat through before serving topped with the green part of the spring onions.

Rice – the universal equalizer

While in Europe the likes of Aesop's Fables have pervaded for millennia as hand-me-down moral tales, children from staunch Afro-Caribbean families may be familiar with the Anansi spider stories. A particular tale reproduced in *365 Folk Tales* springs to mind mainly because it reminds me of my younger self (or even now to be honest). It goes:

"Once there was a drought. Anansi the spider was very unhappy. All his people were starving. He left his village to find food for his people and himself. He walked many miles, until at last he saw smoke from a distant village. When he reached there, the only food he found was cassava.

One cassava asked Anansi, 'Would you like us roasted, fried or boiled?' Anansi told them he had no particular choice, so they roasted themselves. He was just about to eat them when he noticed smoke at a distance. He came to know from the cassavas that the smoke was emanating from the town of rice. 'Rice is much better food. Who wants to eat roasted cassava?' he thought to himself. With this, he trekked towards the town of rice.

When he reached the town of rice, after a similar exchange, he again noticed smoke in the distance. He left the rice village and went towards the smoke hoping he would get something better than rice. But alas! When he reached there, he found it was his own village. And he had no food for his villagers or himself.

His greed had led him nowhere."

The tale focusses on teaching us the shortcomings of ungratefulness, greed and jealousy. However, it also unintentionally touches on the idea that there are times when there's nothing better than a hearty bowl of rice, be it to bolster a meal or served on its own, flavoured with seasonings and vegetables, or perhaps with a generous helping of spiced gravy.

Like the Anansi stories (*Anansi* meaning "spider" in Akan, the principal native language of the Akan people of Ghana), the origin of rice consumption in Jamaica and the rest of the Caribbean can seemingly be attributed to the enslaved West Africans ferried to the island region by European and American colonizers. With the arrival of East Indian people cultivation was revived to the point that rice became a daily food for all classes of Jamaican, including the enslaved. In the scorching heat of the plantations, the production of crops, such as rice, provided important sustenance. While the enslaved were stripped of their names, identity and various facets of their culture, what couldn't be removed was their oral traditions, of which food played a large part.

For me, there's no real difference between folk tales and recipes, only the latter is now often reduced to a strict science and set of rules. In the same way folk tales mutate and morph like a children's game of telephone whispers, so do recipes. I don't really believe there's one correct authentic recipe for any meal. There's a reason why even the most traditional of dishes, like rice and peas, have hundreds of variations from family to family, and island to island. We adapt tales to suit our surroundings in the same way we adapt recipes, while ensuring we keep as true to the fundamental principles as much as possible and honouring those before us.

Rice is a universal equalizer across cultures, from the southern tip of Chile to the most northern part of Japan. For me, there are many simple rice dishes that help to introduce and convey the beauty and depth of Caribbean-inspired cooking and flavours.

Rice & peas

My early morning jaunts to Kumasi Market in Ghana's Ashanti region reminded me of some of the Jamaican dishes I'd grown up eating. While the majority of roadside vendors selling stews or meals like *kenkey* (dumplings) and fish weren't open, the small stalls were. They sold *hausa koko* porridge, baked pastries or a dish called *waakye* (pronounced *wah-chay*): a glorious combination of dried fish, garri powder, perhaps a hard-boiled egg, spicy fish paste and some greens atop a mixture of deep chestnut-brown rice and dark brown beans. This immediately took me back to the Jamaican rice and peas I'd eaten as a young boy.

This coincidence appears to be no coincidence at all. The pairing of rice and beans have their origins in the Akan, Aja, Yoruba and Igbo domains of West Africa, from Senegal to Nigeria. When these people were transplanted to the Americas, both north and south, and the Caribbean, the memory of rice and beans came with them. In Jamaica, rice wasn't as plentiful as root vegetables, hence Hard Food (see p56) replaced rice as a staple filler but on Sundays, a day the enslaved traditionally had off work, rice and beans was on the menu. This veneration of rice and peas lives on today and thanks to innovations like quick rice and canned beans, the dish transitioned from a weekday rarity to an everyday occurrence, though for proper rice and peas you still need to allocate a night for soaking the peas. Before red kidney beans became a popular pairing, the dish was originally known to feature the European-named gungo (deriving from Congo) peas, sometimes known as pigeon peas, and hence the moniker "rice and peas". In many Caribbean islands and diaspora cookshops, the dish is still served this way. Given this history, you can imagine the collective gasps from the Caribbean community the first time we saw rice and peas made with garden-variety green peas.

Of all the Jamaican dishes from my childhood, I admit I found rice and peas the most difficult to get to grips with. This likely stemmed from a pre-existing, mini-phobia of cooking rice (sometimes too soggy, sometimes burnt with blackened-pot bottom, and so on). With my mum using one hand to take her daily 3-hour phone call to her cousin and the other to show me her basically foolproof, mainly open-pot technique for cooking rice, I'm now pleased to say any phobia has since passed. This method may seem bizarre at first, but I'm assured this is how her "olders did it" and the saying at our local football club "trust the process" seems very apt here.

If you're looking for a quick way to make the dish, check out the version with canned, rather than dried, beans instead.

200g (7oz) dried kidney beans, soaked overnight, or 400g (14oz) can kidney beans, not drained
2 spring onions (scallions), left whole
2 sprigs of thyme
2.5cm (1in) piece of fresh root ginger, peeled and thickly sliced
2–3 garlic cloves, sliced
½ white onion, chopped (optional)
200ml (¾ cup) coconut milk
300g (10oz) basmati rice, thoroughly washed and drained
1 Scotch bonnet pepper, whole (optional)
1 tbsp vegan butter (optional)
1 tbsp desiccated coconut, or 1 tbsp coconut cream (optional)

FOR THE SEASONING:

1 tsp All-purpose Seasoning (see p239) (optional)
1 tsp black soy sauce or browning (optional)
1 tsp freshly ground black pepper
1 tsp light soft brown sugar (optional)
1 tsp sea salt
6 pimento seeds (allspice berries), crushed, or ½ tsp ground allspice

"Traditional way" with dried kidney beans

Drain and rinse the soaked dried beans (if using canned beans see the "Quick Way" below.) Put the beans into a saucepan or Dutch pot with 800ml (3⅓ cups) water and bring to the boil over a high heat. Boil the beans for 10 minutes, then turn the heat down to medium, add the spring onions, thyme, ginger, garlic and onion, if using, and cook for 1 hour, until the beans have softened. To check, try to mash a bean with a fork and if it is fairly tender then proceed, if not carry on cooking. If the water has evaporated, top up with an extra 200ml (¾ cup).

Add the seasoning ingredients to the beans. Next, add the coconut milk and rice, then stir (the liquid should be about 5mm/¼in above the rice.) Turn the heat up to high and boil for 3 minutes, then turn the heat down to medium, add the Scotch bonnet, if using, and cook for about 15 minutes, until the liquid has been absorbed. Stir intermittently to ensure the rice doesn't stick to the bottom of the pan. Taste the rice and adjust the seasoning to your preference.

Turn the heat down to the lowest setting, stir in the vegan butter and desiccated or coconut cream, if using. Place foil over the top of the pan or pot to stop the steam escaping, cover with the lid, then cook gently for 15 minutes without lifting the lid.

Finally, turn the heat off, remove the thyme sprigs, ginger and spring onions, fluff up the rice with a fork and leave to rest covered with the foil and lid on for another 10 minutes before serving.

"Quick way" with canned kidney beans

Empty the kidney beans and any liquid in the can into a pan or pot. Add the seasoning ingredients and the spring onions, thyme, ginger, garlic and onion, if using. Add roughly 3 tablespoons water or enough to swill out the can. Bring to the boil over a medium heat and cook for 10–15 minutes, until heated through. Mash some of the beans with a fork.

Next, add the coconut milk and rice, then stir (the liquid should be about 5mm/¼in above the rice). Continue the recipe as instructed above.

Turmeric & pumpkin rice

Just east of Port Antonio, along the coast, lies a small community named Drapers, one of the most magical corners of Jamaica. While the area is peppered with boutique hotels, guesthouses and such, until recently the lack of any cruise ship ports meant that anyone who ended up this side of Portland knew exactly what they were doing there.

Most fresh produce stands have an air of mysticism about them in the Caribbean. Bananas the size of pinky fingers, cashew nuts with the fruit still attached, and a general array of island goods that don't usually make their way across the Atlantic. In Drapers, however, at the foot of a hill a stone's throw from the Caribbean Sea ocean front is Mama Earth fruit stand. To call it a market stall is an understatement since it also provides an educational and medicinal service of sorts to the local populace and those who make the trip across Portland Parish to visit.

As if the seemingly endless assortment of whole foods wasn't amazing enough, the cordial co-owner, who goes by the name of Papa San and his wife, Mama Earth, tell me that if I fancy a meal made with their produce, they can cook it for me the next day. Seeing all the fresh goods, I conceived a meal that I'd never come across before – rice-infused with raw turmeric, glowing orange pumpkin and spices, sweetened with plantain, then complemented with all the hard food trimmings to test their prowess. Papa, without batting an eyelid, asked me what time I wanted it, then told me not to be late.

The next day, having spent it west of Port Antonio in Hope Bay, some 15 miles-away, and requiring a change of route taxi at the petrol station in Port Antonio, I was late. By the time I arrived, another hungry reveller had liked the sound of my glorious invention, so I didn't get to enjoy the full portion, but what I did have stays with me to this day and I often try to recreate it at home.

SERVES 4

250g (9oz) basmati rice,
  thoroughly washed and drained
pinch of sea salt, plus extra for
  the mash
1 tsp ground turmeric

FOR THE PUMPKIN MASH:

2 tbsp coconut oil, or oil of choice
½ onion, finely diced
2 spring onions (scallions), chopped
2 garlic cloves, minced
½ rib of celery, chopped
½ tsp ground turmeric
½ tsp All-purpose Seasoning
  (see p239)
1 tsp finely grated fresh root
  ginger, or ground ginger
300g (10oz) pumpkin, peeled,
  deseeded and diced
½ ripe plantain, peeled and diced
400ml (13.5fl oz) can coconut milk
200g (7oz) can butter beans
  (lima beans), drained (optional)
freshly ground black pepper

Add the rice to your saucepan or Dutch pot and pour in enough water to cover by 1cm (½in). Bring to the boil over a high heat and add the salt and turmeric. After the pot has been boiling for a minute, turn the heat down to low, cover with the lid and simmer for 15–20 minutes, until the water has been absorbed and the rice is tender.

Meanwhile, make the pumpkin mash. Heat the oil in a large pan over a medium heat. Add the onion, spring onions, garlic and celery. Sauté for 2 minutes, then add the turmeric, all-purpose seasoning and ginger, stirring for another 2 minutes.

Next, add the pumpkin and plantain and cook for 1 minute, stirring. Add the coconut milk, turn the heat to high and bring to the boil, then reduce the heat to medium. Cover with the lid and simmer for 10 minutes.

Using a potato masher or fork, lightly mash the pumpkin, leaving some chunks. Stir in the butter beans, if using. Cover for 5 minutes to heat through and season with salt and pepper to taste. At this point, you can either add the rice to the pan and stir to combine, or serve the pumpkin mixture on top of the rice. Serve with Hard Food (see p56) and salad.

Guinea corn salad

From the cotton fields of Mississippi to the sugar plantations of Jamaica, the oral tradition of call and response songs by the enslaved, rooted in their African heritage, were key in getting through the day. Under the thumb of both a non-forgiving enslaver and equally unrelenting sun, the chorus produced solace of sorts. This song was recorded in 1797 based on the words of J.B. Moreton, a British writer who frequented Clarendon in Jamaica, and reproduced in *The Penguin Book of Caribbean Verse in English*. It recalls a longing for the past home comfort – guinea corn.

> *Guinea Corn, I long to see you*
> *Guinea Corn, I long to plant you*
> *Guinea Corn, I long to mould you*
> *Guinea Corn, I long to weed you*
> *Guinea Corn, I long to hoe you*
> *Guinea Corn, I long to top you*
> *Guinea Corn, I long to cut you*
> *Guinea Corn, I long to dry you*
> *Guinea Corn, I long to beat you*
> *Guinea Corn, I long to trash you*
> *Guinea Corn, I long to parch you*
> *Guinea Corn, I long to grind you*
> *Guinea Corn, I long to turn you*
> *Guinea Corn, I long to eat you*

Guinea corn, a grain known as sorghum, or *jowar* in some parts of the world, has existed in Jamaica as far back as the late 1600s, primarily since planters shared knowledge of its prowess in feeding stock. Native to Africa, it is no surprise that African descendants were adept in utilizing it in the likes of nutritionally rich porridges and breads. To keep the spirit of this grain alive, I wanted to create something nutritious and easy, combining an array of fresh produce found both in Jamaica and across the world.

SERVES 2 (OR 4 AS A SIDE)

100g (3½oz) sorghum
½ x 400g (14oz) can chickpeas,
    drained and rinsed
300g (10oz) butternut squash,
    pumpkin or sweet potato,
    peeled, deseeded and diced
3 tbsp olive oil
1 tsp All-purpose Seasoning
    (see p239)
1 tsp freshly ground black pepper
1 tsp paprika or Cajun seasoning
    (optional)
½ red onion, sliced or diced
5–8 cherry tomatoes
25g (1oz) baby spinach leaves,
    or any salad leaf
¼ cucumber, diced
1 tbsp pumpkin seeds
1 tbsp sunflower seeds
1 tsp dried chilli flakes (optional)
1 avocado, peeled, stone removed
    and finely diced (optional)

FOR THE DRESSING:

2 tbsp olive oil
1 tbsp apple cider vinegar
juice of ½ lime
1 tsp light soft brown sugar
½ tsp sea salt

Put the sorghum in a bowl and cover with water. Leave to soak for a minimum of 6 hours, but ideally overnight. When soaked, drain and set aside.

Preheat the oven to 200°C (180°C fan/400°F/Gas 6) and line a baking tray with baking paper.

Put the soaked sorghum in a medium saucepan and cover with water, about 500ml (generous 2 cups). Bring to the boil, then turn the heat down to low and simmer with the lid on. The timing depends on how you like the sorghum: drain after 30–45 minutes for al dente; after 1 hour for regular; and 80–90 minutes for a very soft grain. Put the sorghum in a serving bowl.

In a separate bowl, place the chickpeas and butternut squash, or alternative, and drizzle over the olive oil. Add the all-purpose seasoning, half the black pepper and paprika or Cajun seasoning and toss until everything is coated in the spice mix. Tip onto the lined baking tray and roast for 10 minutes, turning once. Add the onion and tomatoes and cook for a further 5–8 minutes, until softened and starting to colour.

Meanwhile, mix all the ingredients for the dressing together in a bowl.

Add the roasted chickpeas and vegetables to the large bowl with the sorghum. Add the spinach, cucumber, seeds, chilli flakes and avocado, if using. Pour the dressing over and toss until combined.

Spiced lentils

While the likes of dahl and kitchri are a mainstream part of culinary life in the eastern reaches of the Caribbean with sizeable Indian populations, in Jamaica the humble pulse is somewhat less common. In the jerk shacks that line the hills and roadsides, rice is the filler of choice, while at the small Indian-descended, family-owned joints – and especially at the Rastafari Ital food spots – lentils are heavily leaned on to shore up the marvellous feasts packed onto plates or into Styrofoam takeout boxes. With this in mind, this recipe serves as a great main meal, or side dish, nestled between a sauce-heavy curry and rice, or even as a filling for Yatties (see p196).

Although, this lentil dish features a dose of jerk seasoning I won't continue the horror by calling it jerk lentils. My issue with the whole "jerk rice fiasco" a while back wasn't with the idea of people from different cultures finding inspiration in Caribbean food, in fact I wish it happened more often, it's just that sometimes the end result is so misleading that it stands to erase a whole cultural history. In short, you can't just sprinkle some jerk spice on something and call it jerk!

―――

Add the dried lentils to a saucepan or Dutch pot and cover with water (if using ready-cooked lentils skip to the next step). Bring to the boil, then turn the heat down and simmer for 20–30 minutes, until tender. Drain and set aside.

Heat the oil in the pan or pot over a medium heat. Add the onion and 1 spring onion and sauté for 2 minutes, then add the garlic and cook for another minute.

Next, stir in the cooked lentils until combined. Add the jerk seasoning (if you are using shop bought, you'll likely need to add the brown sugar). Stir in the thyme and all-purpose seasoning, if using, then season with salt and pepper to taste. Add 1 tablespoon water, stir and cook for a further 5 minutes. If the lentils need to be cooked a little longer, cover with the lid, turn down the heat to medium-low and cook for another 3–5 minutes, adding a splash more water if needed.

SERVES 4 (OR 6 AS A SIDE)

250g (9oz) dried black or brown lentils, rinsed thoroughly, or 2 x 250g (9oz) packs ready-cooked Puy or beluga lentils
1 tbsp coconut oil, or oil of choice
½ onion, finely chopped
2 spring onions (scallions), finely chopped
2–3 garlic cloves, minced
2 tbsp Jerk Seasoning (see p238), or shop bought
1–2 tsp light soft brown sugar, to taste (optional)
1 sprig of thyme
1 tsp All-purpose Seasoning (see p239) (optional)
sea salt and freshly ground black pepper

Tun cornmeal

SERVES 2 (OR 4 AS A SIDE)

175g (6oz) fine cornmeal
1 tbsp coconut oil
½ white onion, chopped
1 spring onion (scallion), whole
3 garlic cloves, minced
½ tomato, chopped
⅓ red or green bell pepper,
    deseeded and chopped
    (optional)
2 sprigs of thyme
1 tsp All-purpose Seasoning
    (see p239)
1 tsp freshly ground black pepper
200ml (¾ cup) coconut milk
1 tbsp vegan butter
1 tsp sea salt
1 tsp dark soft brown sugar

I remember when I turned thirteen or fourteen and started getting pocket money, I had an epiphany that I could buy and eat cereal whenever I wanted – any time of the day, not just for breakfast. I think many people must have had the same realization with tun cornmeal, a porridge-type dish, steeped in coconut milk and balanced with sugar, salt and spices, and sometimes with added savoury-tasting vegetables. It used to be reserved for the early hours of the day, but it's so delicious that over the years it has found its way onto lunch and dinner menus, often with steamed veg, beside or sometimes mixed with okra and even fish. While not overly common at regular Jamaican and Caribbean eating outfits, at the Rastafari Ital shops its meek, yellow-mashed presence is almost guaranteed.

The term "*tun*", a patois variant of turn, is said to come from the action of turning the cornmeal as it cooks, and while it looks simple to make, the number of variations is surely in the thousands. If you didn't grow up with tun cornmeal and therefore don't have any nostalgic attachment to it made in a certain way, try as many variations as possible, including this one.

———

In a bowl, mix 150ml (⅔ cup) water with the cornmeal to a dry mashed potato-like consistency. Set aside.

Heat the oil in a heavy-based saucepan or Dutch pot over a medium heat. Add the onion, spring onion and garlic and sauté for 3–5 minutes. Next, add the tomato, red or green bell pepper, thyme, all-purpose seasoning and pepper and sauté, stirring, for another 2–3 minutes.

Add the coconut milk and butter, turn the heat up a notch and stir for 1–2 minutes, until the butter melts.

Gradually add the cornmeal-water mix in heaped tablespoons. Stir well between each spoonful and repeat until all the cornmeal has been added. Make sure you do this quickly to stop the cornmeal becoming too stiff and difficult to stir. It may seem too dry, but the steam in the pan will moisten it in time.

Turn the heat down to very low, cover with the lid and simmer for 20 minutes, stirring occasionally. Remove the thyme and spring onion, then stir in the salt and sugar, cover the pan and simmer for another 10 minutes, until a smooth porridge-like consistency.

Steamed vegetables

It's easy to feel overawed by the kaleidoscope of fresh produce in Jamaica and the wider Caribbean. A whole new ABC of ingredients to learn, from ackee and breadfruit to callaloo and beyond can understandably be dizzying for the newcomer. While those superstars of Jamaica's culinary roster are frequently celebrated and reminisced, I'd like to heap praise on the uncomplicated and effortlessly comforting dish of steamed vegetables. Always there, burrowed between rice and curry, tucked behind a stewed fish or underneath a baked chicken, propping up a meal without any fanfare.

Centuries-old accounts of Jamaican cabbage observe it being *"white as Milk, and sweet as a Nut, when eaten Raw; and when boiled not unlike common Cabbage, but much sweeter"*. (J.P. Greene, J. Knight. *The Natural, Moral, and Political History of Jamaica, and the Territories Thereon Depending.*) Beyond the necessities of nourishment, perhaps, its pleasing taste is the reason the dish has continued to be a meal anchor after all these years. Cabbage is the only real requirement in this dish, but feel free to add any other light vegetables you have, such as peas, sweetcorn, broccoli or even okra.

––––––

Soak the cabbage, carrots and red or yellow bell pepper in salted water for 10–15 minutes. Drain, then place in a large bowl with the spring onion, if using, and thyme. Toss the vegetables with your hands, then add the coconut oil and continue mixing with your hands until combined.

Pour 2 tablespoons water into a heavy-based saucepan or non-stick pan, swirl it around and place over a medium heat. (It's best to use a heavy-based saucepan to prevent the cabbage burning.)

Add the contents of your bowl to the pan with the salt and pepper. Cover with the lid and simmer for 10 minutes, making sure the vegetables don't burn or stick. Add an extra tablespoon of water and check the seasoning; try not to let too much steam escape when lifting the lid.

Cover again and cook for a further 5 minutes, until the cabbage has wilted and is slightly translucent. Taste, then remove the pan from the heat, stir in the spinach and leave to sit with the lid on for a further 5–10 minutes, until wilted.

SERVES 2 (OR 4 AS A SIDE)

200g (7oz) white cabbage, shredded
2 carrots, cut into julienne
½ red or yellow bell pepper, deseeded and chopped
1 spring onion (scallion), chopped (optional)
1 tsp dried thyme
2 tbsp coconut oil
½ tsp sea salt
½ tsp freshly ground black pepper
20g (¾oz) baby leaf spinach

Veggie chunks

SERVES 2–4

3 tbsp rapeseed oil

1 tbsp curry powder

1–2 tsp All-purpose Seasoning
(see p239)

200g (7oz) plain soya veggie
chunks or TVP, rinsed and
soaked for 15 minutes in
hot water until rehydrated,
then drained and squeezed
of excess water

6 pimento seeds (allspice berries),
crushed, or ½ tsp ground
allspice

4 sprigs of thyme,
or 1 tsp dried thyme

3 garlic cloves, minced

1 tbsp minced fresh root ginger,
or 1 tsp ground ginger

1 onion, finely chopped

2–3 spring onions (scallions),
finely chopped

¼ red bell pepper, deseeded
and sliced

½–1 Scotch bonnet pepper
(depending on preferred heat)

1 carrot, thinly sliced into rounds

1 tomato, finely chopped

250ml (1 cup plus 1 tbsp) hot water

250ml (1 cup plus 1 tbsp)
coconut milk

½ x 400g (14oz) can chickpeas,
drained

175g (6oz) potato, peeled and
cut into chunks, or Spinners
or Boiled Dumplings (see p57)

sea salt and freshly ground
black pepper

parsley or coriander (cilantro),
to garnish

1 lime, cut into wedges, to serve

The first time I ever had veggie chunks was at the now sadly departed Ital 'n' Vital takeout in Tottenham, North London. Long before vegan food became vogue, here chef-owner Rasta Ramses served up wholesome Ital flavours for decades with his take on Ital stew, ackee and tofu, steamed veg and, of course, all the mandatory hard food additions. One of the more relatively unknown dishes, placed at the bottom of his menu was "chunks", also known as veggie chunks.

Made from soya or textured vegetable protein (TVP), these chunks became the perfect resource for Rastafari sustenance since being dried meant it could be stored with ease, regardless of temperature, for months or years, then soaked and boiled when needed. With its spongy texture, able to absorb the flavours of herbs and spices, it became the perfect vegan conduit to replace meat in the wide array of Jamaican dishes that vegans would otherwise shy away from, such as brown stews and rundowns. Think of this recipe, found in Ital spots from Mandeville to Miami and Manchester, as a vegan version of curry goat of sorts, if you squint your eyes.

———

Mix 1 tablespoon of the oil in a bowl with the curry powder and 1 teaspoon all-purpose seasoning. Add the chunks and turn to coat them in the seasoning. Next, add the pimento or allspice, thyme, garlic, ginger, half the onion and spring onions, the red bell pepper, Scotch bonnet and half the carrot and mix to combine. Cover the bowl and leave to marinate in the fridge for 30 minutes, or ideally a few hours.

Heat the remaining oil in a large saucepan or Dutch pot over a medium heat. Add the veggie chunks and the rest of the contents of the bowl, then add the tomato.

Pour the hot water into the bowl, swish it around to remove any remnants of the marinade and pour it into the pan or pot. Add the coconut milk and let the liquid come to the boil. Stir, then turn the heat down to medium-low, cover with the lid and simmer for 10–15 minutes.

Add the other half of the onion, spring onions and carrot and stir. Add the chickpeas, potato or spinners/dumplings and stir again. Turn the heat down to low and simmer for 15 minutes, until the potato is tender. Check the seasoning, adding more if needed. Garnish with herbs and serve with wedges of lime.

Hard food

Almost every day, no matter the time of year or what else was cooking, my grandmother, Mavis, always had a pot boiling in the afternoon. Submerged in bubbling, boiling water was a combination of yams, potatoes, pumpkin and dumplings that would accompany anything from chicken kiev to roast lamb. To this day, the taste of a lightly salted yam still reminds me of her. Like the sun setting, or the BBC News at 10, it was something I didn't question because it just happened, and most likely would happen the next day. It wasn't until she passed away and that tomorrow stopped that I realized I'd never asked her why, after all those years living in London, this was so entrenched in her daily routine.

"Food" or "hard food", as I've known it, has been the sustenance of Jamaicans for half a millennium onwards. Enslaved Jamaicans mostly lived at subsistence level and in harsh times they faced famine and death, so any way of bolstering meals was literally a matter of life and death. The indigenous Taino peoples were said to rely greatly on root crops, such as the sweet potato. Those of West African descent, especially the Igbo people, looked to highly revered foods, such as yam and cassava. In addition, when flour became a permanent fixture on the island, boiled journey cakes (dumplings) served the same purpose.

Such was the importance of this group of starchy foods that it begot the alias of "food" as simply no meal was complete without it. Others may know this group of foods as "ground provisions" or "provisions". The "provision ground system" that enslaved Africans protested for was an arrangement where areas of land were allocated to them for the production of most of their food, during the time they weren't labouring for the planter. In 1739, Bajan writer, Charles Leslie wrote, *"No Country excels (Jamaica) in a barbarous Treatment of Slaves"*, and with this came the need for maximizing nutrition at every meal, while minimizing the expense.

The produce grown on these plots favoured the vegetables the overwhelmingly West African populace of enslaved people already knew how to cultivate, and which the colonial slave ships transported. Yams were key, but also dasheen and various types of banana joined the roster. As poverty became hereditary for a great deal of Jamaicans after emancipation and independence, the culinary traditions of their ancestors remained, and still does to this day.

Now my grandma's daily routine makes sense to me. She didn't have a yard or balcony in her Hackney flat but if she did, I'm sure she would have attempted to grow the contents of the boiling pot herself. In the same fashion as her, and to save hob space, cook everything in the same pot and remove according to the time suggested. Choose from the following (see right), scooping them out with a slotted spoon once cooked. They all serve about four.

Spinners or Boiled dumplings

125g (1 cup minus 1 tbsp) plain (all-purpose) or
   wholemeal flour, plus extra for dusting
1 tsp sea salt
1 tsp coconut flakes (optional)
1 tbsp fine cornmeal (optional)

Combine the flour with ½ teaspoon salt and
the optional ingredients in a mixing bowl.
Gradually pour in 4 tablespoons water with
one hand, while mixing everything together
with the other to form a dough. If the mix is
too wet add more flour, and extra water if too
dry, until you can roll the dough between your
hands without it leaving any sticky residue.
Wrap in cling film, place in a bowl and chill
for 30 minutes.

Bring a large saucepan or Dutch pot
of salted water to the boil over a high heat.

For spinners, divide the dough into
6–8 equal-sized pieces. Roll each one on
a lightly floured work surface into the shape
and size of your little finger.

For dumplings, divide the dough into
3 equal-sized pieces, each slightly larger than
a golf ball. Roll each one into a ball on a lightly
floured work surface, then slightly flatten the
top with your palm. Using your thumb, lightly
press the middle of each dumpling.

Cook the spinners or dumplings in a large
pan or pot of boiling water for 10–12 minutes,
until they are no longer soft or doughy; don't
overcook them or they will become soggy.
Remove with a slotted spoon and drain well.

Yam, dasheen, pumpkin, potato or sweet potato

250g (9oz) root vegetables of choice,
   peeled and diced to preference
sea salt

Bring a saucepan or Dutch pot of salted water
to the boil over a high heat, then turn the heat
down to medium. Place the vegetables of
choice into the pan and boil for 15–20 minutes,
until tender. Drain before serving.

Green banana

1–2 green bananas, topped and tailed, make
   a skin-deep lengthways cut along the middle
sea salt

Bring a saucepan or Dutch pot of salted water
to the boil over a high heat, then turn the heat
down to medium. Place the green bananas
in the pot and boil for 20–25 minutes, until
tender. Drain, peel and chop before serving.

Breadfruit

Growing up I've seen breadfruit cooked and roasted anywhere heat could be summoned, be it on a grill made from an old car wheel or over a backyard fire. The light green, hard-bodied fruit is placed over a high heat and cooked until jet-black and the shell exterior peels away with a delicate touch, exposing a soft, pillowy interior – not too dissimilar to bread!

Everyone I've met, not from the Caribbean, has ever heard of it confirming, like many other culinary illusions of grandeur, that surely breadfruit MUST be Jamaican. However, when a friend mentioned in passing that her family, who hailed from the South Pacific Islands some 9,000 miles away, regularly ate breadfruit I was intrigued.

Of course, that connection was no coincidence. Late 18th-century tropical storms had devastated Caribbean plantations along with wheat fields and provision grounds used to feed the enslaved with crops like yams and bananas. Without this sustenance the foundations of the sugar pyramid would crumble. Breadfruit, on the other hand, was seen as bread and fruit, without the effort required of either. It was hardy, seasonal for nearly three quarters of the year, used relatively little land and with very little cultivation, which was a fantasy to the British plantation owners.

The French, like the British, had a colonial presence around the globe and had already started transporting breadfruit from French Polynesia to the likes of St. Vincent and the French Guiana.

The British captured a French ship that contained, among other things, breadfruit, however, they discovered the breadfruit tree couldn't be grown from seed. After a failed attempt at transporting the tree in 1789, which led to the famous tale of Captain William Bligh and the Mutiny on the Bounty, a few years later, records suggest that *"347 plants of the breadfruit arrived on 5 February 1793"*, on Bligh's HMS Providence, brought from Otaheite (Tahiti) and *"distributed through the island"*.

Ironically, breadfruit was initially shunned by the enslaved population and was used only for animal fodder until it grew in popularity after the emancipation.

Today, breadfruit in Jamaica is mainly eaten in the same way as it was back then – baked, fried and grilled – served with Ackee & Saltfish (see p158) as a traditional breakfast or as a side to any dish.

Bake

Preheat the oven to 200°C (180°C fan/400°F/Gas 6).

Using a sharp knife, cut an X into the base of the breadfruit to prevent it bursting when baking. Cut out the stem and discard. Coat the breadfruit in 1 tablespoon oil, then place directly on the oven rack and bake for 1½ hours, until steaming and the skin browns. (If using less than a whole breadfruit, wrap in foil to prevent the inside drying out and burning.) Leave to cool slightly.

Remove the skin with a knife, like peeling a potato, then cut the breadfruit in half and cut out the core. Cut each half in two, then cut each one lengthways into 2 or 3 slices. Alternatively, cut the slices into bite-sized chunks.

Fry

Cut out the stem of the breadfruit and discard. Remove the skin with a knife, like peeling a potato, then cut the breadfruit in half and cut out the core. Cut each half in two, then cut each one lengthways into 2 or 3 slices.

Heat 1 tablespoon oil in a large frying pan over a medium-high heat. When the oil starts to sizzle, turn the heat down to medium. Place as many slices in the pan as you can fit without overcrowding and fry for 4–5 minutes on each side, until golden yellow. Remove from the pan and drain on kitchen paper.

Grill

Using a sharp knife, cut an X into the base of the breadfruit to prevent it bursting when cooking. Cut out the stem and discard. Place the breadfruit directly on the flames of a medium gas ring and cook for 20 minutes, until blackened. Using tongs, turn the breadfruit to cook another section of it for 20 minutes, then rotate until all sides are blackened (or do this under a grill or on a barbecue). Leave to cool slightly.

Remove the skin with a knife, like peeling a potato, then cut the breadfruit in half and cut out the core. Cut each half in two, then cut each one lengthways into 2 or 3 slices. Alternatively, cut the slices into bite-sized chunks.

SERVES ABOUT 4

1 breadfruit, washed, about 500g (1lb 2oz) in total
coconut, vegetable or sunflower oil

Plantain

Heated debates in Afro-Caribbean communities around the world fiercely differ over how to pronounce the name of this staple fruit. Even the word "fruit" seems to undersell the prowess of plantain. The sound of "*plarn-tin*" or "*plann-tayne*" immediately raises ire on the opposing side. Though for the "*banana*" and "*plátano*" sayers of the world, the argument draws more bemusement than anything else.

I grew up in a proudly Caribbean family, so you can probably guess my political leaning on the matter. Technical linguistics aside, the real answer to this dilemma is whoever is serving it (and however they say it), I need to ensure I am doled out the maximum amount of plantain possible. I have to admit, I can be utterly shameless in the way I pronounce it, switching depending on whether I'm in a yard takeout or a Nigerian *buka*.

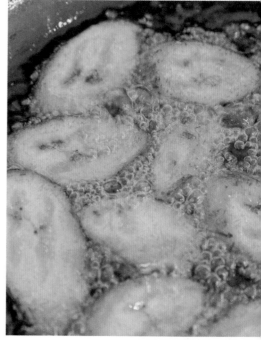

A whole tome could be written about plantain and its global movement around the world. The voyage from Southeast Asia to Africa, then Europe and the Caribbean, provides a fascinating backdrop to study migrant pathways over the last few centuries and accounts for why the plant is so renowned globally.

Originally seen as just another starchy food in the array of Hard Foods (see p56) to bolster meals, generation after generation have managed to conjure novel ways to use it However many ways there are to pronounce this wondrous food, there are tenfold ways to cook it and, like a pyramid scheme, there are dozens of ways to prep it, depending on its ripeness and with varying end results. The only time I don't add plantain to a dinner plate is if I'm making something like soup, or trying a different cuisine where plantain doesn't quite fit, but mainly it's because I've eaten it all. Depending on how I feel and what I'm cooking, these are the most frequent methods I follow.

Bake

1 plantain (yellow)
1 tbsp coconut oil, or oil of choice

—

Preheat the oven to 200°C (180°C fan/
400°F/Gas 6) and line a baking tray with
baking paper.

Top and tail the plantain, then make
a cut lengthways down the skin, not into the
fruit, to open it, and peel. Turn it on its side
so both ends point upwards and slice into
3 lengthways.

Brush with oil and bake for 20–25 minutes,
turning halfway, until golden and slightly
browned. Serve with most meals. This method
is especially useful when all four rings are
occupied and/or I want to cut down on
frying. You can also cut it into thin slices
for plantain chips.

Boil

1 plantain (yellow)
½ tsp sea salt

—

Bring a pan or pot of water to the boil over
a high heat, then turn the heat to medium.

Top and tail the plantain, then make a cut
lengthways down the skin, not into the fruit.

Add the salt to the pan, stir, then add the
plantain and boil for 15 minutes, until you
can pierce it easily with a fork. Drain, then
peel the plantain. Serve for breakfast/brunch
with other Hard Food (see p56).

Fry

1 plantain (yellow), unpeeled
2 tbsp coconut oil, or oil of choice

—

Top and tail the plantain, then make a cut
lengthways down the skin, not into the fruit,
to open it, and peel. Cut the plantain into
diagonal slices and set aside.

Heat the oil in a large frying pan over
a medium heat. Add the plantain and fry for
3 minutes on each side, or until it has changed
from yellow to golden and slightly brown.
Serve with most meals.

Press

1 plantain (green)
2 tbsp coconut oil, or oil of choice

—

Top and tail the plantain, then make
a cut lengthways down the skin, not into
the fruit, to open it, and peel. Cut into 2
or 3 slices, then halve each one lengthways.

Heat the oil in a large frying pan over
a medium heat. Add the plantain and fry for
3 minutes on each side, until the colour turns
deep yellow.

Using a spatula, lift out the plantain and
drain on kitchen paper. When cool enough
to handle, place each piece of plantain on its
side and gently squash with the flat bottom
of a bowl or plate until flattened to about 1cm
(½in) thick. Don't press too hard or quick or
it will break. Return the plantain to the pan
and fry for a further 2 minutes on each side.
Serve with fried fish dishes.

Callaloo & spinach

As great as good old-fashioned spinach is, the reduction of the native Jamaican water leaf, callaloo, to "like-spinach" is akin to comparing Harry Potter to *Lord of the Rings*, or American football to rugby. A British bureaucrat who travelled to Jamaica in the mid-1700s noted that spinach wasn't plentiful, however, *"this want is supplied by the Calliloo, which is much the same, and when picked and well dressed cannot be distinguished."* (J.P. Greene; J. Knight, *The Natural, Moral, and Political History of Jamaica, and the Territories Thereon Depending.*) I would completely disagree. Yeah, it's sort of the same if you squint, but the flavour is very different. That being said, with careful seasoning, you can create a dish with spinach that replicates this traditional callaloo recipe.

An observation the bureaucrat made that does ring true, however, is that *"it grows everywhere wild".* It's said you can grow anything in the Caribbean – just chuck some seeds down and wait. I witnessed this first-hand as some errant callaloo seeds bloomed into willowy weeds in my yard. Since the callaloo plant has historically been seen as a pest, I think our ancestors would shudder at the amount of money their offspring now have to part with to buy a can of it.

Interestingly, in Haiti, the word "callaloo" refers to okra; in other parts of the Caribbean *callalou* is made with taro leaves; and in the often-forgotten hotbed of the slave trade, Brazil, the similarly named *caruru-azedo* refers to hibiscus, known in Jamaica for its use in Sorrel (see p254).

The hearty callaloo leaf, while used to bolster a variety of dishes, makes a nourishing meal in itself, especially combined with other vegetables. This dish can be imagined as a warm salad of sorts, but it's more often served as a side to Ackee & Saltfish (see p158) or Hard Food (see p56) or as a filling for Yatties (see p196). Don't let the green fool you, this dish can be surprisingly spicy. If you cannot find callaloo, then the spinach alternative provides a more than ample green substitute.

Callaloo

Heat the oil in a large saucepan over a medium heat. Add the onion and garlic and sauté for a few minutes until slightly golden. (Some prefer to add the all-purpose seasoning and salt and pepper here, but it's optional.)

Add the carrot and cook for a few minutes, then stir in the red and green bell peppers until everything is combined.

Empty the can of callaloo into the pan, stir, then add the tomato and thyme. Cover with the lid, turn the heat down a notch and simmer for 10 minutes.

Remove the lid, take in a waft of the already amazing smell, add the all-purpose seasoning (if you haven't added it already), then season with salt and pepper to taste. Add the butter, if using. Simmer for a further 5–10 minutes, until warmed through. When ready, remove the thyme and serve.

––––

NOTE   *To make a smaller quantity, use a 280g (9½oz) can and halve the quantity of the other ingredients.*

SERVES 2 (OR 4 AS A SIDE)

1 tbsp coconut oil
½ onion, finely chopped
3 garlic cloves, minced
1 tsp All-purpose Seasoning (see p239)
1 small carrot, diced
1 bell pepper (½ red and ½ green), deseeded and diced
540g (19oz) can callaloo, drained
1 tomato, diced
1–2 sprigs of thyme
1 tbsp vegan butter (optional)
sea salt and freshly ground black pepper

Coconut spinach

Heat the oil in a large saucepan over a medium heat. Add the garlic and spring onions and sauté until slightly golden. Add the red bell pepper and carrot, if using, and cook for 1 minute, stirring, before adding the spinach. Turn the heat down slightly and keep stirring until the spinach begins to wilt.

Now, add the nutmeg, all-purpose seasoning and salt and pepper to taste. Add the coconut milk and Scotch bonnet, cover with the lid and cook for another 5 minutes, until the coconut milk and water from the spinach have almost evaporated and the leaves are tender, then serve.

SERVES 2 (OR 4 AS A SIDE)

½ tbsp coconut oil
2–3 garlic cloves, minced
2 spring onions (scallions), finely chopped
½ red bell pepper, deseeded and diced (optional)
1 carrot, cut into julienne or diced, or sliced into rounds (optional)
450g (1lb) spinach leaves, tough stalks removed, leaves chopped and washed
pinch of freshly grated nutmeg
pinch of All-purpose Seasoning (see p239)
4 tbsp coconut milk
1 Scotch bonnet pepper, whole
sea salt and freshly ground black pepper

Fritters

Rastaman Rev's guesthouse is a beautiful, multi-coloured construction off a quiet lane in Port Antonio, run by the humble but wickedly funny elder statesman, who also goes by the name of Ellery. Upstairs, amid the red, gold and green motif, a view of the blue sea peeps between the gently swaying skyline of trees. At breakfast time, between 6 and 7am, before the noise of the traffic, the seemingly everlasting construction work, dancehall-filled booming speakers and the rooster calls, the sound of the ocean gently fills the airwaves.

I stayed so long at Rev's that he entrusted me with free rein to his usually locked outdoor kitchen and shed of tools. After enquiring if I liked certain fruits, including bananas and so on, and sugar cane, he replied, "Good!" then pointed to the bushy green rampart surrounding the back of the guesthouse and told me if I wanted anything I was free to pick it myself.

Often, I watched Rev as he summoned a bag of flour contained in a twisted plastic bag, gathered whatever fruit or veg was nearby, grated it, then engaged a small gas tank to power his outdoor kitchen; a process that felt like it transcended centuries. Oil was then poured into jet-black pans and within minutes fritters were produced in all their non-uniform, imperfect goodness. Little did I know fritters were deep rooted in history. The West African process of pounding the main ingredient in a pestle, forming it into a patty with the hands and deep-frying it in vegetable oil was observed as far back as the mid-1300s in Mali.

Fritters, frittas or flittas, as some of my aunties call them, and always strictly banana or saltfish, were a weekend staple as a kid. I was often punished with stinging hands and lips for my impatience when taking them from their kitchen-paper perch while still piping-hot. Anything beyond these two styles of fritter were non-existent in my family, but at numerous Rasta outposts the fritter experimentations inspired me to try new flavours. Use the following recipes overleaf as a template for any fritter ideas you may have.

Beetroot fritters

MAKES ABOUT 8

300g (10oz) raw beetroot, peeled and finely grated
   or blended
100g (¾ cup) plain (all-purpose), or wholemeal flour
3 garlic cloves, minced
1 spring onion (scallion), finely chopped
2.5cm (1in) piece of fresh root ginger, peeled
   and minced
1 tsp sea salt
1 tsp All-purpose Seasoning (see p239)
90ml (⅓ cup) plant milk of choice, or water
3 tbsp coconut oil, or oil of choice, plus
   extra if needed

_____

Place the beetroot in a large bowl, then add
the flour and mix until combined and the
mixture turns slightly pink. Next, add
the garlic, spring onion, ginger, salt and
all-purpose seasoning and mix again. Finally,
slowly add the milk or water, and combine
until the mix turns to a thick batter.

Heat 1 tablespoon of the oil in a large
frying pan over a medium heat. Using a wet
spoon, place 1 tablespoon batter into the pan,
then add a second tablespoon of batter on top
of the first. Use the back of the spoon to
spread the batter out to a round fritter, about
6cm (2½in) diameter.

Repeat to cook a few at a time, adding
more oil when needed. Cook for 3 minutes,
then flip over and cook for a further
2 minutes, until lightly browned. Drain
on kitchen paper, keep warm, and repeat
to make about 8 fritters in total.

Spinach & tomato fritters

MAKES ABOUT 8

125g (1 cup minus 1 tbsp) plain (all-purpose),
   or wholemeal flour
50g (1¾oz) spinach leaves, tough stalks
   removed and finely chopped
2 garlic cloves, minced
1 spring onion (scallion), finely chopped
1 tomato, finely diced
½ onion, finely chopped
½ Scotch bonnet pepper, deseeded finely
   chopped (optional)
1 tsp All-purpose Seasoning (see p239), or
   sea salt
1 tsp vegan butter (optional)
½ tsp baking powder
½ tsp freshly ground black pepper
3 tbsp coconut oil, or oil of choice, plus
   extra if needed

_____

Mix together the flour with 175ml (¾ cup)
water in a large bowl. Whisk in the rest of the
ingredients, except the coconut oil.

Heat 1 tablespoon of the oil in a large
frying pan over a medium heat. Using a wet
spoon, place 1 tablespoon batter into the pan,
then add a second tablespoon of batter on top
of the first. Use the back of the spoon to
spread the batter out to a round fritter, about
6cm (2½in) diameter.

Repeat to cook a few at a time, adding
more oil when needed. Cook for 3 minutes,
then flip over and cook for a further
2 minutes, until lightly browned. Drain
on kitchen paper, keep warm, and repeat
to make about 8 fritters in total.

Pumpkin fritters

MAKES ABOUT 8

300g (10oz) pumpkin, squash or sweet potato,
    peeled, deseeded and cut into pieces
3 tbsp coconut oil, or oil of choice, plus
    extra if needed
125ml (½ cup) plant milk of
    choice, or water
1–2 tbsp granulated sugar
pinch of sea salt
¼ tsp ground nutmeg
a few drops of vanilla extract
½ tsp ground cinnamon
250g (1¾ cups plus 2 tbsp) plain (all-purpose),
    or wholemeal flour

———

Steam the pumpkin, squash or sweet potato until soft like butter. Mash in a bowl, then leave to cool.

Place the pumpkin in a large bowl. Mix in 1 tablespoon of the oil. Whisk or beat in the milk or water, sugar, salt, nutmeg, vanilla, cinnamon and flour to make a smoothish batter. Set aside to rest in the fridge for 10 minutes.

Heat 1 tablespoon of the oil in a large frying pan over a medium heat. Using a wet spoon, place 1 tablespoon batter into the pan, then add a second tablespoon of batter on top of the first. Use the back of the spoon to spread the batter out to a round fritter, about 6cm (2½in) diameter.

Repeat to cook a few fritters at a time, adding more oil when needed. Cook for 3 minutes, then flip over and cook for a further 2 minutes, until lightly browned. Drain on kitchen paper, keep warm, and repeat to make about 8 fritters in total.

Banana fritters

MAKES ABOUT 8

3 ripe bananas, peeled
200g (1½ cups) plain (all-purpose),
    or wholemeal flour
4 tbsp plant milk of choice, or water
1–2 tbsp granulated sugar
½ tsp ground cinnamon
¼ tsp ground nutmeg
a few drops of vanilla extract
pinch of sea salt
3 tbsp coconut oil, or oil of choice, plus
    extra if needed

———

Place the bananas in large bowl and mash them with the back of a fork. If they aren't mashing easily, soften them in the oven at 180°C (160°C fan/350°F/Gas 4) for about 5 minutes, or for a minute or so on high in the microwave. When mashed, mix in the flour until combined. Next, stir in the rest of the ingredients, except the coconut oil, and mix to make a smoothish batter.

Heat 1 tablespoon of the oil in a large frying pan over a medium heat. Using a wet spoon, place 1 tablespoon batter into the pan, then add a second tablespoon of batter on top of the first. Use the back of the spoon to spread the batter out to a round fritter, about 6cm (2½in) diameter.

Repeat to cook a few at a time, adding more oil when needed. Cook for 3 minutes, then flip over and cook for a further 2 minutes, until lightly browned. Drain on kitchen paper, keep warm, and repeat to make about 8 fritters in total.

Plantain porridge

Whether it's a grey winter morning in London with the sound of wind and rain, or a spring morning in Jamaica with the encroaching sun and waking roosters, a bowl of porridge equally fits the bill. Hanging out at my friend Greg's food shack, off Ochi's Milford Road, I'd spend hours just observing. On weekdays, from the crack of dawn, school kids, office clerks, local retirees and taxi drivers alike pass by for their cup of the day's chosen porridge.

A year or so after, seeking breakfast in the Spintex Road area of Ghana's Accra, I find an eerily similar, almost identical, occurrence as school kids, taxi drivers, fancy foreign jeeps pull up, non-stop, at a humble makeshift shack with tarpaulin roof, to collect their morning *hausa koko* porridge. For centuries, in this region, starchy plants, like plantain and yam, as well cereals such as sorghum, fonio, millet and later maize (cornmeal) were placed in wooden mortars and ground into flour before being combined with boiling water.

Colonial forces noted these meals and provided heavily reduced versions, akin to gruel, to the prisoners of the transatlantic slave ships. Once in the New World, however, West African descendants of these enslaved reconstituted these porridges and restored them to their former glory after centuries of degradation.

All varieties of porridge are so popular that no place dares to serve only one type, and like Greg's shack, prefer to rotate the different favourites daily. Some days it's peanut porridge, other days hominy corn, and sometimes there's nothing better than a regular oat porridge. The most hearty and effective in getting me through the early hours of the day, were those using plantain and/or green banana as their base. You can attempt to use regular bananas as a substitute, but although delicious it's not going to be exactly the same.

SERVES 2

3 medium-ripe plantains, firm enough
   to grate, topped and tailed
400ml (13.5fl oz) can coconut milk
150ml (⅔ cup) hot water
½ tsp ground cinnamon
½ tsp ground nutmeg
½ tsp ground turmeric (optional)
1 tbsp maple syrup
2 tbsp oil of choice
80g (2¾oz) dairy-free dark chocolate,
   broken into small pieces
1–2 tsp peanut butter
1 handful of chopped nuts

———

Using a sharp knife, cut the plantains lengthways down the middle. Remove and discard the skins, then coarsely grate 2 of the 3 plantains (set aside the third for now).

In a pan or pot, add the coconut milk, grated plantain and the hot water, and warm over a medium-high heat. Once hot, turn the heat down slightly, add the spices and maple syrup and simmer for 5–10 minutes, stirring frequently to allow the flavours to combine. It is ready to take off the heat when the porridge has thickened to your liking.

Meanwhile, cook the remaining plantain. Cut it into slices slightly thinner than the width of your little finger. Heat the oil in a large frying pan over a medium heat. Add the plantain and fry, turning once, until golden. Set aside to serve as a topping.

Set aside 6 small pieces of chocolate and place the rest in a heatproof bowl set over a pan of gently simmering water (the bottom of the bowl should not touch the water). Let the chocolate melt over a low heat (you can also melt the chocolate in a microwave).

To serve, spoon the porridge into 2 bowls and top with the fried plantain, melted chocolate, chocolate pieces, peanut butter and the nuts.

RAW

"Such is the Rasta way of life, maximizing all of the earth's natural resources."

Redemption Ground, a Rastafari commune in the town of Great Pond, seems a million miles away from the hustle and bustle of the tourist resort hotels and cruise liners that dominate just a couple of miles south in the city of Ocho Rios. As such, the residents here have managed to strike a fine balance between their recluse-like lifestyle and taking commercial advantage of the city.

One year, while attending Grounation Day, a Rastafari holy day, I slept on the veranda of one of the Redemption Ground buildings with only my bag as a pillow and a sheet, along with others who had made a similar intentioned pilgrimage. The tropical skies had opened, but the warm air and pulsating vibration of the traditional Nyabinghi celebratory ceremony radiating from the tabernacle, eliminated any of the usual malaise that accompanies rain in Europe.

By morning, signs of the tropical downpour had all but evaporated as the blazing sun breached the clouds. In usual fashion, youngers and elders, side-by-side, began to prepare the day's meal. A firewood shortage was spotted and, as a healthy young man, I was summoned to the open-top rear of a bright orange truck to help source some more timber for the fire. Hanging on for dear life we eventually passed a rural construction site and our assistance in removing wood was warmly welcomed: such is the Rasta way of life, maximizing all of the earth's natural resources.

On our return, the firewood was laid out and heat applied to the concrete-built stove. Provisions were secured and the almost meditative state of peeling, grating and chopping began. A second group huddled in a shack to the side preparing another concoction. I heard the word "sip" bandied about so I assumed they were preparing the next batch to meet the flame when this one was finished.

Sitting on a tree stump in the now radiant sunshine, I daydreamed to the sound of metal cutlery meeting wood and the mild flicker of burning timber. Out of nowhere I was handed a halved and hollowed-out coconut shell, the contents of which I had no idea. Evidently seeing the intrigue on my face, "Live sip," a Rasta remarked. "Live. It's alive," he added.

While the idea of livity for many refers to the sanctity of life for animals and mammals, for others, including the Rastafari, the notion extends to plant foods. As discussed by numerous health-food advocates, raw vegans and smaller subsets, like fruitarians, juicearians or sproutarians, etc., the beauty and completeness of herbs, fruit and vegetables already exists in their natural state. Save from some processes to break them down, like blending or lightly cooking, the need to apply excessive levels of heat (above 70°C/150°F) to many plant foods is unnecessary in order to consume and appreciate them.

"The sun exists as a natural oven – if the biggest star in the sky has determined it is cooked, then it is cooked."

For the likes of Rasta Prof-I, one of the patriarchal figures at Redemption Ground, and Aris Latham, an acclaimed culinary innovator, this produce is "sun-fired". The sun exists as a natural oven – if the biggest star in the sky has determined it is cooked, then it is cooked.

This chapter doesn't aim to enter the debate for or against raw food, nor does it suggest a full adoption of its diet. Rather the idea is to simply celebrate the produce of the Caribbean and such produce is so enviably plentiful it's taken for granted. Having faced the horror of the price of canned ackee in London and New York to see school children nonchalantly kicking the fruit along the street in my time in Jamaica, will always be slightly envy-inducing. Yet the indifference towards fruit and vegetables (unlike myself and the streams of tourists who spend hours taking photos of market stalls) appears to be generational.

You can barely travel anywhere in Jamaica without seeing fruit and vegetables and this appears not to have changed over the centuries. As detailed in C. Walker's book *Jamaica Ladies: Female Slaveholders and the Creation of Britain's Atlantic Empire,* which mentions that in 1727 an anonymous author waxed lyrical, "*The proliferation of Amerindian, European, and African produce in Jamaica, a place where English herbs and peas, African eddoes, plantains, and yams grew together with soursops, custard apples, star apples, avocados, guavas, bananas, coconuts, melons, and fields of pine-apples, the most delicious fruit under heaven.*"

On a cold winter's day, I often yearn for those roadside fruit vendors and miss the pleasure of being on the road and spotting a stall in the distance, it coming into frame and the rush of rustling up some change, striking up a bargain, and having a quick banter all in a matter of a few seconds, in the name of a small scandal bag of fresh produce.

The appreciation of fresh produce is in no way limited to ardent Rastafari followers. I was constantly blown away by the knowledge of local flora and fauna shown by many. Discussions about the intricacies of different mangoes and coconuts completely went over my head. My ignorant London-self had rarely contemplated there were different types.

The yard in my old complex as far as I was concerned simply came with a bush. Little did I know how diverse that bush was, full of dozens of different fruit-bearing trees. I'd soon listen in awe at how my neighbour, Magnus, would name each tree with just a quick glance at the leaves, followed by recalling their fruit-bearing schedule; fruit that everyone in the yard was free to reap. I was overwhelmed when another neighbour, Daphne, came out and doled out bonus information.

"Intuitively, nature becomes part of everyday life"

Over the months, visiting numerous farms and volunteering at schools, even kids young enough to be my children could quiz me under the table when it came to their knowledge of nature. What struck me was that this knowledge clearly wasn't from any books they'd read or studied: it was simply the way of life. With age, family and neighbours naturally emit information, stories and tales about the trees, plants and so on, which are then passed down to future generations. Walking home from school, day-after-day, kids see the change in seasons, the leaves turning, the fruits changing colour and eventually dropping or shrivelling. Intuitively, nature becomes part of everyday life.

Some days I was hard-pressed to cook when I had a bevy of custard apples, naseberries, guineps, papayas and soursop at my disposal. Some of the most dazzling, exciting, experimental takes on Jamaican food I discovered were raw, and what follows in this chapter is my take on this cuisine. The connection with plant foods, for those like myself once completely detached, simply leads to an appreciation of produce in its natural, unadulterated form. Raw soups are often the order of the day (see the chapter on Soups for more details and recipes), sustained with "power" smoothies packed with nutrient-rich fruit, vegetables, nuts and oats. Hydration usually comes from fresh spring water or coconut water (jelly wata), in addition to the numerous combinations of leafy greens and fruit blended into tantalizing fresh juices.

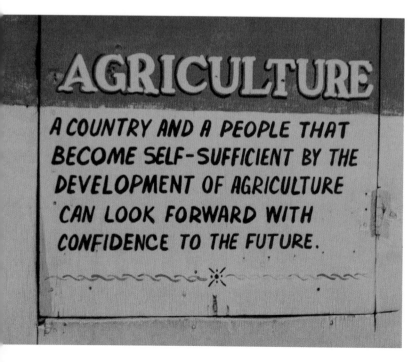

AGRICULTURE

A COUNTRY AND A PEOPLE THAT
BECOME SELF-SUFFICIENT BY THE
DEVELOPMENT OF AGRICULTURE
CAN LOOK FORWARD WITH
CONFIDENCE TO THE FUTURE.

Plantain, seaweed & berry curry

Jamaican food, and that of the wider Caribbean region, is steeped in history and tradition. As a result, a great deal of people are not fans of divergence from the norm and time eating out in Jamaica, or at local cookshops in the diaspora, is usually spent eating a small handful of old favourites on rotation. Most of the cookshops are sort of strong-armed by the community into serving the same roster of foods as the next, except for maybe a few specialities.

The Ital shops, however, provide a safe space where experimentation and deviation are more than welcomed – menus differ widely from place to place. Along the northern coast, on the way to Oracabessa from Ocho Rios at the junction that takes you up to Blue Hole called Exchange Road, lies one of these places – a market stall named Everbless. Here, green bananas and plantains are sold by the branch, whole jackfruits are loaded into trunks and many of the route taxis that pass everyday make a pit stop to allow punters to shout their fruit orders out of the car window; it's almost akin to a fast-food drive through.

When I visit, I note a menu painted on the back wall and enquire about availability. In true Jamaican fashion, the good-humoured Rasta told me he didn't have anything listed, but not to worry because he would make me something else if I held on for a minute. One minute turned to ten, but I wasn't fazed as there's no better entertainment in the world than people watching in Jamaica. Soon after, he handed me a calabash of something so different from anything I'd ever seen served in the country that it was almost indecipherable to me. Reeling off the ingredients, one-by-one, he told me everything was grown locally in St. Ann Parish. It was Jamaican food, prepped by a Jamaican in Jamaica, with Jamaican-grown ingredients, and yet I'm not sure anyone would classify it as such, as I imagined the reception it might get at one of my old local yard shops in Dalston. Regardless, I was blown away and this is my close re-enactment of it.

SERVES 2 (OR 4 AS A SIDE)

FOR THE CURRY SAUCE:

1 ripe black plantain, about 200g (7oz) in total, peeled
100g (3½oz) tomatoes, chopped
50g (¾oz) raw cashew nuts
6–8 tbsp coconut milk
2.5cm (1in) piece of fresh root ginger, peeled and chopped, or ½ tsp ground ginger
½ garlic clove (optional)
1 tsp ground turmeric
1 tsp nutritional yeast flakes (optional)
1 tsp paprika or dried chilli flakes
½ tsp sea salt
pinch of ground cumin

FOR THE SALAD:

150g (5½oz) iceberg lettuce, shredded
50g (1¾oz) cucumber, diced
½ bell pepper (¼ red and ¼ green), deseeded and diced
30g (1oz) almonds, lightly crushed
2 tbsp dried red berries, such as goji, barberries or cranberries
1 sheet nori, cut into thin strips

Chop two-thirds of the plantain (saving the remaining third) and place in a blender or food processor with the rest of the curry ingredients, then pulse until smooth.

Dice the remaining plantain and place in a serving bowl with the rest of the salad ingredients and toss gently. Spoon the curry sauce into the middle and serve immediately. Alternatively, toss all the ingredients together to coat the salad in the curry sauce.

Raw platter

Free from the extensive bureaucracy and red tape that hampers food businesses in some countries, in Jamaica the line between homemade and commercially made is often blurred. You'll find small convenience stores on front porches, makeshift lunchtime cookshops in driveways, and jerk cookouts in backyards. Uptown in the Barbican area of Kingston, Tehuti Maat extends his nutritional education and welfare to a humble cafe run out of his home and veranda. Tehuti's Café uses the plethora of locally available fruit and vegetables to form an ever-changing daily menu of raw vegan dishes, illustrating that the foods of Jamaica and the Caribbean are more than meat, stews and hard food. No plate exemplifies this more than the rainbow-coloured mini-buffet of dishes, which shows that raw eating can be more exciting than a simple green salad. This isn't a replica, but rather a homage using ingredients that can be found in most European supermarkets. Enjoy eating these dishes together as a platter, or use them individually to add a blast of colour to any feast.

SERVES 2 (EACH RECIPE)

Squash noodles with curry sauce

300g (10oz) butternut squash (use the long part without the seeds), peeled
½ recipe quantity of Curry Sauce (see p76)

———

Using a spiralizer, turn the butternut squash into thin noodles. If you don't have a spiralizer, use a vegetable peeler and slice the squash into long, thin slices.

Spoon the curry sauce over the butternut squash noodles and mix gently to combine.

Courgette noodles with callaloo pesto

85g (3oz) courgette (zucchini)
4 cherry tomatoes, quartered

FOR THE CALLALOO PESTO:

100g (3½oz) canned callaloo, drained, or fresh spinach, leaves roughly chopped
20g (¾oz) basil or parsley leaves
15g (½oz) pine nuts (optional)
1 garlic clove, minced
2 tbsp olive oil
1 tbsp lemon juice
1 tsp nutritional yeast flakes (optional)
½ tsp light soft brown sugar (optional)
pinch of sea salt
pinch of freshly ground black pepper

———

Using a spiralizer, turn the courgette into thin noodles. If you don't have a spiralizer, use a vegetable peeler and slice the courgette into long, thin slices.

Place your choice of ingredients for the callaloo pesto in a food processor or blender and blend to a paste. Spoon the pesto over the courgette noodles and mix gently to combine. Serve topped with the tomatoes.

Scotch bonnet beetroot hummus

400g (14oz) can chickpeas, drained, saving 2 tbsp
    aquafaba (chickpea water)
75g (2½oz) raw beetroot, peeled and roughly
    chopped
juice of ¾ lemon
2 tbsp olive oil
1 tbsp tahini
2 tsp coconut sugar, or light soft brown sugar
¼–½ Scotch bonnet pepper, deseeded, or 1½ tsp
    cayenne pepper
1 tsp ground coriander
1 tsp ground cumin
pinch of sea salt
¼ tsp sesame seeds
pinch of freshly ground black pepper

Place all the ingredients for the hummus,
except the sesame seeds and black pepper,
into a blender or food processor and pulse
to a thick, coarse purée. Sprinkle with the
sesame seeds and black pepper and serve.
Store in an airtight container in the fridge
for up to 3 days.

Salad with hot marinara sauce

150g (5½oz) white cabbage, thinly sliced
60g (2oz) cucumber, cut into julienne
60g (2oz) courgette (zucchini), cut into julienne

FOR THE HOT MARINARA SAUCE:

1 red bell pepper, deseeded and sliced
30g (1oz) sun-dried tomatoes in oil, drained
    and chopped
½ Scotch bonnet pepper, deseeded and sliced
1 tbsp mixed herbs
1 garlic clove, minced
½ tsp All-purpose Seasoning (see p239)
pinch of freshly ground black pepper
pinch of cayenne pepper

Place all the ingredients for the hot marinara
sauce in a food processor or blender and blend
to a thick paste.

Mix the cabbage, cucumber and courgette
in a serving bowl and top with the hot
marinara sauce.

Spiced nut "cheese" stuffed tomato

2 beef tomatoes, or large tomatoes

FOR THE NUT "CHEESE":

150g (5½oz) raw cashew nuts, soaked in warm water
    for 1 hour, drained
1 tbsp olive oil, or grapeseed or coconut oil
1 tbsp maple syrup
1 tsp apple cider vinegar
1 tsp garlic powder
½ tsp sea salt or All-purpose Seasoning (see p239)
pinch of freshly ground black pepper
snipped chives, to garnish

To prepare the tomatoes, cut off the tops
(save to make lids), scoop out the seeds, then
leave to drain upside down until needed.

To make the nut "cheese", put all the
ingredients in a blender or food processor
with 5 tablespoons water and blend to a thick,
coarse purée.

Spoon the cashew nut "cheese" into the
hollowed-out tomatoes, then sprinkle with
chives before serving. Top with the lids.

NOTE   *If you don't have time to soak the
cashews, place them in a pan and just cover with
water. Bring to the boil, then turn the heat down
and simmer for 30 minutes, half-covered with the
lid, until softened, then drain and use as above.*

Raw pizza

American exceptionalism, as seen in the tale of Fried Chicken (see p146), began to fully take hold in Jamaica by the 1980s, supplemented by the growing American-Jamaican diaspora travelling back and forth between the two regions. Subsequently, pizza parlours and burger joints now decorate American-style plazas across the country, much to the chagrin of many elders and Rastafari I talk to.

Those in health food circles have started to look at these popular international foods as a base for new and exciting types of Ital and vegan food, simultaneously reframing and re-imagining what Jamaican food is, and can be. For those in the know, a certain raw vegan pizza has become a cult icon in cities like Ochi Rios and Kingston. My version is based on one served to me by my friend and amazing chef, Vita, and serves primarily as a way to give him a shout-out. It utilizes ingredients that can be found with ease in European supermarkets and "cooked" in a basic oven, rather than a professional dehydrator. This does mean the dish takes a few hours to make, but it's worth it for the wow factor alone.

Preheat the oven to its lowest setting and line a baking tray with baking paper.

To make the pizza crust, put all the ingredients into a food processor and process to a coarse paste. Spoon the mixture onto the lined baking tray, then using the back of a spoon or spatula, smooth out into a round, about 26cm (10½in) diameter and 5mm (¼in) deep, ensuring the base is level with a smooth edge. Bake for 2½ hours, leaving the door slightly ajar to let the moisture escape. Carefully flip the crust over, using a plate to help, and bake for a further 2½–3 hours, until dry and crisp. If the base isn't dry or crisp enough for your liking, leave it in the oven for an extra 20 minutes, otherwise the texture should be like a thin-crust dough, and shouldn't fall apart if handled with care.

Just before the crust is ready, make the cashew "cheese". Put all the ingredients into a food processor or blender with 120ml (½ cup) water and pulse until the mixture is smooth like hummus, then set aside.

Place the crust on a board or pizza plate and spread the cashew "cheese" over the top. Top with lettuce leaves and your toppings of choice. Finish with chilli flakes and serve.

MAKES 1

FOR THE PIZZA CRUST:

200g (7oz) courgettes (zucchini), grated
100g (3½oz) sunflower seeds
50g (1¾oz) whole flaxseeds
2 tbsp dried basil, or 1 large handful of basil leaves
1 tbsp olive oil or coconut oil
1 tsp sea salt
½ tomato

FOR THE CASHEW "CHEESE":

150g (5½oz) cashew nuts, soaked in warm water for 1 hour, drained
1 spring onion (scallion), chopped
¼ courgette (zucchini), chopped
2 garlic cloves
2 tsp apple cider vinegar
1 tsp lemon juice
pinch of sea salt

FOR THE TOPPINGS – CHOOSE FROM:

lettuce leaves (enough to cover the base), such as iceberg, shredded
mango, peeled and diced
nori seaweed, finely chopped
plantain, peeled and finely chopped
red bell pepper, deseeded and finely diced
sun-dried tomatoes, finely chopped
1 tsp dried chilli flakes

Raw salads

Salads, as they are known in the West, have not played a historical part of the Jamaican diet. Most historical references to the island's salads include a combination of greens, but they are often cooked, rather than the more usual raw. Given that salads wilt in even mild weather, you can imagine what happens when they are exposed to the heat of the tropical sun. As access to refrigeration may be more recent in some parts of Jamaica than others, and still a great expense to many, the lack of a salad culture makes sense. More so, on a trip to Jamaica you're warned not to drink the tap water, so with water sanitation kind of a prerequisite when preparing salads, vegetables are usually eaten either preserved in vinegar or steamed to oblivion.

That said, at organic farmers' markets with coolers in tow, health food shops and modernized diners, innovative, interesting salads are becoming more plentiful. The best I found were the simple, effortless salads featuring three or four elements at the most. Here, the proprietor may not be trying to impress but actually ends up doing so.

Rather than an actual dish, salads were often made in the same vein as the slaws (see p89), as decorative sides to stews and curries. Like the slaws, the natural sweetness of the island's plant foods had me devouring every last leaf.

These two salads are favourites, especially when coated in their lively Caribbean dressings. Both are simple to make, offer a combination of crunch and chew, while adding a splash of colour to often, admittedly, brown and beige meals.

Beetroot, tomato & kale with coconut dressing

Line a serving bowl with the kale or lettuce, then sprinkle over the vinegar and top with the beetroot. Add both types of tomato with the walnuts, then toss gently.

To make the dressing, put all the ingredients in a mini food processor or blender and pulse for about 10 seconds until combined. Pour the dressing over the salad and gently toss, then finish with a sprinkling of the salad topper.

SERVES 2 (OR 4 AS A SIDE)

75–100g (2½–3½oz) kale,
    tough stalks removed,
    or lettuce leaves
1 tsp apple cider vinegar or white
    wine vinegar
50g (1¾oz) raw beetroot, peeled
    and thinly sliced
1 medium tomato, sliced
4 cherry tomatoes, halved
10g (¼oz) walnuts, roughly
    chopped
salad topper (shoots),
    for sprinkling

FOR THE DRESSING:

150ml (⅔ cup) coconut milk
1 tbsp apple cider vinegar
    or white wine vinegar
½ shallot, chopped
½ tsp finely chopped fresh root
    ginger, or ground ginger
juice of ½ lime
1 garlic clove, chopped (optional)
2 tsp cane sugar or light soft
    brown sugar
1 tsp sea salt
½ tsp mixed herbs

Avocado & mango

SERVES 2 (OR 4 AS A SIDE)

1 semi-ripe mango, peeled, stone
  removed and diced
1 semi-ripe avocado, peeled, stone
  removed and diced
½ red onion, finely chopped
½ red bell pepper, deseeded
  and diced
1 tsp freshly ground black pepper
1 tsp sugar (optional)
½–1 tsp All-purpose Seasoning
  (see p239)
¼ tsp sea salt
juice of 1 lime or lemon
few sprigs of dill, fennel fronds,
  or coriander (cilantro), to serve

Add the fruit, vegetables and seasonings to a serving
bowl, and toss together. Squeeze the citrus juice over,
toss again, and finish with a scattering of dill, fennel
or coriander before serving.

Sun-dried salad with plantain dressing

Sun-drying fruits for future use has been in existence in Jamaica for centuries. Spanish buccaneers arriving in 1494 noted the Taino peoples cultivated the fruit of what we now know as pimento, and sun dried it to season and preserve meat; a technique the Spanish adopted soon after. Likewise, the West Africans dried cocoa pods in the process of creating early iterations of chocolate and, as far back as 1894, European traders were noted as saying in The Royal Botanic Gardens' *Kew Bulletin*, "*The dried banana is no novelty to us, as for several years past West India merchants have endeavoured to introduce it to the London market.*"

Sun-dried fruits and vegetables are praised for their nutritional value, and innovations like the dehydrator have made the process easier. Although, if you're fortunate to live around the equator then nothing works better than the good old-fashioned sun. If neither are available, then it's possible to dehydrate produce over a period of a few hours in an oven set at the lowest temperature.

When in Jamaica, I often crave something between a light salad and the dense starchy meals served at the Rasta Ital cookshops. I've found dried fruit and vegetables are the answer and discovered this mish-mash of dried goods in a large supermarket in Kingston's Half Way Tree, and the market vendors that line the streets a stone's throw away also serve my purpose well.

Preheat the oven to its lowest setting and line a large baking tray with baking paper, or use a dehydrator if you have one.

Bring a large pan or pot of water to the boil and fill a large bowl with cold water. Blanche the vegetables for drying – red bell pepper, courgette, carrot and beetroot – in batches by putting them into the pan of hot water for 10 seconds, then scooping out and placing in the bowl of cold water for 10 seconds. Drain and pat dry with kitchen paper.

Arrange the blanched vegetables, evenly spread out, on the lined baking tray and place in the oven (or place directly on the rack of your dehydrator). Leave the oven door ajar and cook for 4–5 hours. After each hour, gently turn over the vegetables. When dried and crisp, remove from the oven (or dehydrator).

SERVES 2 (OR 4 AS A SIDE)

FOR THE DRIED VEGETABLES:

1 red bell pepper, deseeded and sliced
1 courgette (zucchini), thinly sliced into rounds
1 carrot, thinly sliced into rounds
1 raw beetroot, peeled and thinly sliced into rounds

FOR THE SALAD:

100g (3½oz) kale, tough stalks removed and leaves sliced
100g (3½oz) rocket (arugula) leaves
1 handful of dill
1 handful of basil leaves
2 tbsp sliced spring onions (scallions) or chives
250g (9oz) sun-dried tomatoes in olive oil, or 250g (9oz) sun-dried tomatoes mixed with 2 tbsp olive oil, halved
400g (14oz) can chickpeas, drained and rinsed
pinch of sea salt
pinch of finely ground black pepper
2 tbsp dried barberries, raisins, cranberries or goji berries
1 avocado, peeled, stone removed and sliced
2 tbsp almonds or walnuts

FOR THE PLANTAIN DRESSING:

½ ripe black plantain, about 85g (3oz) in total, peeled
2 tbsp coconut oil or alternative
1 tbsp apple cider vinegar
juice of ½–1 lime
1 tsp honey
½ tsp freshly ground black pepper

To make the salad, place the kale, rocket, herbs and spring onions or chives in a serving bowl.

In a separate bowl, add the sun-dried tomatoes with the 2 tablespoons of oil, the chickpeas and salt and pepper, then mix until combined. Add this to the kale salad and toss. Add the dried fruit, avocado, nuts and dried vegetables and gently toss the salad again.

To make the plantain dressing, blend all the ingredients in a blender or mini food processor until smooth. Alternatively, mash the plantain and mix with the rest of the dressing ingredients. Serve the dressing spooned over the salad.

RAW

Three slaws

Red slaw

¼ red cabbage,
  about 400g (14oz) in total
1 carrot
1 cucumber
1 red onion
50g (1¾oz) raw beetroot, peeled
2 tbsp apple cider vinegar
1 tsp caster (superfine) sugar

Pepper slaw

⅓ white cabbage, about 500g
  (1lb 2oz) in total
1 large carrot
⅓ red bell pepper, deseeded
⅓ cucumber
1 tomato, finely diced
1 tbsp apple cider vinegar
1 tbsp coconut oil, melted
2 tsp caster (superfine) sugar

Mixed cabbage slaw

⅓ white cabbage, about 500g
  (1lb 2oz) in total
100g (3½oz) red cabbage
1 large carrot
1 tomato, finely diced
1 tbsp apple cider vinegar
1 tbsp coconut oil, melted
2 tsp caster (superfine) sugar

The term coleslaw is said to derive from the Dutch *koosla*, which roughly translates as cabbage salad. Given the centuries-old popularity of cabbage in Jamaica, such as Steamed Vegetables (see p52), it's inevitable that cabbage is also enjoyed in its raw form across the island. While I'm accustomed to the mayonnaise-coated form of coleslaw in England and the US, in Jamaica, perhaps because of the heat, versions containing dairy aren't usual.

For some, a slaw is an unloved addition to the plate that ends up as part of the last remnants of a meal, alongside meat bones, corn cobs and bare thyme stems. Yet, for me a meal isn't complete without them. On my travels, I became obsessed with the variety of slaws from different cookshops. Cabbage was cut in so many different shapes and sizes: sometimes white cabbage formed the base with a cameo of red cabbage; sometimes vice versa; and sometimes playing equal roles in a tag team.

At some places to make the dish last more than a few days and perhaps free-up fridge space, a more vinegar-heavy preserved version was served, nearly akin to pickled onions. On other occasions, the slaw was essentially a cabbage salad, plated dry with the idea that the sauce from the curry would provide the means to saturate it. Whatever the location, whatever the vegetable, from carrots to bell peppers and so on, all were just referred to as coleslaw or slaw, and on a maiden trip anywhere I never knew how it would arrive. Referencing low-res photos snapped on my phone, these three are some of my favourites that I like to eat at almost every lunch or dinner.

——

Using a mandoline, grater or sharp knife, cut your vegetables of choice into thin slices or julienne. When prepared, put all the ingredients into a large serving bowl and toss together.

Serve the slaw straightaway or store in an airtight container in the fridge for up to 2–3 days.

Coconuts on the veranda

Magnus, a neighbour a few doors down from me in the yard complex in Great Pond, is who I'd like to be in thirty years' time. He has the ability to identify fruit trees and plants with only a cursory glance at their leaves, complete with a recollection of seasonal schedules and suggested recipes to boot. After a lifetime spent here Magnus's effortless knowledge of the yard's greenery makes complete sense.

One day I hear a noise emanating from the yard, the sound of some kind of carpentry job. On inspection, I see that it's Magnus on his white-tiled, pastel-orange veranda in shorts and sandals grating fresh coconut with a half-metre-long, corrugated metallic grater.

Both coconuts and a veranda represent life in Jamaica to me. Time spent on the veranda is like TV and social media-feed rolled into one: seeing the day go by; people watching; and observing the changes of the surrounding foliage. The perfect place to sit back or partake in chores, like harvesting coconuts, while covered from the elements, be it the roasting afternoon sun or tropical downpours.

I often say there are no secret ingredients in Caribbean food, however, there's no comparison between a freshly harvested coconut versus a shop-bought one: the former is so vibrant in texture and flavour compared to its retail alternative that the term secret ingredient seems apt, if only for the fact that it's hardly a secret. For Magnus, who harvests coconuts from his own plot near his home, shop-bought ones are definitely a last resort.

Throughout much of the Caribbean, West Africa and Asia everyone is skilled at handling coconuts. They are deftly caressed like a Harlem globetrotter basketball and swiftly decimated with a handy blade, with the floor (usually cement) often used for the final crack. In Jamaica, the piles of used and discarded husks that line highways and residential avenues alike go some way to illustrate the popularity of the coconut. There they are left for nature to slowly consume them – and the cycle repeats itself.

It's likely that if you're in Europe you may not have the time or resources to acquire a dozen coconuts, or so. Although, admittedly, coconut products are relatively cheap and now widely available. If you do find yourself with a bounty, make the most of them, I'm sure you won't regret it.

As you may notice in the recipes in this book, anywhere coconut can be shoehorned into a dish it is, be it the simple water or jelly; desiccated dried flesh; ground into flour; blended into creamy milk; or cooked down to an oil or butter.

CRACKING A COCONUT

If using coconuts with a yellow/green outer layer, use a large knife to cut it away and expose the white or brown inner shell. Grip the coconut in one hand with your thumb and fingers facing the sky. In the other hand, use a hammer to tap the shell. Turn the coconut horizontally while continuing to tap it equatorially until it's cracked all the way round, then prise the two halves open – or if you're not being fancy just crack it against a concrete wall or floor – taking care not to lose the coconut water inside. Open the coconut over a bowl and pour out the water through a funnel into a bottle and keep in the fridge for up to a couple of days, or drink immediately.

DESICCATED COCONUT

Using a small, sharp knife, prise the white flesh away from the cracked brown coconut shell. Coarsely grate the coconut flesh. Spread out on a lined baking sheet and place in the oven, set at the lowest temperature (or in the hot sun) for 3–4 hours, until dried. (You can also use a dehydrator.) When dry, leave to cool. It will keep in an airtight container for up to 1 month.

COCONUT MILK

Using a small, sharp knife, prise the white flesh away from the cracked brown coconut shell. Cut the flesh into small chunks and place in a blender with the coconut water from inside the coconut, then pulse until smooth and milky – it will take about 3 minutes. If you have a cheesecloth, tip the blended coconut into the middle over a bowl, gather up the sides and twist into a bundle. Squeeze to release the milk from the coconut. Alternatively, use a sieve: pour the blended coconut into the sieve over a bowl, then use the back of a spoon to press it through the sieve and squeeze out as much milk as possible. Discard the pulp in the cheesecloth or sieve, or use to make coconut flour, right. Pour the coconut milk through a funnel into a bottle and keep in the fridge for up to 1 week, or use immediately.

Fresh juices

Drinks in the Caribbean that derive from Taino and West African heritage have a tradition of both fermentation and non-fermentation. Apart from the use of citrus and, of course, the famed tropical coconut, most drinks appear to rely on roots and plants, as opposed to fruit. For example, there are tonic wines, such as Sorrel (see p254), Ginger Beer (see p250) and an Eastern Caribbean favourite known as *mauby*, made from tree bark among other things. In addition, there are a number of alcoholic drinks akin to moonshine. These drinks usually rely on some form of preservation, unlike blended fresh fruits, which quickly go off in the island heat.

The development of juices appears to coincide with the cultivation of sugar and molasses by enslaved West Africans for colonial powers, and the industrial revolution that followed. More so, Europeans in the Caribbean favoured cool drinks as a response to the heat. Orange juice was the go-to fruit juice, especially made from Seville oranges, and as it was concentrated it could be kept without the need of a fridge. When fridges started to become the domestic norm from the 1960s onwards, fresh juices became more popular.

The legacy of sugar persists to an unfortunate degree in the supermarket boxed juices that we enjoyed as kids. Likewise, the premade juices at cookshops are loaded with so much processed sugar it's hard to discern the actual taste of the fruit. Probably one of the best things to happen in recent years in Jamaica is the Rastafari getting their hands on blenders. Armed with a knowledge of Jamaican produce, their juices make drinking commercially made ones a complete no-no.

At Ibo Spice Yard, an almost magical open-air Rasta cookshop on Kingston's legendary reggae hub Orange Street, the crew produce an ever-changing roster of fresh juices, meaning there's always something new to wow you. The rich variety of herbs, fruits and native spices only found on the island, mean it's quite hard to perfectly reproduce the ones found there, but these three juices – red, gold and green – certainly attempt to replicate the spirit.

———

Place all the ingredients in a blender and blend until smooth. Strain the juice through a sieve or piece of cheesecloth into a jug, then pour through a funnel into a bottle. Seal with a lid and chill for 10 minutes to 1 hour before drinking. Serve with ice, if you like.

SERVES 1 (EACH RECIPE)

Alkaline green-fire

125ml (½ cup) coconut water or water
20g (¾oz) young callaloo or spinach leaves, tough stalks removed
1 rib of celery, sliced
½ cucumber, chopped
2.5cm (1in) piece of fresh root ginger, peeled and chopped
½ green bell pepper, deseeded and chopped
¼–½ green chilli or green Scotch bonnet pepper, deseeded if you prefer

Pine & ginger

250g (9oz) pineapple, peeled and diced
240ml (1 cup) coconut water or water
80–100g (2¾–3½oz) fresh root ginger, peeled and chopped
juice of 1 lime

Watermelon, beetroot & ginger

300g (10oz) watermelon, skin removed, deseeded and chopped
200g (7oz) raw beetroot, peeled and chopped
125ml (½ cup) coconut water or water
50g (1¾oz) fresh root ginger, peeled and chopped
juice of ½ lime or lemon (optional)

Soursop juice

Apart from the custard apple, the closely related soursop, known in some regions as *korosol* or *guanabana*, is one of those foods that I live in eternal envy of those who get to eat it regularly. The fruit's prickly green exterior with the semblance of a shell is nothing but a facade played by nature, which you'll find out if you caress the soursop. In fact, you'll find it's a complete charade as caressing the fruit too firmly can make it burst, such is its softness when ripe. As soursop is an indigenous Jamaican fruit, the same hereditary knowledge of dealing with jackfruit seeds applies here in order to navigate the black pips and their thin, translucent lining buried deep within the creamy, cotton-esque flesh interior.

Unless I'm at an Ital food joint, I rarely have soursop juice as I find it's usually loaded with too much sugar and dairy milk, or even condensed milk, all of which I tend to shy away from. Additionally, on the occasion I find myself in possession of a soursop, there's almost no way it will survive long enough to make it home to be juiced. That said, every so often a great homemade soursop juice, which tastes like a natural milkshake, makes a wonderful surprise for my family, and I'm sure it will be for yours too.

Soursop with milk

SERVES 2

1 ripe soursop fruit, about 360–450g (12½–14oz)
  in total
100ml (⅓ cup plus 1 tbsp) milk of choice
½ tsp ground nutmeg
½ tsp ground cinnamon
1 tsp vanilla extract (optional)
2 tbsp sugar or honey

————

To prepare the soursop, with clean hands
or wearing disposable gloves, peel off the skin
and place the fruit in a sieve set over a bowl.
Discard the skin. If the soursop is really ripe,
it should fall away with minimum effort. Use
your thumbs to scrape any flesh hanging onto
the skin into the bowl.

Tear the soursop apart to expose the heart
(the light brown spine running down the
middle) and discard this. Pour 250ml (1 cup
plus 1 tbsp) water into the bowl and use your
hands to squeeze the flesh until it dissolves
into the water. You should start to see the
white juice and translucent pulp with black
seeds inside. Press the pulp to expose the seeds,
then discard the seeds, keeping the pulp.

Using a blender: pour the contents of
the bowl and the pulp into a blender. Add the
milk, nutmeg, cinnamon, vanilla, if using,
and sugar or honey, then blend for 30 seconds,
until the pulp dissipates. For a smoother
consistency, add an extra 1–2 tablespoons
water or milk and blend again until smooth;
it should have a thick milk consistency. Chill
for 30 minutes to 1 hour before serving.

Without a blender: strain the mixture
through a sieve over a bowl. Using the back
of a spoon or your hands, firmly press the pulp
through the sieve to crush it and extract more
juice. You can eat any remnants of pulp left
in the sieve afterwards. Add the milk, nutmeg,
cinnamon, vanilla, if using, and sugar or
honey and whisk. For a smoother consistency,
add an extra 1–2 tablespoons water or milk
and whisk again until smooth. Chill for
30 minutes to 1 hour before serving.

Soursop with water

SERVES 2

1 ripe soursop fruit, about 360–450g
  (12½–14oz) in total
juice of 1 lime
2.5cm (1in) piece of fresh root ginger,
  peeled and chopped, or 1 tsp
  ground ginger
2 tbsp sugar or honey

————

To prepare the soursop, with clean hands
or wearing disposable gloves, peel off the skin
and place the fruit in a sieve set over a bowl.
Discard the skin. If the soursop is really ripe,
it should fall away with minimum effort. Use
your thumbs to scrape any flesh hanging onto
the skin into the bowl.

Tear the soursop apart to expose the heart
(the light brown spine running down the
middle) and discard this. Pour 250ml (1 cup
plus 1 tbsp) water into the bowl and use your
hands to squeeze the flesh until it dissolves
into the water. You should start to see the
white juice and translucent pulp with black
seeds inside. Press the pulp to expose the seeds,
then discard the seeds, keeping the pulp.

Using a blender: pour the contents of the
bowl into a blender with 325ml (1¼ cups)
water. Add the lime juice, ginger and sugar
or honey, then blend for 30 seconds, until the
pulp dissipates. For a smoother consistency,
add an extra 1–2 tablespoons water and blend
again until smooth; it should have a thick milk
consistency. Chill for 30 minutes to 1 hour
before serving.

Without a blender: strain the mixture
through a sieve over a bowl. Using the back
of a spoon or your hands, firmly press the pulp
through the sieve to crush it and extract more
juice. You can eat any remnants of pulp left
in the sieve afterwards. Add 325ml (1¼ cups)
water, the lime juice, ginger and sugar or
honey and whisk again until smooth. Chill for
30 minutes to 1 hour before serving.

Protein-rich smoothies

I can usually tell when a conversation on the main road in Jamaica is about to turn into a sales pitch for a certain type of drink as the salesman-to-be will ask if I have a girlfriend or wife. After this, a collection of drinks will appear from nowhere and I'm told I absolutely NEED these drinks to increase my stamina for this supposed significant other's sake and mine. These drinks on offer usually come in two forms: roots tonic wines and thick, protein-rich smoothies, loaded with oats, nuts and seeds.

When I first properly met Prince Nyah, an affable Rasta residing in the hills of Great Pond, he jumped, latching himself onto a nearby tree branch, and proceeded to bang out a dozen pull-ups before asking me to guess his age. I was off by some years, as it turned out he was only a few years younger than my own grandad. When I asked what was his secret, Nyah said it was his drinks, of course. At his Honey Lodge shop, a wooden and corrugated steel structure, Nyah spends the early part of the day concocting his smoothies.

This theme revealed itself again on a visit to the School of Visions Rasta commune in the Blue Mountains to the west of Kingston. A cut, muscular figure, probably a few years older than me, told me he usually didn't consume anything other than a smoothie during the whole day while farming and traversing the one-hour-round-trip up and down the hill that separates the commune and the nearest main road. Upon my astonished reaction, he told me to try it for myself.

I'm in awe that these visually beige drinks are loaded with so much flavour, depth and sustenance, and since this visit to Jamaica I've incorporated my own versions of them into my daily morning routine.

—————

Place all the ingredients in a blender and blend until smooth. Pour the smoothie into a glass and serve.

SERVES 1 (EACH RECIPE)

Seed power

250ml (1 cup plus 1 tbsp) soya milk, or milk of choice
3 tbsp rolled oats
2 tbsp pumpkin seeds
2 tbsp sunflower seeds
1–2 tbsp honey or sweetener of choice
1 tbsp hemp seeds
1 tbsp peanut butter or 1–2 tsp raw peanuts
1 tbsp Sea Moss (see p246)

Protein strongback

250ml (1 cup plus 1 tbsp) soya milk, or milk of choice
30g (1oz) almonds
30g (1oz) raw cashew nuts
5–6 dried pitted dates, roughly chopped
20g (¾oz) pumpkin seeds
½–1 banana, chopped, preferably frozen
1 tbsp peanut butter or 1–2 tsp raw peanuts
1 tbsp Sea Moss (optional) (see p246)

Irish moss

220ml (1 cup) almond milk or oat milk
40g (¼oz) rolled oats
4 tbsp Sea Moss (see p246)
2 tbsp light soft brown sugar or honey
2 tbsp peanut butter or 30g (1oz) raw
    peanuts (optional)
1½ tbsp ground flaxseeds
1 tsp ground allspice
1 tsp vanilla extract (optional)
pinch of ground cinnamon
pinch of ground nutmeg

Plantcado smoothie

Researching the drinks that people of West African descent drank across the Caribbean from 1500 onwards is intriguing, especially considering the non-existence of electrical kitchen equipment that we have today. One account tells of the *"experimental"* drink concoctions such as *"mobbie [mauby], brew'd with potatoes, water and sugar; kowwow of molasses, water and ginger,"* as well as *"pine drink"* and *"plantain drink"*. (A.E. Yentsch, *A Chesapeake Family and Their Slaves: A Study in Historical Archaeology.*)

Having grown up only knowing plantain fried, boiled or baked, the idea of eating it raw has barely crossed my mind – let alone drinking it. Venturing across Jamaica, at the numerous Ital vegan eating posts many seem keen to experiment. Here, the abundance of plantain means they are thrown into the blender without a second thought to make a bevy of incredible drinks. The first time I tried this thick, rich smoothie I held the bottle up at a 180-degree angle trying to eke out every drop. If you don't have the patience for a drink that moves at the speed of a snail, nor have a squeezy bottle, feel free to add a tad more water.

***

Put the plantain, avocado, coconut water or water and spices, if using, in a blender and blend until smooth. It should be thicker than the usual smoothie and if stored in the fridge, it will become thicker still and more yogurt-like. Serve in a glass or bowl.

SERVES 1

1 overripe black plantain about 200g (7oz) in total, peeled and chopped
½ avocado, peeled, stone removed and chopped
170ml (¾ cup) coconut water or water
⅛ tsp ground allspice (optional
⅛ tsp ground cinnamon (optional)
⅛ tsp ground nutmeg (optional)

Spirulina smoothie

Spirulina in its natural form is an algae that grows in lakes in the warmer regions of the planet. Bitter in taste and with the aroma of what you might expect from an algae, it usually comes as a deep-green powder. It's celebrated for its various health benefits thanks to a concentration of vitamins and minerals among other things: such is the nutrient density of spirulina that it was used by NASA as a dietary supplement for astronauts on space missions.

In the West, spirulina is slowly traversing its way on the well-trodden "superfood" path, from scientific journals and health food circles to the mainstream. Its consumption, however, is said to go back over a thousand years with use estimated as early as the 9th century in the westerly reaches of Africa in Lake Chad, between the namesake country of Chad and Nigeria. Across the Atlantic, it was registered in the 1300s in a region that now comprises Mexico.

In parts of Africa, where it is known as *dihé*, women carry out the traditional method of harvesting with a filter process that uses a dense thicket of reeds and papyrus satchels. The algal biomass is then dried on the sandy shores of the lake before it is further sun-dried on mats. This legacy may explain why the Rastafari of Jamaica took to it when an English businessman and co-founder of the Jamaican Agriculture Industrial Party introduced his commercial spirulina endeavour to the island, one of his numerous interactions with the then ostracized Rastafari community in the 1950s. Since that time, spirulina-infused food and drinks have become a fixture in Ital cookshops across the country. My take is this rich, thick smoothie, packed with fruit, spices and with the added boost of a hit of spirulina.

－－－－

Place all the ingredients in a blender and blend until smooth. Pour the smoothie into a glass and serve.

SERVES 1

250ml (1 cup plus 1 tbsp) milk of choice
1 ripe banana or plantain, about 200g (7oz) in total, peeled and chopped, chilled or frozen
50g (1¾oz) frozen mango pieces
50g (1¾oz) frozen pineapple pieces
1 tbsp desiccated coconut
1 tsp blue spirulina powder or spirulina powder
1 tsp hemp powder (optional)
pinch of ground cinnamon (optional)
pinch of ground nutmeg (optional)

SOUP

"No amount of financial resources or secret ingredients can improve the best simple homemade soups."

While the likes of jerk chicken, ackee and saltfish, and rice and peas have become commonplace Caribbean dishes in the diaspora, there's no doubt for me that soups make the island go round.

Costing less than a few dollars to buy, soups cross all social divides in Jamaica, where the same stallholder might serve a hand reaching out of a tricked-out American motor just moments after serving a local homeless person. The ability of these vendors to cram a multitude of flavours and textures into one hand-held vessel makes them a true unifier: be it a Rastafari vegan Ital sip made with fresh produce up in the Blue Mountains; a light broth, known as fish tea, that makes the most of whatever seafood is available; or the chicken-loaded cock soup. All are boosted by an array of herbs and spices and bolstered by a plethora of starch and vegetables.

No amount of financial resources or secret ingredients can improve the best simple homemade soups. Home-cooked pots of soup feed families for days, while the cauldron-like vessels on roadsides sell out by sundown, giving taxi and route bus drivers, and the labourers, tourists and school kids they convey, a quick fuel pit stop. In all corners of the island, in every nook and cranny from hills to downtown, junkyards to the beachside, rain or shine, break of dawn or late into the night after a rave, anywhere, every day of the year, you'll never be far from a pot of soup bubbling away.

There are no tricks. The key to a good soup is often entirely personal, with years of selective bias influencing an attachment to the textures and profiles of certain ingredients or additions. This may be the comforting spinners or dumplings, or slowly dissolving pumpkin, particular cuts of chicken, or substantial chunks of yam. There is perhaps an ancestral lineage. In B.W. Higman's book *Jamaican Food: History, Biology Culture*, he quotes scholars as revealing, *"The enslaved people of Jamaica had learned to add small amounts of salted meat and fish to their 'soup' of vegetables and ground provisions in order to make it palatable and to eke out the meagre allowances they received from their masters."* More so, those enslaved had come from a long lineage of both native Latin American and West African soup consumers over centuries and maybe millennia: generations figuring out the optimal way to maximize the humble soup and from this we benefit today. Like the winds that blew across the oceans, fanning the sails of the middle passage slave ships so do the memories and cultures of the captees on board. With the arrival of the ancestors of West Africans across the world came their rich, plentiful soups, which continue to be a fundamental part of everyday life.

"Soups are life, death and beyond in Jamaica."

While water or stock are at the heart of most soups, where other traditional ingredients and cookware could not be transported and replicated the essence of them was, and still is, used instead: earthen pots became Dutch pots; *ewedu* became callaloo and then spinach; and *swallows* became spinners. The leaves, grains and names may have changed but the spirit remains, and so does a soup's ability to provide solace in a new land whatever the ingredients.

Soups are life, death and beyond in Jamaica. During burial ceremonies of the newly arrived, and the descendants of, West Africans, particularly Ghanaians, libations were offered to higher powers with a soup placed at the head of the deceased. There are also stories of the miscellaneous appearance of poisoned soups making the perfect conduit for the attempted assassination of their enslavers by female enslaved, who often prepared the food for both house and field. The usual punishment for this was hanging.

In the classic Anansi tale of *Tiger Soup* (retold by F. Temple in *Tiger Soup: An Anansi Story from Jamaica*) an enraged tiger looks to tear a cunning Anansi limb from limb after the swindling monkey tricks him into diving into a lagoon-like blue hole to nab the soup the tiger had been painstakingly curating. After being found out, a panicked Anansi hurriedly flees and upon reaching a small village he teaches a small group of monkeys a self-incriminating song to shift the blame onto them. On hearing the song, the tiger is enraged to hear that the monkeys have eaten the soup: *"And now,"* he bellows, *"the Tiger is going to eat – you!"* This tale surely must have emanated from an irked mother who had spent hours labouring over a soup only to later find an empty pot and minimal appreciation from her spouse and kids. (With age, I can fully understand this rage and can only apologize profusely to my own mum.) Today, the soups sold by the higglers and roadside stands in Jamaica are sometimes the difference between eating and not eating on a given day.

In the same way the spirit of soup travelled from the African continent to the Caribbean region and its surroundings, it moved with the peoples before, during and after the Windrush Generation (the half a million people who arrived in the UK from the Caribbean between 1948 and the early 70s), again travelling on boats to a new foreign land. In the diaspora, making a pot of flavoursome soup to stretch for days often meant that children could feed themselves in the evenings with the press of a microwave button or switch of a hob while parents and family worked second jobs. In a land where wages were never guaranteed based on the colour of one's skin, payment could go towards the ingredients to make a soup that would feed many, and simultaneously provide warmth in the British winter. On Saturdays, often a soup day for Caribbeans, you could be sure that wherever you were, friends or family nearby had a soup on the go. This story isn't mine alone and I know from talking to Caribbean cookshop owners and chefs across the country that many people from a similar background share the same memories and sense of pride.

> ## "While Caribbean and Jamaican cuisine is embedded in tradition, the spirit of a recipe is ultimately more important than strictly following the ingredient's list."

The joy of now having the time and resources to cook soup for myself means no longer being disappointed when I've only been dished out a few (or NO) dumplings or the root vegetable, dasheen, and having to feign my best Oliver Twist sad face to get a few more select chunks. Like other recipes in this book, the main consideration when making these soups is the denseness and water content of the vegetables used, particularly the starchy ones. The more starchy, dense and less watery ones, like yam, go into the pot earlier and take longer to cook, while leafy greens, like spinach or callaloo, should be added much later as they need less time to cook. With this information, do experiment with whatever produce is available to you. While Caribbean and Jamaican cuisine is embedded in tradition, the spirit of a recipe is ultimately more important than strictly following the ingredient's list.

In your local West African, Indian or Caribbean grocery shop or even the international food section of your nearby supermarket, you may spot Caribbean soup packs, such as cock soup mix or fish tea-base, which are a flavour staple for many popular soups in the region. Due to their rarity outside certain metro hubs, I've mainly opted to avoid them, however, should you get your hands on these soup mixes feel free to make the most of them in your own homemade soups.

Raw sip

The Nyabinghi (often called binghi) celebrations at the numerous Rastafari communes in Jamaica are special occasions that, like any other meditative gathering, can only be truly understood by attending. The atmosphere, set by smoke from the firepit and chalices alike, permeates the breeze gliding through the open-air tabernacle. Non-stop, throughout the night, dreadlocks fly free while drums alternate between tempos, fast and slow, underpinning hours of song, dance, chanting and prayer until sunrise. To keep the head clear, the majority of Rastas abstain from eating throughout the entire session, meaning they go without consuming anything from sundown to sunrise.

In the morning, after prayers, the sound of wood crackling and pots clattering pre-empts the impending break in the fast, usually with a piping hot Ital Sip (see p112), filled to the brim with vegetables and Hard Food (see p56).

In eager anticipation after a binghi at Redemption Ground in Great Pond, north of Ocho Rios, I'm handed a calabash full of soup. Confused as I expected the sip not to be ready for another hour or so, the elder registers my confusion and tells me, "Everything (a)bout it alive!", while another from a distance shouts "raw sip!" I knew that Prof-I, a patriarchal figure at the commune and some of the others didn't eat cooked food, but I hadn't witnessed any raw meals being made. In the calabash handed to me was a soup with a base of natural coconut water, warm in the way that the juice of a coconut naturally is without being chilled. The coconut water had been spiced with a variety of home-grown spices and in the place of starchy root vegetables was a light, crunchy vegetable salad. Admittedly, being lighter it didn't fill me up in the same way a ground provision-based stew would have but it was incredible nonetheless and I've yet to see it anywhere else since. It's another dish I've attempted to recreate from blurry photos and taste bud memory, and one which provides great refreshment in the summer. It's now possible to find fresh coconuts in most major cities, however, you can also use organic coconut water (not the processed preserved cartons in supermarkets) instead.

Savoury sip

SERVES 2

1 fresh coconut or 500ml (2 cups plus 2 tbsp)
   coconut water
1 tbsp fresh coconut meat, chopped
1 rib of celery, chopped
1 handful lettuce, sliced into 1cm (½in) strips
½ carrot, sliced into thin rounds or strips
½ spring onion (scallion), finely chopped
⅓ onion, finely chopped
¼ red bell pepper, deseeded and finely chopped
½ sheet nori, cut into thin strips (optional)
1 tsp All-purpose Seasoning (see p239)

———

If using a fresh coconut, carefully crack it open
(see p90) and decant the water inside into a jug.

Pour the coconut water into a larger bowl
and add the coconut meat, the vegetables and
the nori, if using. Stir before adding the
all-purpose seasoning, then stir again. Leave
to rest for 2–3 minutes before serving to allow
the vegetables to absorb the flavour of the
coconut water and spice.

Serve in 2 bowls (or the hollowed-out
coconut shell) or share 1 large bowl.

Sweet sip

SERVES 2

1 fresh coconut or 500ml (2 cups plus 2 tbsp)
   coconut water
1 tbsp fresh coconut meat, chopped
10 strawberries, hulled, sliced or chopped
50g (1¾oz) peeled mango, sliced or chopped
2 tbsp blueberries, fresh or frozen
1 tbsp sliced or chopped peeled pineapple,
   fresh or frozen
pinch of granulated sugar
pinch of ground cinnamon
pinch of ground nutmeg

———

If using a fresh coconut, carefully crack it
open (see p90) and decant the water inside
into a jug.

Pour the coconut water into a larger bowl
and add the coconut meat and all the fruit.
Stir before adding the spices, then stir again.
Leave to rest for 2–3 minutes before serving
to allow the fruit to absorb the flavour of
the coconut water and spices.

Serve in 2 bowls (or the hollowed-out
coconut shell) or share 1 large bowl.

Avocado, okra & spirulina sip

Comparing avocados sold on the high streets of Britain with those dangling from garden trees in Jamaica, you'd think they were two entirely different fruit. In Jamaica, like the US, the avocado is known colloquially as alligator pear, or pear for short. The name likely arose as a lost-in-translation take on its Spanish descendant name of *aguacate* from Mexico. Although, some surmise it's a reference to both the shape of the fruit and it's knobbly, dark green skin, like an alligator. The pear part of the name is said to be a reference to a male's, erm, let's say, reproductive satchel and derives from the Aztec root of the Spanish word. However, the avocado wasn't originally native to the island. European references to it appear in the late 1600s and given that Spanish rule existed a few decades before that date, it seems the Spanish saw the island as a place to cultivate produce sourced from the Americas.

Avocados are so cheap, plentiful and consistently delicious in Jamaica, I've found myself often inspired by conversations with (the not self-proclaimed, but essentially) raw, vegan rasta, Prof-I. By blending avocados, I like to make creations both sumptuous in flavour and nutritionally rich without cooking. I had come across both hot and cold avocado-based soups before in the UK, though most were usually a bit bland. The arsenal of variety in the Caribbean larder means there is no such blandness, in fact rather the opposite. Spirulina (see p99) is something of an acquired taste so if this is your first time, do reduce the quantity to find out if it's for you.

Pour the water into a food processor or blender, then add the rest of the ingredients, except the black pepper and sesame seeds, then blend until smooth. Pour into a bowl and top with a grinding of black pepper, the sesame seeds and extra desiccated coconut.

SERVES 1

240ml (1 cup) ice-cold water
1 large ripe avocado, halved, stone removed and flesh scooped out
1 rib of celery, chopped
1 okra, topped and tailed, chopped (optional)
1 tbsp desiccated coconut, plus extra to serve
1 tbsp maple syrup or light soft brown sugar
1 tbsp soy sauce
2 tsp spirulina powder
1 tsp ground coriander
juice of ½ lime
pinch of All-purpose Seasoning (see p239)
freshly ground black pepper
sesame seeds, to garnish

Gungo peas soup

SERVES 6

200g (7oz) dried gungo peas, soaked overnight, or 400g (14oz) can gungo peas
800ml (3⅓ cups) hot vegetable stock
6 pimento seeds (allspice berries), crushed, or ½ tsp ground allspice
1 recipe quantity Spinners or Boiled Dumplings (see p57) (optional)
1 white onion, chopped
2–3 garlic cloves, chopped
1 sprig of thyme, or ½ tsp dried thyme
250g (9oz) white or yellow yam, or cocoyams (taro) or sweet potato, peeled and cut into chunks
250g (9oz) potato, peeled and cut into chunks
1 red bell pepper, deseeded and finely diced
1 carrot, sliced into rounds, then halved
400ml (13.5fl oz) can coconut milk
3 spring onions (scallions)
1 Scotch bonnet pepper, whole
½ tsp sea salt or All-purpose Seasoning (see p239)
½ tsp freshly ground black pepper

At this point I should highlight something I've not mentioned before, like a redacted FBI document. There are many people who don't consider rice and peas made with kidney beans to be the "true" rice and peas. While the scale of affinity towards a particular legume shifts from island to island, it feels wrong to definitively say, for example, kidney beans are Jamaican-style and gungo peas are Trini-style as you'll likely aggrieve someone. Although, for many, the presence of gungo peas (or Congo peas of Congolese origin and often called pigeon peas) in a wide array of dishes elicits waves of nostalgia.

At Ital cookshops across Jamaica, these peas, as well as split peas and the optically similar lentil, form the base of many curries and stews. For those on the go, a slightly lighter Ital sip comes in the form of gungo peas soup, which relies on the peas, rather than a bevy of ground provisions to fill the belly. By the time the peas are cooked down, they almost disintegrate in the mouth and with the addition of coconut milk this could almost be called a hot smoothie.

———

If using dried gungo peas, drain and place in a large saucepan or Dutch pot with the vegetable stock. Bring to the boil and cook for 30 minutes, until starting to soften. Add the pimento or allspice and canned beans, if not using dried.

While you wait, this is a good time to make the spinners or boiled dumplings, if using.

Next, add the onion, garlic and thyme to the pan and cook over a medium-high heat for 30 minutes. Add the yam, potato, red bell pepper and carrot, cover and simmer for 20 minutes.

Add the coconut milk, spring onions, dumplings, if using, stir and turn the heat up to medium high. When the pot starts to bubble, turn the heat down to low.

Add the Scotch bonnet, cover with the lid and simmer for a final 15 minutes, until everything is cooked and tender. Season with salt or all-purpose seasoning and pepper.

Red pea soup

Red pea soup, or stew peas, is an institution practically everywhere in Jamaica, from uptown diners to roadside stalls. Growing up, this or Cock Soup (see p117) were staple dishes made by my mum as soon as the days began to get shorter and colder. I never knew which one it was going to be until I was summoned from my bedroom with a loud shout, and I was always a bit more excited if it was red pea soup – something about the slow-cooked kidney beans and coconut milk, combined with the seasoning is fantastic.

A single pot would magically last several days, especially when bolstered with extra starch and vegetables that make an ample filler on their own without the need for meat or poultry. This dish usually comes loaded with pork, chicken or beef, which you can feel free to add at the initial cooking stage. Fortunately, this soup is easy to make vegan and still tastes great.

─────

If using dried kidney beans, drain and rinse them. Place the beans in a large saucepan or Dutch pot, cover with water and bring to the boil over a high heat. Boil the beans for 10 minutes, then turn the heat down to medium and simmer for 45 minutes to 1 hour, until tender. Drain, then mash half of the beans.

While you wait, this is a good time to make the spinners or boiled dumplings.

Put the cooked/mashed beans (or the canned beans) back in the pan with the hot water. Add the garlic, onion, potato, cayote, carrot, sweet potoato or yam, corn, if using, and spring onions to the pan with the Scotch bonnet and cook, covered with the lid, for 20–25 minutes.

Add the coconut milk, pimento or allspice, thyme, all-purpose seasoning, salt and pepper and stir until combined. Add the dumplings and simmer for another 15 minutes, until the vegetables are tender and the dumplings are cooked through. If the stew is too thick, add extra water and heat through. Alternatively, if using canned beans and you would like your soup thicker, combine the cornflour with a little water, then mix into the soup and cook until thickened to your liking. Let the soup rest off the heat for 10 minutes before serving. You can add a dash of Scotch Bonnet Hot Sauce (see p240), if you like.

SERVES 4–6

350g (12oz) dried red kidney beans, soaked overnight, or 2 x 400g (14oz) cans kidney beans, not drained and half mashed
1 recipe quantity Spinners or Boiled Dumplings (see p57)
1.5 litres (6 cups plus 4 tbsp) hot water
3 garlic cloves, minced
1 small onion, finely chopped, or 3 tsp onion powder
1 white potato, peeled and diced into 3cm (1¼in) chunks
1 chayote, about 200g (7oz), peeled and diced
1 carrot, sliced into rounds
150g (5½oz) sweet potato or yam, peeled and cut into chunks
1 corn on the cob, cut into 4cm (1½in) rounds (optional)
2 spring onions (scallions), green part only, finely chopped
1 Scotch bonnet pepper, whole
400ml (13.5fl oz) can coconut milk
6 pimento seeds (allspice berries), crushed, or ½ tsp ground allspice
3 sprigs of thyme
1 tbsp All-purpose Seasoning (see p239)
1 tsp sea salt
1 tsp freshly ground black pepper
1 tsp cornflour (corn starch) (optional)

Ital sip

Time seems to stand still at the top of the Blue Mountains. The raucous noise of the weekend Nyabinghi meditation ceremonies is replaced by tranquility during the weekdays. The slight breeze meandering through the forest of trees, the roving cattle and tinny projection of radios can be heard at a distance. The peacefulness of the moment doesn't match the hard work going on behind the scenes in the Rastafari settlements. While they emit an aura of a leisurely lifestyle, the energy and exertion required to live off-grid needs work and all manner of elbow grease, from farming and plumbing to carpentry and masonry. This combined with the overnight ceremonies requires ample sustenance, especially when meat is off the cards. Enter Ital sip, "sip" being a Rasta-ism for soup.

Essentially, this is a vegetable soup but to reduce it to such basic terminology, strips it of its magic. In all the different Rastafari settlements, guesthouses and eating outposts I visited, the preparation of the meal is a familial affair and evidently rooted in West African lineage. The youngers are summoned to gather produce from the plots, while the elders configure the makeshift outdoor fireplaces, do the chopping and begin the meal. At this point, all the hard work – months of farming and food prep – has been done. All that is needed is a huge pot, wood and fire.

After leaving Jamaica, I longed for those Ital sips and I recreated this meal based from memory on a mish-mash of different ones I'd tried, relying on Spanish and Jamaican supermarkets in Lauderhill, South Florida, a place that only Brixton or Harlesden in the UK can match for its plethora of Jamaican enterprise.

You may struggle to find all the produce for this meal in your local supermarket, however, many towns have small markets or food shops run by a variety of global diasporas that mostly sell everything, while the seasonings are commonplace. That said, every time I saw Ital sip being made by the Rasta it seemed to be as much about a lifestyle and philosophy than a strict recipe, and while it has its common roster of ingredients nothing is set in stone, so do vary this depending on what you have available.

SERVES 6

200g (7oz) yellow split peas, rinsed

1 recipe quantity Spinners or Boiled Dumplings (see p57)

3 garlic cloves, chopped

1 small onion, chopped

250g (9oz) cocoyam (taro), peeled and diced

1 corn on the cob, sliced into 6 rounds

250g (9oz) sweet potato or pumpkin, peeled, deseeded and diced

1 Scotch bonnet pepper, whole

400ml (13.5fl oz) can coconut milk

200–300g (7–10oz) callaloo or spinach, chopped

2 white potatoes, peeled and diced

1 carrot, chopped

1 chayote, about 200g (7oz), peeled and diced (optional)

2 spring onions (scallions), left whole

1 sprig of oregano

1 sprig of thyme

1 tsp ground ginger

6 pimento seeds (allspice berries)

1 tbsp All-purpose Seasoning (see p239)

½ tsp freshly ground black pepper

4 okra, topped and tailed, sliced

1 rib of celery, finely chopped

In your largest pan or Dutch pot, add the split peas with 700ml (3 cups) water and bring to the boil over a medium-high heat. Turn the heat down to medium and simmer, half-covered, for 20 minutes, until the split peas are half cooked.

While you wait, this is a good time to make the spinners or boiled dumplings.

Add the garlic, onion, cocoyam, corn, sweet potato or pumpkin and Scotch bonnet to the pan and stir with a wooden spoon. Add half the coconut milk, stir, and cook for 10 minutes.

Next, add the dumplings, callaloo or spinach, potatoes, carrot, chayote, spring onions, herbs, ginger, pimento, all-purpose seasoning and pepper, stir and cook for 10 minutes. Pour in the rest of the coconut milk. Add the okra and celery, half-cover with the lid, and simmer for 5 minutes, until the vegetables are tender and the dumplings cooked through, then serve.

Higglers – marronage & mangoes

"How do they know I'm not from here?" I jest to a fellow British Jamaican, referring to the market vendors hollering, "Yo foreign!" at us. "They just know," she jovially replies.

For a summation of Jamaican agriculture, commerce, history, religion, culture and complex social structure, you need look no further than the higgler. A higgler is defined as "one who peddles"; and who "sells anything – food, cloth, even scrap iron". While market selling in Jamaica has been documented since the time of the Taino peoples in the late 15th century, the informal economy took on an entire new significance during colonialism and slavery.

On Sundays, the enslaved were allowed to sell excess produce from their ground provision plots for their own gain. They sold to freed people, travellers, merchants and so on who frequented new hubs in places like Kingston's Port Royal and the former capital Spanish Town.

Christian missionaries saw these spaces as effective in dispersing the words of the Bible, and the urban planning that followed centred on these spaces. On Sundays, the mass confluence of people – that would otherwise have been separated by plantations spread hundreds of miles apart – acted as an early form of social media. Here, the enslaved could *"share information about the most recent developments in their struggle for freedom".* (Davorbailey, *The Origins and Growth of the Jamaican Higgler.*)

The trust network established by higglers provided a system reminiscent of the underground railroads in the southern US, where runaways were able to cover long distances using points of contact along the escape routes. The community and kinship fostered in the markets also made this possible. Maroons, or escaped slaves, were able to plan their break for freedom as they sourced food and resources from the higglers. Adverts for lost slaves were common and featured frequently in the media of the day, such was the dexterity of these absconders.

Trust is still of great importance today. As shown in Winnifred Brown-Glaude's book *Higglers in Kingston,* with its look into the life of higglers revealing that they trust each other before they trust a system that has never looked out for them. This system of trust is what makes the market unique and wonderful in a world of supermarket self-checkouts. You can't run anything past the all-seeing eyes of the vendor: hours spent journeying, toiling and vending – they've seen more than most of us can forget.

Much maligned, parodied, and most often defeminized Black women, these entrepreneurial people are the ones that for centuries have propped up the image and ecosystem of the country that we know today. The innovation needed to attract customers among fierce competition, be it colourful stands, fruit dangling on strings, and the aesthetics of laying out produce (aka food styling) are all there to see. Life at the markets is an education in itself. So much can be learned at markets: a quick maths lesson while bartering; new cookery skills thanks to the oral exchange of recipes; not to mention general life skills.

Some prefer the perceived hassle-free, quiet and uniform convenience of the new type of big box supermarkets found the world over, and also springing up in Jamaica. Others live for the rapport with their go-to vendor, as renowned reggae artist Junior Reid sang on his track "Higgler Move": *"Every Higgler them have them customer hey."* For them, continued support for the street vendors is a must. Not just for the higglers, but for the network of local farmers, producers, bakers, apiarists, oil makers, and those up in the rural areas who toil the land and can't conceivably make it to the market themselves. All rely on the increasingly displaced higgler.

Cock soup

Going to a university in a relatively small city compared with London, my desire for home-cooked comfort food intensified as the sun set on autumn, the days became shorter and the college green was blanketed in frost. There was a small Jamaican bar in town called Hi-Lo's that was always great for a late-night rum, but unfortunately didn't replicate my mum's homely soups that I'd enjoyed after school in the years before.

Samuel Selvon's 1956 novel, *The Lonely Londoners,* set in the wake of the Second World War's mass migration of people from the Caribbean to the UK, speaks frequently about the unforeseen cold weather in this new homeland. I often wonder if my grandparents and their elders ever conceived the coldness that they would have to endure in the likes of Toronto, Harlem and Hackney. What once had been reserved for Saturdays in the shade of the island heat: soup of all types became an everyday solace in the soot-ridden, industrial heartlands of the diaspora.

After Red Pea Soup (see p110), my favourite mum soup was (and still is) chicken soup or cock soup (when yard roosters were used), loaded with chicken bits, soft potatoes and cooked-down pumpkin, which turn the soup a vivid orange. I have a sneaky feeling that my mum would purposefully overdo the Scotch bonnet, sending peppery smoke billowing through the house to prevent us from finishing the whole pot of soup in one sitting.

A couple of years back when I was living in Ochi, the stars aligned on Mother's Day of all days when an effervescent neighbour, Ms Daphne, some years older than my mum, saw me hanging out in the yard and invited me to come and have soup – chicken no less – with her and her mother. This recipe is borne out of a memory of those soups but, sadly for a certain group of people, without the chicken foot that is often used to shore up this dish.

SERVES 4–6

1.5 litres (6 cups plus 4 tbsp) hot vegetable bouillon/stock or water
1kg (2¼lb) chicken legs or skin-on, bone-in chicken thighs
300–400g (10–14oz) pumpkin, peeled, deseeded, and cut into 3cm (1¼in) chunks
6 pimento seeds (allspice berries), crushed, or ½ tsp ground allspice
3 garlic cloves, minced
1 onion, finely chopped
5 sprigs of thyme
2 spring onions (scallions), finely chopped
1 recipe quantity Spinners or Boiled Dumplings (see p57) (optional)
200g (7oz) yellow yam or sweet potato, cut into 2cm (¾in) chunks (optional)
2 ribs of celery, sliced
1 turnip, cut into chunks (optional)
1 carrot, sliced into rounds
1 Scotch bonnet pepper, whole
1 potato, cut into 2cm (¾in) chunks
1 chayote, about 200g (7oz) in total, peeled and cut into 2cm (¾in) chunks (optional)
sea salt and freshly ground black pepper

Bring the stock or water (if using water, season with salt) to the boil in a large, heavy-based saucepan or Dutch pot. Add the chicken, pumpkin, pimento seeds or allspice, garlic, onion, thyme and spring onions. Return to the boil, then turn the heat down to medium, cover with the lid, and simmer for 30 minutes.

While you wait, this is a good time to make the spinners or boiled dumplings, if using.

Mash half the pumpkin in the pan, then add the spinners or dumplings, yam, celery, turnip, if using, carrot, Scotch bonnet, potato and chayote and cook for another 15 minutes on a medium-high heat.

Turn the heat down to medium-low and cook for 10 minutes. Taste and season with salt and pepper to taste, then turn the heat down to low and simmer for a final 5–10 minutes, until the chicken is cooked through and the vegetables are tender.

Pepper pot

Everywhere the ancestors of Black African women travel, soups of some kind follow. Links to the motherland may have been severed and names altered, yet throughout the diaspora one name that crops up again and again is pepper pot. That said, pepper pot means different things to different people. In the easterly Caribbean shores, pepper pot was the pot-liquor in which cassava roots were boiled to free them of their toxicity, known to the Carib Indians as *casiripo* and to the Guyanese as *cassareep*. This silky, jet-black dish, however, never quite made it as popular fare in Jamaica.

In the US, tales of pepper pot have become American lore, rather than African-American lore, with founding father George Washington's "revolutionary" troops surviving on a stew of meat innards, vegetable scraps and spices. The sustenance and warmth of this soup helped them persevere through the winter against the British in the push for independence. What is usually omitted from this story is the culinary influence of the West African descendants and Caribbean migrants who populated the north eastern region of the US.

At that time, the Jamaican pepper pot was not too dissimilar from the version you'd find in Philadelphia. It had a base of cows' or pigs' tails, leaves and, of course, some form of ground provisions, be it a single potato or an amalgamation of Hard Food (see p56). A 1698 Oxford English Dictionary entry for the Jamaican dish notes, *"They make a rare Soop they call Pepper-pot; it is an excellent Breakfast for a Salamander…"* Evidently, these early colonial itinerants couldn't handle a bit of heat, if you are so inclined feel free to omit the Scotch bonnet peppers from this simple soup.

SERVES 4–6

3 tbsp oil of choice
1 white onion, chopped
6 pimento seeds (allspice berries), crushed, or ½ tsp ground allspice
3 garlic cloves, chopped
1 spring onion (scallion), finely chopped
5 sprigs of thyme
500–600g (1lb 2oz–1lb 5oz) beef short ribs, chopped into 4cm (1½in) thick slices
1.2 litres (5 cups) hot beef stock
6–8 okra, topped and tailed, and sliced into 5mm (¼in) rounds
150g (5½oz) yam or white potato, peeled and cut into 2cm (¾in) dice
1 recipe quantity Spinners or Boiled Dumplings (see p57) (optional)
250g (9oz) callaloo or spinach leaves finely chopped
150g (5½oz) black kale (cavolo nero), stems discarded, leaves finely chopped
½ tsp sea salt or All-purpose Seasoning (see p239)
1 tsp freshly ground black pepper
400ml (13.5fl oz) can coconut milk
1 Scotch bonnet pepper, whole (optional)
250g (9oz) sweet potato, peeled and cut into 2cm (½in) dice

Heat the oil in a large saucepan or Dutch pot over a medium-high heat. Add the onion and sauté for 1 minute before adding the pimento or allspice, garlic, spring onion and thyme. Sauté for 3 minutes, then add the beef and cook for another minute.

Add the stock to the pan or pot and bring to the boil. Turn the heat down to medium-low, cover with the lid and cook for 1–1½ hours, occasionally skimming off any white froth that rises to the surface. Add the okra and yam or potato. Cover again with the lid and cook for another 45 minutes.

While you wait, this is a good time to make the spinners or boiled dumplings, if using.

Next, add the callaloo or spinach, black kale, salt or all-purpose seasoning, black pepper and coconut milk. Bring to the boil and when the soup starts to bubble, turn the heat down to medium-low, cover with the lid and simmer for 15 minutes.

Add the Scotch bonnet, if using, sweet potato, and spinners or dumplings. Put the lid back on and simmer for a final 20–25 minutes. Test the beef, if it's tender and cooked to your liking turn off the heat and serve.

Fish tea

In a country of limited economic fortunes, soup has been a lifeline for people over the centuries. While cookshops (even a humble shack) need a certain level of infrastructure to operate, soup vendors can pop up anywhere: in the corner of a barber shop; beside a pool table in a game hall; or, of course, at a late-night rave.

Meaty soups can be quite heavy, so many looking for a quick pick-me-up favour seafood versions. While conch soup is a favourite with locals and tourists alike, the taste and texture of the mollusc can be quite divisive. Fish tea, however, is widely popular, which more than likely explains its presence everywhere across Jamaica. It is essentially a broth, although since its base stock is light it has become known by the name fish tea, and even abbreviated to simply "tea". Since tea is used as a catch-all for many things in Jamaica, do ask for clarity if someone offers you tea! Those of central or south American descent may also recognize it as *chupe*, *caldo* or *sopa de pescado*.

Fish tea, long seen as affordable nourishment, traditionally featured the undesirable parts of a fish, including the head, as well as whatever odd assortment of small fish available to the vendor or family member cooking it. In true Jamaican fashion, it is heavily supplemented with a treasure trove of starchy roots and vegetables of which the ratio, selection and chunk-size is completely up to you.

———

Using a fish scaler or sharp knife, give the fish a once over to remove any remaining scales. Place the fish in a bowl and rinse with water. Drain, then add fresh water and squeeze over the lemon or lime. Use the squeezed-out citrus halves like a sponge to clean the fish, then rinse again with water.

To make a broth, bring 500ml (2 cups plus 2 tbsp) water to the boil in a large, heavy-based saucepan or Dutch pot, then turn down the heat to a simmer. Place the fish in the pan with the garlic, salt and pepper and simmer for 30 minutes. Strain the fish through a colander or sieve over a bowl and save the broth. Leave the fish to cool, then flake into large pieces, discarding the head, skin, tail and bones.

To make the tea, pour the broth and 1 litre (4 cups plus 3 tbsp) water into the pan or pot and bring to the boil over a medium-high heat. Add the pumpkin, yam,

SERVES 6

2–3 medium-sized fish, about 600g (1lb 5oz) in total, such as snapper, scaled, gutted and cleaned
1 lemon or lime, halved
3 garlic cloves, cut in half
pinch of sea salt, plus extra to season
pinch of freshly ground black pepper, plus extra to season

FOR THE TEA:

300–350g (10–12oz) pumpkin, peeled, deseeded and cut into bite-sized chunks
150g (5½oz) yam, peeled and cut into bite-sized chunks
1–2 green bananas, peeled and chopped
1–2 carrots, sliced into 1cm (½in) rounds
1 potato, peeled and cut into bite-sized chunks
6 pimento seeds (allspice berries)
1 Scotch bonnet pepper, whole
3–4 sprigs of thyme, or 1 tsp dried thyme
½ tsp All-purpose Seasoning (see p239) (optional)
1 corn on the cob, sliced into 4cm (1½in) rounds
1 small bell pepper (choice of colour), deseeded and chopped
2½ spring onions (scallions), chopped
2 ribs of celery, chopped (optional)
7–8 okra, topped and tailed, halved lengthways or sliced into thin rounds
1 tbsp soy sauce (optional)
1 tbsp coconut milk, or butter (optional)

bananas, carrots and potato and stir. Next, add the pimento, Scotch bonnet and thyme. Season with more salt or the all-purpose seasoning, if using, and pepper to taste and cook, stirring occasionally, for 3 minutes. Add the corn, bell pepper, 2 of the spring onions and celery, then turn the heat down to medium-low and simmer for 10 minutes.

Add the fish, okra, soy sauce, coconut milk or butter, if using, cover with the lid, and simmer for another 10 minutes. Leave to cool slightly before serving. Garnish with the remaining spring onion.

Langoustine soup

A common theme in Jamaican food is discovering the most incredible dishes created from a collection of simple ingredients in the most unexpected of places. Harking back to the duality of Jamaican life (see p153), where beauty can turn to chaos at the flip of a switch, I once had my movements limited in Kingston when the area I was staying in was placed under a temporary state of emergency, complete with the arrival of the military guard. This is a semi-regular makeshift response to rising crime that can turn a usually bustling locale into a ghost town, reminiscent of an American spaghetti western with swinging saloon doors and tumbleweed blowing down the street.

Trying to make the most of my time, I ended up hanging out with some taxi drivers at an unofficial depot where they nourished themselves from a giant steel cauldron using a giant ladle. Nobody seemed to bat an eyelid when I reached for a polystyrene cup to find out what everyone was knocking back. Inside the cauldron was a deep, silky-orange soup with an intensity of colour that only pumpkin can create and with small bright-red crustaceans bobbing their heads above the surface. The drivers referred to it as simply langoustine, shorthand for langoustine soup.

While it is not quite in the upper echelons of Jamaican soups, langoustine is still renowned on the island given the relatively easy access to shellfish. Others, especially those from the French Caribbean islands of Martinique and Guadeloupe, may recognize this as bisque, a creamy soup that relies on a blitz of its own ingredients for substance, rather than being bolstered with an array of root vegetables like many other soups on the island. In this soup, duality strikes again as the coconut milk tames the heat of the Scotch bonnet pepper, creating a fine balance, which is brought to life with an acidic hit from a liberal squeeze of lime.

Langoustines may be hard to come by, if your local fishmonger doesn't sell them and you don't fancy a dawn trip to your wholesale fish market. In such an event, large prawns are more than an adequate replacement.

SERVES 4

500g (1lb 2oz) raw langoustine
   or prawns, deveined and
   shelled (shells saved)
2 spring onions (scallions),
   chopped (white and green
   parts separated)
1 tsp Jerk Seasoning (see p238),
   or shop bought (optional)
1 Scotch bonnet pepper, deseeded
   and chopped (optional)
4 tbsp oil of choice
½ onion, finely chopped
1 carrot, diced
2 ribs of celery, finely chopped,
   plus extra to garnish (optional)
3 garlic cloves, minced
5 sprigs of thyme
450–500g (1lb–1lb 2oz) pumpkin,
   peeled, deseeded and cut into
   bite-sized chunks
½ tsp All-purpose Seasoning
   (see p239)
2 tbsp tomato purée (tomato paste)
juice of 1 lime
120–200ml (½–¾ cup) coconut milk
1 tbsp butter
1 handful of basil leaves,
   to garnish (optional)

FOR THE SHELLFISH STOCK:

2 tbsp coconut oil or butter
shellfish shells (saved from the
   peeled langoustine/prawns)
1 litre (4 cups plus 3 tbsp) hot water
½ onion
½ tsp sea salt
½ tsp freshly ground black
   pepper, plus extra for seasoning

To make the shellfish stock, heat the coconut oil or butter in a large saucepan or Dutch pot over a medium heat. Add the reserved shells and sauté for 3–5 minutes. Add the hot water and onion. Season with salt and pepper, then turn the heat down and simmer for 30 minutes to 1 hour, depending on how strong you like your stock. Strain the stock into a jug.

While the stock is cooking, put the peeled langoustine or prawns into a large bowl with the green part of the spring onions, the jerk seasoning and half the Scotch bonnet, if using. Season with pepper, cover and set aside in the fridge until needed.

Warm half the oil in the pan or pot over a medium heat, add the onion and the white part of the spring onions and sauté for 3 minutes. Next add the carrot, celery and garlic and continue to cook for 3 minutes. Add the remaining Scotch bonnet, if using, thyme, pumpkin, all-purpose seasoning, ½ teaspoon black pepper and stir. Cover with the lid and simmer for 20 minutes.

Turn the heat down to medium-low, stir in the shellfish stock, tomato purée and half the lime juice. Cook, covered, for a further 20 minutes. Decant into a large blender or leave in the pan if you have a hand-held blender. Add the coconut milk, saving a little to serve, and the butter, then blend until smooth. Return the mixture to the pan and simmer for 5–10 minutes over a medium-low heat, until heated through.

Heat the remaining olive oil (or swap for butter) in a frying pan over a medium heat, add the langoustine or prawns and any marinade and fry for 3–5 minutes, until pink. Remove from the pan with a slotted spatula and set aside on a plate, saving the flavoured oil.

To serve, ladle the soup into bowls. Top with basil, if using, a drizzle of coconut milk, the reserved oil, and the langoustine or prawns. You can also add celery as a garnish.

NOSE
-TO-TAIL

"Apart from the shock exclamation of 'Gordon Bennett' and the patience-inducing 'better safe than sorry' adages, that of 'waste not, want not' sticks with me the most."

While the physical things that my grandmother left behind may lie in shoeboxes and storage, the things that she and other elders said live with me, and now I frequently find myself uttering them in the same vein as I get older. When you're a kid, they come as an annoyance but like most other things that those before us do, there is a lightbulb moment when they make complete sense. Apart from the shock exclamation of "Gordon Bennett" and the patience-inducing "better safe than sorry" adages, that of "waste not, want not" sticks with me the most.

As a kid, most years we would visit family in the hills of St. Ann Parish, north of a bustling market town called Brown's Town in Jamaica. On one occasion, about two decades ago when I was about ten years old, there was a goat in the garden. It was most probably purchased due to family coming from "foreign" (abroad). I remember clearly the goat was a friendly, docile animal and I'd often play with it, throwing sticks and such, and helping to feed it daily.

On the day before our departure, we had an absolute feast: curry, soup, dumplings, rice and peas – all the trimmings. The next day upon leaving, it took me a moment to realize the goat in the garden was missing. In my youthful ignorance, I thought it had gone to play with the other goats we'd often see grazing down the road. It was some years later that I had the stark realization that we'd eaten it. Curry goat, mannish water (goat soup), the whole goat in all its glory. On future trips, I witnessed my neighbours in Ochi carrying goat carcasses home over their shoulders, or beheading chickens on tree stumps in their front yards before cooking up chicken foot soup. At the time, I was pretty indifferent to it. The appreciation of and connection to the animal, particularly in the UK and the US, is incredibly disjointed.

Up until the mid-20th century, cattle grazing pens were a pivotal part of the Jamaican food system and in the decades before that were arguably the most lucrative non-sugar agrarian activity in rural Jamaica. If you've ever wondered the origin of Jamaican place names that include the word "pen", such as May Pen and Grants Pen, then they derive from this. The vast plains of St. Catherine Parish were especially arable and open, hence the high concentration of "pens" there.

Meat has now become a packaged commodity as accessible as any other inanimate consumer good, and since the Jamaican pens have declined more meat is unfortunately imported instead of locally reared. Moreover, we've glorified and marketed certain cuts of meat so much that food waste has rocketed, with non-desirable parts going into processed food or discarded. I've always believed that if you're going to eat meat it is ridiculous to be pretentious about what animals you eat and which parts. For the early people of the Caribbean, animals were hunted and were mainly boar. Perhaps, this is why to this day there is still such a reverence and lore of jerk pork in Jamaica. For the enslaved, no such liberty of choice was available. Like in serfdom Europe and beyond, meat was a rarity for the everyday person and was predominantly the domain of slavers and the elite classes. In Jamaica, the meat given, if at all, to the enslaved people were the parts deemed unsavoury for the upper echelons of society, such as offal, innards, hoofs, tails, heads, and so on.

The disdain towards those who were so stingy in distributing meat is possibly at the root of the infamous Jamaican duppy legend of the rolling calf, the spirit of a cantankerous male butcher from the afterworld. This huge, calf-like creature is said to roll along the road, blocking the way of late-night revellers, and chasing them with wicked intent. Various descriptions of the spirit mention its blazing red fiery eyes and a loud clanking chain, which is dragged behind it.

Superstition says to escape the rolling calf, the victim can do one of several things: drop objects for it to count (most supernatural creatures in Jamaican folklore can be evicted this way); get to a road junction before it; or open a pen knife and stick it into the ground. The calf is also said to be terrified of being beaten with a tarred whip held in the left hand, not wanting to be at the receiving end of the punishment. Ironically, the rolling calf is fond of sugar, since in our household, like many others, their real-world counterpart often ends up being submerged in a swimming pool of seasoning, including brown sugar, molasses or the sweetened browning sauce.

Many still perceive off-cuts as slave food and even when prepared with an array of seasonings are completely shunned. Others, however, look to celebrate and reclaim the legacy of these cuts of meat and for many they remain among the most affordable means of sustenance. Across Jamaica, colourful posts and signboards advertise every inch of an animal, from cows' and pigs' heads to necks and tails. With this constant demand, meat wholesale stores can be truly hectic as people choose from the varying list of offal and cuts for the week. Navigating the baying crowds bartering through grilled windows and the out-the-door queues is not for the faint-hearted, particularly on especially hot days.

"Besides maybe Marmite, I've never seen anything as polarizing as certain cuts of meat."

Among my family and friends, there is no uniform agreement on different parts of an animal. Besides maybe Marmite, I've never seen anything as polarizing as certain cuts of meat. Some people, like my cousin, have dibbed the turkey neck for thirty Christmases in a row, while others at the table are completely glad to be rid of its presence. Some savour the chicken foot swimming among the array of vegetables in soups, and some are repulsed by it. Despite its growing popularity, some are even offended by the idea of oxtail.

"If we consume meat, I believe we should be prepared to celebrate all parts of the animal: 'waste not, want not'."

It is, of course, all about how off-cuts are cooked and seasoned. If the task at hand was to eat them just cooked or boiled with absolutely no seasonings, I too would be as disinclined to eat them. But this is Jamaican food, so that is obviously not the case. An heirloom of culture, from indigenous Indians, Africans and indentured Asians, ensure that herbs, spices and seasonings are liberally added to every dish. The flavour of aromatic spring onions, garlic and ginger seep into a fatty cartilage, while pieces of meat cut a merry dance when coated in spices, such as paprika, cayenne, allspice and turmeric, with an added Scotch bonnet pepper to boot. On top of this, the leisurely process of stewing, currying and jerk barbecuing perform an almost switcheroo magic trick: it's sometimes hard to believe that the contents of the pot when you take off the lid are the same basic ingredients you started with.

That said, whenever I return to Jamaica, I don't actually eat much meat. Something about the tropical climate draws me more to the produce of the water, trees and earth. In retrospect, the peak of my meat consumption when it comes to Jamaican and Caribbean food is concentrated in the diaspora during the cold winter months – especially in London, Toronto, New York and South Florida, the international havens of Caribbean food.

Given all this, there are a few meals that are difficult to resist when it comes to special occasions like birthdays, weddings and so on, or from one of my hallowed Jamaican takeouts (JB's in Peckham and Smokey Jerkey in New Cross, South London), or when I return to my mother's house in the short, dark English winter days. As a result, there are ten or so must-have recipes for me. Each one lauds the anatomy of an array of animals and with this in mind, if we consume meat, I believe we should be prepared to celebrate all parts of the animal: "waste not, want not".

Welcome to
CHOSEN RESTAURANT

Ph. 334-3360

Breakfast

ACKEE & SALT FISH... 250
BAKE BEAN & SALT FISH. 350
350
OKRO & SALT FISH 250
(ONLY ON FRIDAYS) 350
STEW CHICKEN / CALLALOO
LIVER / KIDNEY......
SALT MACKEREL ....
FRY DUMPLIN......
TEA · MILO · COFFEE
NATURAL Fruit Juice

Place Orders Here

FRIGIDA

Lunch / Dinner

CHICKEN
BAKE \ FRY \ CURRY

BROWN STEW FISH
STEAM FISH TO ORDER
COW HEAD
COW FOOT
STEW BEEF

SOUP
Cold DRINKS

SOLD HERE
100% JUICE

Summer Blow-Out Prices

- NECK & BACK   75
- TURKEY NECK
- GRUNT (GI)   149
- CB CHICKEN   197
- LOCAL COWFOOT   199
- MANG-FRYERS   199
- BABY KINGFISH FRYERS 199
- MULLET   199
- PORK STEW   295
  BETTY MILK   221
  LASCO FOOD DRINK   118

Package Deal

• 3 PK. DEAL $526	• 5 PK. DEAL $857	10 PK. DEAL $1490
3 LB. RICE	5 LB. RICE	10 LB. RICE
3 LB. FLOUR	5 LB. FLOUR	10 LB. FLOUR
3 LB. SUGAR (DAFA)	5 LB. SUGAR (DAFA)	10 LB. SUGAR (DAFA)

The Best Dressed Chicken PRICE LIST

The Best Dressed Chicken PRICE LIST

PLEASE CHECK
GOODS BEFORE
LEAV...

ORDER
HERE

OPEN SUNDAY
7 A.M. – 12 NOON

Oxtail & butter beans

Of all the animals eaten in Jamaica, my grandmother's rule of making the most of all foods seems most appropriate to the cow (used interchangeably with ox). The animal was so lauded it found its way into many of the island tales of enslaved people stealing food from their enslaver, including one where parents deceived their own kids by feeding them salted fish to not blow the ruse of the hidden butchered cow led astray the night before.

Cows were literally eaten from nose-to-tail with different parts partitioned to different levels of society: ox cheeks, jars of pickled tripe, and calves' tongues and calves' feet in jelly in assorted flavours were said to appeal to upper-class tastes. Meanwhile, innards such as tripe and kidney and even cow skin, were used as a filler of sorts to stretch out meals. For a complex number of reasons, from butchering know-how to limited access, the more familiar meaty cuts of beef never really entered the Jamaican culinary lexicon over the generations.

One part of the cow that did enter lore was the tail. Coveted (there is only one per cow afterall), it became a delicacy once seasoned overnight and slow-cooked. This method of cooking oxtail creates a rich dish with sweetness, saltiness and spice; the loosened parts turning into a meaty jelly. The accompanying softened butter beans (lima beans) dissolving into the meaty gravy, producing an incomparable texture that many cannot imagine living without.

———

Mix all the ingredients for the marinade in a large bowl. Add the oxtail and, using your hands, turn the meat in the marinade until coated. Cover the bowl and leave to marinate in the fridge for at least 1 hour, ideally overnight.

Heat the oil in a large, heavy-based saucepan or Dutch pot (or you could use a pressure cooker) over a medium heat. Remove the oxtail from the marinade, reserving the marinade for later. Add the oxtail to the pan or pot and brown on all sides; this will take about 5 minutes. (Do this in batches to ensure the meat browns, rather than steams, adding more oil if needed.)

Return all the browned meat to the pan or pot. Pour the hot stock or water into the marinade bowl, stir, then pour it into the pan to cover the meat. Add all the

SERVES 4

1kg (2¼lb) oxtail, trimmed and chopped into 5cm (2in) chunks (ask your butcher to do this for you)
5 tbsp oil of choice
1 litre (4 cups plus 3 tbsp) hot beef stock or water
400g (14oz) can butter beans (lima beans), drained
½ Scotch bonnet pepper, deseeded and chopped
1 tsp cornflour (corn starch) (optional)

FOR THE MARINADE:

6 pimento seeds (allspice berries), crushed, or ½ tsp ground allspice
5 sprigs of thyme
3 garlic cloves, minced
2.5cm (1in) piece of fresh root ginger, peeled and minced
2 spring onions (scallions), roughly chopped
1 onion, finely chopped
1 tbsp Jerk Seasoning (see p238) (optional), or shop bought
1 tbsp mixed herbs
1 tbsp Worcestershire sauce
½-1 tbsp soy sauce
1 tsp All-purpose Seasoning (see p239)
1 tsp Cajun seasoning
1 tsp freshly ground black pepper
1 tsp paprika
½ red bell pepper, deseeded and finely chopped
pinch of sea salt

FOR THE GRAVY:

125ml (½ cup) stout of choice
2 tbsp browning
2 sprigs of thyme
1–2 tbsp light soft brown sugar
1½ tbsp Worcestershire sauce
1 tbsp brown sauce or
    oyster sauce
1 tbsp tomato ketchup (optional)
1 Scotch bonnet pepper, whole
1½ tsp soy sauce
1 tsp tomato purée (tomato paste)
½–1 tsp sea salt

ingredients for the gravy and stir. Bring to the boil and cook for 5 minutes, then turn the heat down to low, cover with the lid and simmer for 1½ hours, stirring occasionally (or 45 minutes to 1 hour in a pressure cooker).

Add the butter beans and Scotch bonnet and cook, covered, for another 30 minutes. To test the meat is ready, pierce with a skewer; it should be soft like butter

To thicken the gravy if needed, mix the cornflour with a little water and cook, uncovered, until thickened. Alternatively, if the sauce is too dry add 3–5 tablespoons water and heat through.

Curry chicken

The famous vinyl cover of reggae artist, Dr. Alimantado's album *The Best Dressed Chicken in Town* features a cut dreaded figure waltzing across downtown Kingston's legendary Parade. The album gives a cutting insight into Jamaica in the 1970s, but listening to the record I'm not sure we literally find out who is the best dressed chicken in town. Is it jerk chicken, chicken soup or brown stew? I reach my limits quite quickly with fried chicken and similarly jerk. Meanwhile, brown stew I find best reserved for the gelatinous cartilage of cowfoot and oxtail, and so that leaves curry chicken.

North of the Parade, up Orange Street and Old Hope Road to Half Way Tree, a makeshift restaurant in the front drive of a house confirms my love of curry chicken. Every weekday lunchtime, the family of the house fashions a dive with a few tables, benches and a tarpaulin to shelter from the sun. Under the cover, food is dished out from Dutch pots and drinks are kept perfectly just above freezing point in an ice box. Curry chicken is simple, but it can vary so much: sometimes, it's as thick as a stew, while at other times the sauce is as fluid as soup. It can be deep brown in colour or even a pale orange. Here, it's somewhere in the middle of the spectrum, deeply spiced with black pepper, but the option to kick the heat up a notch is left to customers with small bowls of hot pepper sauce passed from table to table.

Even though I often wax lyrical about enjoying the presence of bones in a dish, this is one where I hypocritically call for their absence – bones also add a few split seconds to the time it takes me to devour a whole pot. Some meals should be left alone to cook, but here I recommend a continual taste test to get it to your liking.

———

To make the marinade, mix the onion, garlic, Scotch bonnet, pimento, ginger, all-purpose seasoning, spring onions, 2 tablespoons curry powder and 1 teaspoon of the soy sauce in a large bowl. Add the chicken, season with salt and turn the chicken in the marinade until coated. Cover the bowl and leave to marinate in the fridge for at least 30 minutes, ideally overnight.

Heat the oil in a large, heavy-based saucepan or Dutch pot over a medium heat. Remove the chicken from the marinade, reserving the marinade for later.

SERVES 4

700g (1lb 9oz) skinless, boneless chicken thighs, cut into bite-sized chunks
4 tbsp oil of choice
3–4 sprigs of thyme
1 tsp cumin seeds (optional)
1 tsp ground turmeric
2 carrots, thickly sliced
½ large potato, peeled and cut into large bite-sized chunks
300ml (1¼ cups) hot water
100ml (⅓ cup plus 1 tbsp) coconut milk
1 tsp browning (optional)
50g (1¾oz) frozen peas (optional)
1 tsp cornflour (corn starch) (optional)
sea salt and freshly ground black pepper

FOR THE MARINADE:

1 onion, chopped
3 garlic cloves, minced
1 Scotch bonnet pepper, chopped (deseeded for less heat)
6 pimento seeds (allspice berries), crushed, or ½ tsp ground allspice
1 tsp fresh root ginger, peeled and minced, or ground ginger
2 tbsp All-purpose Seasoning (see p239)
2 spring onions (scallions), thinly sliced
3 tbsp curry powder
4 tsp dark soy sauce

Add the chicken to the pan or pot and brown on all sides; this will take about 5 minutes. (Do this in batches to ensure the meat browns, rather than steams, adding more oil if needed.)

Return all the browned meat to the pan. Stir in any remaining marinade in the bowl, plus the thyme, remaining 1 tablespoon curry powder, cumin, if using, and turmeric. Next, add the carrots and potato.

Pour in the hot water and coconut milk to cover the chicken, stir, then add the rest of the soy sauce and browning, if using. Season with salt and black pepper to taste. Bring to the boil, then turn the heat down to low, cover with the lid and cook for 40 minutes, stirring occasionally. If using the frozen peas, add them after 35 minutes and cook for another 5 minutes.

To thicken the gravy if needed, mix the cornflour with a little water and cook, uncovered, until thickened. Alternatively, if the sauce is too dry add 3–5 tablespoons water and heat through.

Curry goat

"You eat GOATS!" a fellow classmate wailed in horror as I recounted the joy of a recent meal of curry goat during a primary school conversation. Something about the way she added the "s" at the end made it sound insidious, like my family were cave-dwelling beasts. In the absurdly titled *They Eat That? A Cultural Encyclopedia of Weird and Exotic Food from Around the World,* this sentiment is echoed when the author mentions, seemingly with a literary nudge-nudge, wink-wink, that *"Curry goat is actually one of the national dishes of Jamaica,"* likely to the shock and dismay of its readers.

In retrospect, both point to the same Western reverence and sanctity towards eating certain animals, and the seeming disgust of consuming others. While goat is widely available at local butchers across Britain, particularly in areas with a high ethnic population, it has never fully entered the British culinary repertoire and it's likely this prejudice is the reason. Although goat (and mutton) was favoured during the Tudor period of British history, especially in pies, it doesn't seem to have caught the national imagination since.

Things are different in Jamaica, where meat options were once markedly more limited. Versions of curry goat have been so popular for nearly a century that it was once in contention for the honour of national dish. Writers as far back as the 1600s revealed that goat was preferred to mutton by people of West African descent, and the remnants of this are clear today. As popular as curry goat is in the Caribbean, goat-laden pepper soup is equally adored by those from Sierra Leone to Nigeria, hence our shared nonchalance at the thought of eating goat. The indentured Indian community who arrived in late-19th century Jamaica must have revelled at the reception to their native slow-cooked goat curries, often made from rationed mutton on the weekends. With this meeting of peoples, Caribbean curry goat was born.

While the likes of tikka masala and green Thai curry have reached mass awareness in Britain, curry goat lags behind. The reason? Perhaps, the lack of affinity to bones. Popularized high-street Caribbean chains attempt a substitution with bone-free lamb, yet for curry conservatives (small "c") many of Caribbean heritage stay steadfast in their support of the presence of goat bones. While some ethnic cuisines have diverged from their cultural origins to crossover, put simply Caribbeans aren't having any of it!

I'd very much suggest using this recipe as an introduction to the joy of bones. The search for the last piece of wonderfully seasoned gristle hidden in the crevice of a bone is like a treasure hunt and the ability to strip a bone to its gleaming white core will hold you in good stead with many Jamaican elders.

SERVES 4

1kg (2¼lb) goat meat on the bone,
cut into bite-sized pieces

5 tbsp oil of choice, such as
rapeseed or coconut

1.5 litres (6 cups plus 4 tbsp)
hot beef/lamb/goat stock
or hot water

1 tsp light soft brown sugar
(optional)

5 sprigs of thyme

1 tsp curry powder

2 tbsp coconut milk,
or coconut cream

1 Scotch bonnet pepper, whole

1 large potato, peeled and cut into
bite-sized pieces

½ bell pepper (colour of choice),
deseeded and chopped
(optional)

FOR THE MARINADE:

6 pimento seeds (allspice berries),
crushed, or ½ tsp ground
allspice

5 sprigs of thyme

3 tbsp curry powder

3 garlic cloves, minced

2.5cm (1in) piece of fresh root
ginger, peeled and minced

2 spring onions (scallions),
finely chopped

1 tbsp Jerk Seasoning (see p238)
(optional), or shop bought

1 tsp mixed herbs (optional)

1 tsp soy sauce (optional)

½ bell pepper (colour of choice),
deseeded and chopped
(optional)

½ onion, finely chopped

pinch of freshly ground
black pepper

pinch of sea salt

Mix the ingredients for the marinade in a large bowl.
Add the goat and, using your hands, turn the meat
in the marinade until coated. Cover the bowl and leave
to marinate in the fridge for at least 30 minutes, ideally
overnight – or even 72 hours is welcome.

Heat the oil in a large, heavy-based saucepan
or Dutch pot over a medium heat. (If using a pressure
cooker, see Note below.) Remove the goat from the
marinade, reserving the marinade for later. Add the goat
to the pan or pot and brown on all sides; this will take
about 5 minutes. (Do this in batches to ensure the meat
browns, rather than steams, adding more oil if needed.)

Return all the browned meat to the pan. Pour 1 litre
(4 cups plus 3 tbsp) of the hot stock or water into the
marinade bowl, stir, then pour it into the pan to cover the
meat. Bring up to the boil, then turn the heat down to
low, cover with the lid, and cook for 45 minutes to 1 hour.

After 45 minutes check the pan. Add the remaining
stock or water if the curry looks too dry and stir to
ensure it isn't sticking to the bottom of the pan. Taste
and add extra salt and pepper to taste and the brown
sugar, if using. Add the thyme, curry powder and
coconut milk or cream and cook for 5 minutes. Add the
Scotch bonnet, turn the heat down to low and simmer,
covered, for 30–45 minutes.

Add the potato and bell pepper, cover and simmer for
30 minutes. Taste the meat, if it's not as soft as you'd like,
cook for a further 20 minutes, or if the sauce is too dry,
add 3–5 tablespoons water and heat through. Turn off
the heat and let sit for 20–30 minutes before serving
with Rice & Peas (see p44) or Syrian Flatbread (see p206).

NOTE *If you have a pressure cooker, brown the meat
as described, above, then transfer the browned meat to
a pressure cooker with the stock and marinade and cook
for 30 minutes. Transfer the contents of the pressure cooker
back to the pan. Season with salt and pepper, add the sugar,
if using, thyme, curry powder, coconut milk or creamed
coconut and Scotch bonnet and simmer for 45 minutes,
then continue as mentioned above.*

Tripe

Tripe falls into that category of foods in the UK that even mention of it prompts instant divisive reaction. Yet, in continental Europe, tripe is at the heart of many celebrated meals. The tomato-heavy Italian *trippa alla romana* celebrates its namesake Rome, and likewise, *callos Madrileña*, a Spanish dish paired with chorizo sausage, has been lauded for centuries in Madrid.

Around the world, market equilibriums have commonly determined entrails to be the cheapest part of an animal to buy, and so it makes sense countries with storied feudal pasts are as embedded with tripe as much as those with histories of slavery.

In Jamaica and other Caribbean islands, tripe features, like most meat, in a curry with plenty of spices such as this richly flavoured, slow-cooked dish. Where the West African staple of stews may have been the early method of choice, the island's intersection of African and Indian culture rears itself here.

_____

Put the tripe in a large pan, cover with water and add the salt. Bring the water to the boil and boil for 20 minutes, then drain and rinse.

Mix together all the ingredients for the marinade in a large bowl. Add the tripe and, using your hands, turn it in the marinade until coated. Cover the bowl and leave to marinate in the fridge for at least 1 hour, ideally overnight.

Heat the oil in a large, heavy-based saucepan or Dutch pot (or you could use a pressure cooker) over a medium-high heat. Add the onion and sauté for 3 minutes, then stir in the spring onions, ginger and garlic and cook for 2 minutes. Add the tripe and the marinade and cook, stirring, for 3 minutes.

Pour in about 500ml (2 cups plus 2 tbsp) water to just cover the tripe. Stir, then add the pimento or allspice, ketchup or tomato, thyme, Scotch bonnet and sugar, if using. Cook, covered with the lid, for 2–2½ hours over a medium heat (or for 30 minutes in a pressure cooker).

Remove the lid and add the red bell pepper and butter beans. Turn the heat down a notch, season to taste before cooking for a further 10 minutes.

To thicken the gravy if needed, mix the cornflour with a little water and cook, uncovered, until thickened. Alternatively, if the sauce is too dry add 3–5 tablespoons water and heat through. Garnish with herbs to serve.

SERVES 4

1kg (2¼lb) cleaned cow tripe, trimmed of excess cartilage, cut into thin strips, rinsed well
1 tbsp sea salt
2 tbsp coconut oil, or oil of choice
1 white onion, chopped
2 spring onions (scallions), chopped
2.5cm (1in) piece of fresh root ginger, peeled and minced, or 1 tsp ground ginger
3 garlic cloves, chopped
6 pimento seeds (allspice berries), crushed, or ½ tsp ground allspice
1 tbsp Scotch Bonnet Ketchup (see p243), or tomato ketchup, or 1 tomato, chopped
1 sprig of thyme
1 Scotch bonnet pepper, whole
1 tsp light soft brown sugar (optional)
1 red bell pepper, deseeded and chopped
400g (14oz) can butter beans (lima beans), drained
2 tsp cornflour (corn starch) (optional)
parsley or coriander (cilantro) leaves, chopped, to garnish

FOR THE MARINADE:

2 tbsp curry powder
1 tsp All-purpose Seasoning (see p239)
1 tsp sea salt
½ tsp freshly ground black pepper

Liver & onions

SERVES 4

500g (1lb 2oz) calves', lambs'
or chickens' liver, membrane
removed, trimmed and cut
into 10cm (4in) long strips
milk or salted water mixed
with 1 tsp apple cider vinegar
5 tbsp oil of choice
½ large onion, thinly sliced
¼ bell pepper (colour of choice,
deseeded and thinly sliced
1 tomato, diced
2 tbsp Scotch Bonnet Ketchup
(see p243), or tomato ketchup
1 tbsp dark soy sauce or browning

FOR THE MARINADE:

6 pimento seeds (allspice berries),
crushed, or ½ tsp ground
allspice
2 spring onions (scallions),
chopped
4–5 sprigs of thyme
3 garlic cloves, minced
2.5cm (1in) piece of fresh root
ginger, peeled and minced,
or 1 tsp ground ginger
2 tsp All-purpose Seasoning
(see p239)
1 tbsp soy sauce
1 Scotch bonnet pepper, whole
1 tsp freshly ground black
pepper

In true island fashion, generation upon generation have prepared this dish, or similar, which is full of flavour and immerses the liver in an array of spices, sweet peppers and a rich gravy. Admittedly, the texture of liver may somewhat be an acquired taste for those not raised on it, but this dish could win you over. The gravy is great mopped up with a batch of crisp Fried Dumplings (see p202).

———

Put the strips of liver in a shallow dish and pour over enough milk to cover, or use salted water mixed with vinegar instead of the milk. Cover the dish and leave to soak for 30 minutes to 1 hour in the fridge. (The soaking will help to get rid of any bitterness in the liver.) Drain, rinse, then place the liver on kitchen paper and pat dry.

Mix all the ingredients for the marinade in a bowl. Add the liver and, using your hands, turn it in the marinade until coated. Cover the bowl and leave to marinate in the fridge for at least 30 minutes, ideally overnight.

Heat the oil in a large frying pan over a medium-high heat. Remove the liver from the marinade and place it in the pan (take care as it may spit). Fry for about 2–3 minutes on each side, until browned and browned on the outside but pink in the middle.

Add the onion, bell pepper and tomato and sauté for 2 minutes, stirring. Add the ketchup and soy sauce or browning and continue to cook for 1–2 minutes, turning the meat and vegetables until coated in the gravy. Serve or turn the heat down to low, cover the pan and simmer for another 5 minutes for a thicker gravy.

Peppered steak

Having ventured into what must be hundreds of Caribbean food institutions across the UK, I'm frequently asked, "Who has the best food?", or "Who has the best *this*?", or even "Who does the best *that*?", and so on. Since it's all a matter of personal taste and opinion I don't like to give an answer in public, but I will always say that if you find yourself somewhere in the southwest London triangle of Brixton, Clapham and Streatham then a trip to True Flavours on Acre Lane is an absolute must. There's a good reason why people double park and queue out the door, waiting in anticipation at the chance to get their order in, especially for chef-owner Junior's peppered steak. Well-prepared meat is layered with a silky sweet and tangy sauce and balances perfectly with subtly salted rice or pasta and Steamed Vegetables (see p52).

Perhaps another reason for this unrivalled patience, I've also seen at Peppers & Spice in Dalston, is that peppered steak is not a common fixture at Caribbean food institutions. Looking at the ingredients for this recipe, the multiple waves of Chinese migrants over the centuries to Jamaica are ever-present, and you are perhaps more likely to find an exquisite peppered steak at your local Chinese eatery than your local Caribbean joint. If neither are available, this elementary recipe is simple enough to arouse joy.

_____

Heat 1 tablespoon of the oil in a wok or large frying pan with a lid over a medium heat. Add the onion and stir-fry for 3 minutes, then add the white part of the spring onion, garlic and ginger and stir-fry for 2 minutes. When browned and slightly translucent transfer to a bowl, increase the heat to medium-high, add the steak, salt or all-purpose seasoning and pepper and stir-fry for 8–10 minutes, until browned on all sides. Remove from the pan and set aside in the bowl with the onions, ginger and garlic.

Turn the heat down to medium and add the remaining oil, stock or hot water, soy sauce, sugar, vinegar, if using, Scotch bonnet ketchup or hot sauce and stir for 30 seconds. Return the contents of the bowl back to the wok or pan, along with the bell peppers and tomatoes. Cover with the lid, turn the heat down to medium-low and simmer for 3 minutes.

In a small bowl, mix the cornflour with 3 tablespoons water, then add to the pan, stir, and simmer for 2 minutes, until the gravy thickens. Serve with rice.

SERVES 4

2 tbsp coconut oil, or oil of choice
1 white onion, thinly sliced
1 spring onion (scallion), white and green parts separated, finely chopped
3 garlic cloves, minced
2.5cm (1in) piece of fresh root ginger, peeled and minced
500g (1lb 2oz) beef steak, such as tenderloin, sliced into 1cm (½in) wide strips
½ tsp sea salt or All-purpose Seasoning (see p239)
½ tsp freshly ground black pepper
200ml (¾ cup) hot beef stock or water
4 tbsp soy sauce
2 tsp light soft brown sugar
1 tbsp apple cider vinegar (optional)
1 tsp Scotch Bonnet Ketchup (see p243), or hot sauce (optional)
1½ bell peppers (mix of colours), deseeded and cut into thin strips
2 tomatoes or 6 cherry tomatoes, chopped or halved
2 tsp cornflour (corn starch)

The blacker the dutchy, the sweeter the stew

True Flavours in South London's Brixton is one of those joints that's so good that queues out the door are just accepted: customers place an order, go about their business, and return in the hope it's ready. Seven days a week until the late hours of the night, Junior and crew churn out homely Jamaican food to veteran locals, who still buy vinyl records from Supertone across the road, in addition to third and fourth generationers who've probably never even been to the Caribbean. More so, the new stream of uni students and grad scheme employees moving to the area seem less daunted about exploring the goings on there than when I first visited some years ago.

Serving hundreds of customers every day, something must keep them coming back, especially as there isn't exactly a dearth of alternative options in the area. As Junior invites me into the kitchen around the back, I find the answer. Not only are the staff jovially bandied together in a Ford-esque conveyor belt of food-to-box-to-customer, but nigh on everything on the menu is cooked in a Dutch pot, and the reason orders take slightly longer is that they won't serve anything until it's at the apex of readiness. While many cookshops prep food and have it sitting in the window in covered bain-maries (which is perfectly fine), Junior permits no such act. Everything, from peppered steak to fish and rice are cooked in Dutch pots, which occupy all four rings of multiple adjacent cookers at the same time. There are Dutch pots of different sizes and different shades of metal, from reflective silver to pitch black.

This is quite rare as Dutch pots tend to be the preserve of the home-cooking arsenal of the sentimental unwavering diaspora elder. Of my generation, although familiar with these silver rotund pots, not many own one themselves. The dedication to Dutch pots (or dutchies, dutchy maids, Dutch ovens...) is hereditary.

Since plantation owners dispensed these portable cast-iron pots to the enslaved, they, and the offspring that followed, learned to cook each and every meal in them, be it fried, boiled or baked (the flat top and ridges were used to balance coals). Many of those from West Africa likely had experience of cooking in these large cauldrons before, which perhaps explains the large number of one-pot meals, such as curries, soups and stews, common in West African and Caribbean cooking.

In my mother's cupboard dutchies are stacked like Russian dolls. Different sizes for different meals and occasions. The hue of a pot is the equivalent to the rings of a tree trunk, or human wrinkles. Preference is always given to the darker, more tenured, and this has been written into lore with the Anansi tale of the *Magic Pot*.

In the tale, the sly protagonist, Anansi, stumbles across a magical talking pot, black and rustic, that on command grants him all manner of feasts from rice and peas to chicken and salted fish, and hard food. The only request made by the pot is that it's never washed or cleaned. After someone stumbles on Anansi's secret, they summon a feast and then make the disastrous error of cleaning the pot, erasing its magic. Angry that his meal ticket is over, when he stumbles across a magical talking whip Anansi exacts his revenge on the kitchenware criminal.

I'm not sure if there's a scientific reason why everything cooked in a Dutch pot, especially an extremely cultured one, tastes better, maybe it's related to its perfect thickness and curvature, or the even distribution of heat, but I doubt you'll find many people to debate this with. The Dutch pot is like a stabilizer, occasionally we may cheat on it, resorting to a pressure cooker to save time when cooking certain cuts of meat, but then always return to it to finish the job.

Brown stew cowfoot

Andrea Levy's novel, *Small Island*, depicts a harrowing account of transitory life for those for whom the world wars irreparably altered their lives and sent them thousands of miles away from home. In the chapter, "Gilbert", a Jamaican British Royal Air Force recruit, agonizingly waxes lyrical about missing home cooking and his disdain for the Brit's propensity to boil every single modicum of flavour out of their food. Beyond lust and the horrors of war he tells, *"There was hardship I was prepared for – bullet, bomb and casual death – but not for the torture of missing cowfoot..."*

Leaning on the writings of the everyday citizen, Jamaican Yvonne Shorter Brown in her recollection of 1950s island life says, *"The poor people would buy the cow foot, cow tail, and cow head to 'make up' with dry broad or lima beans or green Congo peas for their Sunday dinner. The rich only ate these meals as an economic measure, not out of necessity."*

The people who love cowfoot defend it in the same way football fans defend their favourite team. To attack one is an attack on the self, and those who can't understand this vehement support remain confused. Mouths drool, eyes widen and nostrils flare at the thought of the gelatinous cartilage clinging to the bone. As my mum teaches me how to make cowfoot, she recalls the same techniques, particularly that of "swingeing" the meat first (see below), that her elders taught her, and no doubt their elders before them. For someone to turn their nose up at a generationally transcending meal like this one is comparable with turning one's nose up at a family heritage. What's also clear is that those ancestors could make the least desirable parts of an animal taste amazing when slow-cooked in a brown stew of molasses, bell peppers and spices.

———

As my mum would say, "swinge" the meat. If any piece of cowfoot still has hair on it, hold it with tongs over the flames of a hob, slowly rotating the piece and scalding it for about 20 seconds. Leave to cool on a plate before scraping off the hair and any other excess. (Ask your butcher to do this for you if preferred, or you don't have a gas hob or blow torch.)

Place the cowfoot pieces in a large pan and pour in enough water to cover. Bring to the boil, then boil for 10–15 minutes over a high heat. When you start to see

SERVES 4

1kg (2¼lb) cowfoot pieces, trimmed and cleaned
juice of 1 lime
2 tbsp apple cider vinegar
4 tbsp oil of choice
1.3 litres (5½ cups) hot water
½ onion, chopped
3 sprigs of thyme, or 1 tsp of dried thyme
2 tbsp Scotch Bonnet Ketchup (see p243), or tomato ketchup
400g (14oz) can broad beans (fava beans), drained, half of the beans mashed with a fork
1 tsp light soft brown sugar
1 tsp dark soy sauce
1 tsp All-purpose Seasoning (see p239)

FOR THE MARINADE:

3 garlic cloves, minced
3 sprigs of thyme, leaves picked, or 1 tsp of dried thyme
2.5cm (1in) piece of fresh root ginger, peeled and minced
2 spring onions (scallions), finely chopped
1 tsp olive oil or coconut oil
½ onion, diced
¼ bell pepper (colour of choice), deseeded and diced
6 pimento seeds (allspice berries), crushed, or ½ tsp ground allspice
1 tbsp browning
1 tsp light soft brown sugar
1 tsp sea salt
½ tsp freshly ground black pepper

white froth rise to the surface of the water, turn off the heat and discard the cooking water. Put the now large, white-looking pieces of cowfoot in a colander and rinse in cold water to remove any remaining froth.

Place the cowfoot in a large bowl with the lime juice and vinegar and toss. Use the lime halves as a sponge to clean each piece. Rinse the meat again in the bowl with water to remove any excess.

In a food processor or blender, blend the first seven ingredients of the marinade until smooth. Mix with the rest of the marinade ingredients and add to the bowl of cowfoot. Turn the meat, using a spoon, clean hands or wear gloves until the meat is coated. Cover the bowl and leave to marinate in the fridge from 30 minutes to overnight; a long marinade isn't totally necessary.

Heat the oil in a large, heavy-based saucepan or Dutch pot (or you could use a pressure cooker) over a medium heat. Remove the cowfoot from the marinade, reserving the marinade for later. Add the cowfoot to the pan or pot and slightly brown on all sides; this will take about 5 minutes. (Do this in batches to ensure the meat browns, rather than steams, adding more oil when needed.) Return all the meat to the pan or pot.

Add 1 litre (4 cups plus 3 tbsp) of the hot water to cover and bring to the boil. When the water starts to boil, add 2 tablespoons of the reserved marinade, stir and cover with the lid. Cook for about 2 hours, topping up with more hot water in roughly 40-minute intervals to ensure the meat is covered and the stew doesn't dry out (or cook for 45 minutes to 1 hour in a pressure cooker).

To test the meat is ready, use tongs to grab a piece and with a sharp knife or skewer, pierce the meaty part of the cowfoot, if your utensil pierces the meat with no resistance, like a cake, then it is done, if not continue cooking – about 10 minutes in a pressure cooker or 30 minutes in a pan or pot.

I prefer to cook this last stage in a pan or pot as there is more room to stir the stew. If using a pressure cooker, tip the stew into a pan/pot. Stir in another 1–2 tablespoons of the marinade into the pan, When it starts to bubble, add the onion and thyme, then cover with the lid and simmer for 5 minutes. When ready, you'll notice the liquid thickens and you may need to use some force to stir it. You can add the extra 100–300ml (⅓ cup plus 1 tbsp–1¼ cups) hot water if you prefer a looser sauce, but I prefer to leave as it is.

Turn the heat down to low, remove the lid, stir to ensure the stew isn't sticking to the bottom of the pan, then add the ketchup, broad beans, brown sugar, soy sauce and the all-purpose seasoning. Season with extra salt and pepper to taste and stir to combine. Cover and simmer over a low heat for a final 10–15 minutes, until the beans are tender, adding 3–5 tablespoons water if the sauce is too dry. Serve with Rice & Peas (see p44) and Plantain (see p60).

Braised pork

At a Jamaican funeral service, the melancholy of the memorial slowly evaporates and the events of the day inevitably turn into a joyous celebration of life that often lasts long into the night, complete with swooning reggae classics, drink and dance. This tradition appears deep-rooted in West African rites that made their way to Jamaica.

Hoping to quell any joy that the enslaved could create, in the 1800s night funerals were prohibited by colonial law. Owners who permitted them were liable to a penalty of fifty pounds (the equivalent of five thousand pounds today). The festivities back then very much mirror those of today with live instruments in place of a sound system and, of course, an array of foods available. The coffins were reputedly not laid until the crack of dawn, and such was the reverence for pork in Jamaica that it was known to be placed on the coffin of the deceased along with yam and rum for their voyage to the afterlife.

Pigs (or boar), being one of the few land-roaming animals native to Jamaica, the British cartographer Richard Blome observed in *A Description of the Island of Jamaica* in 1672, *"Jamaican pigs were far better tasting, more nourishing, and much easier to be digested than those of Europe"*, and later in the 18th century, Charles Leslie, an English archivist, declared the meat of Jamaica's pigs, *"so sweet and delicate, that nothing can equal it"*. (B.W. Higman, *Jamaican Food: History, Biology, Culture.*)

As the number of wild boar dwindled and there was no sizeable commercial culture or market for pork, for a long time it was usually reserved for jerk-style cooking. Yet, over the last century or so as Asian, and particularly Chinese cuisine, have made their way into mainstream Jamaican cooking, a host of pork dishes have emerged.

The first thing I ate in Jamaica after being away for nearly a decade was a variation of braised pork, simply called "pork". I don't usually eat much pork and only ended up ordering it as it was late (3pm) and everything else on the menu had sold out or wasn't available. This was unlike any pork I'd ever eaten before: somewhere on the spectrum between auburn and golden brown, steeped in an opulent, sweet, thick soy sauce, crispy on the first bite but succulent and tender on the inside. You can tell it left a lasting impression. Unfortunately, the next time I ordered it I received a staunch, "We nuh have that today!" and so I've tried to recreate it here.

SERVES 4

500g (1lb 2oz) pork belly, cut into
large bite-sized pieces
juice of 1 lime
2 tbsp apple cider vinegar
2 spring onions (scallions), sliced
5cm (2in) piece of fresh root
ginger, sliced
2 tbsp oil of choice, such as
coconut, rapeseed or sunflower
3 tbsp dark brown sugar
3 tbsp light soy sauce
2 tbsp dark soy sauce
¼ Scotch bonnet pepper, thinly
chopped, deseeded if preferred
(optional)
1 cinnamon stick, or ½ tsp
ground cinnamon

Place the pork in a bowl with the lime juice and half the
vinegar and mix to combine, rinse it in water, then drain.

Put the pork in a large saucepan with the spring
onions and half of the ginger. Cover with 300ml
(1¼ cups) water and bring to the boil for 5-10 minutes,
scooping off any froth that rises to the surface. Place a
colander or sieve, over a bowl and drain the pork, saving
the cooking water. Set aside the ginger and spring onion.
Rinse the pork under cold running water and set aside.

Heat the oil in a large, heavy-based saucepan or
Dutch pot over a medium heat. Stir in ½ teaspoon sugar
and the pork and quickly brown on each side. Add the
remaining vinegar and both types of soy sauce and stir.
Next, pour in the reserved cooking water, saved spring
onion and ginger, the rest of the ginger and the Scotch
bonnet, if using, and stir to combine.

Turn the heat to medium-high and when it starts to
bubble, turn it down to low, cover and simmer for 1 hour.
Stir, turn the heat to medium, add the cinnamon and the
rest of the sugar, then boil until the liquid reduces to a
dark, rich, sticky consistency. Serve with rice or Spinners
or Boiled Dumplings (see p57) and Pepper Slaw (see p89).

Fried chicken

When people tell you that KFC tastes different in Jamaica, they aren't lying; however, I've yet to meet anyone who can fully explain why. Some say it's the oil, some say it's the island poultry, others claim it's the sweetness of the island air. It's probably more likely to be the sweetness of the sugar or corn syrup! I've seen those who would scarcely be seen at a European chicken shop in awe of the luminescent, fire-orange hunks of fried chicken served across Jamaica. Should you make the mistake of trying to source some of this island fry on a bank holiday, then say goodbye to a good hour or two of your life while you queue.

Fried chicken plays an interesting role in Jamaica, particularly in its high-street guise. As American culture began to permeate the void left by the British exodus in the early 20th century, American brands by way of radio and television became seen as aspirational – as they did the world over. In the same way American denim jeans in Soviet Eastern Europe were seen as a signal of freedom and prosperity so were, and arguably still are, Colonel-faced bags and pizza boxes in Jamaica. The rise of the aspirational element of "foreign" foods has likely played a hand in the denigration of more traditional meat dishes. A clerk of an Americanized food chain in Marlon James's *A Brief History of Seven Killings* refers to jerk as "ghetto food", the very phrase that much of Jamaican cuisine is now working to shed.

Beyond the multinational chains in Jamaica, at most local shacks fried chicken has become a staple, nestled among jerk and curry chicken on the menu. One thing is for sure, be it in South America or South Korea, everyone understands fried chicken and this version dubbed by many as "Jamaican fried chicken" laden with herbs and spices is vying for the world champion crown.

––––––

Preheat the oven to 90°C (70°C fan/175°F/Gas ¼) and place a wire rack on a baking tray.

Mix all the ingredients for the seasoning in a bowl. Add the chicken thighs and drumsticks and, using your hands, turn in the seasoning until coated. Cover the bowl and leave to marinate in the fridge for at least 30 minutes, ideally overnight.

In a bowl, mix all the ingredients for the batter, except the egg, if using, and milk. Mix the egg, if using, and milk together in a separate bowl.

SERVES 4

4 skin-on, bone-in chicken thighs and 4 drumsticks, about 1kg (2¼lb) in total
500–600ml (2 cups plus 2 tbsp–2½ cups) groundnut (peanut) or sunflower oil

FOR THE SEASONING:

3 garlic cloves, minced
2 spring onions (scallions), finely chopped
½ onion, finely chopped, or 1 tbsp onion powder
2 tbsp All-purpose Seasoning (see p239)
2 tsp paprika
6 pimento seeds (allspice berries), crushed, or ½ tsp ground allspice
½ Scotch bonnet pepper, deseeded and chopped

FOR THE BATTER:

125g (1 cup minus 1 tbsp) plain (all-purpose) flour
2 tbsp cornflour (corn starch) (optional)
1 tbsp All-purpose Seasoning (see p239)
2 tsp paprika
1–2 tsp freshly ground black pepper
1 tsp ground ginger (optional)
1 tsp mixed herbs (optional)
½ tsp ground turmeric
½ tsp sea salt
1 egg, lightly beaten (optional)
150ml (⅔ cup) milk of choice

FOR THE HONEY MUSTARD:

5 tbsp runny honey
3 tbsp Dijon mustard
1 tbsp lemon juice
½ tsp cayenne pepper
½ tsp freshly ground black pepper

Heat the oil to 175°C/350°F in a large, heavy-based saucepan or deep-fat fryer, if you have one, over a medium-high heat.

Meanwhile, spoon about 5 tablespoons of the dry batter mix into a sealable kitchen bag or lidded container. Submerge a piece of chicken into the milk/egg mixture for a few seconds, place it in the bag or container, then shake to coat the chicken. Repeat the milk/egg and dry batter process for a second time. Repeat to coat the rest of the chicken, adding more of the dry batter as needed, just before frying.

Turn the heat of the hob down to medium. Place 2 pieces of the coated chicken in the hot oil and fry for 10 minutes on each side, until deep golden and crisp, and the chicken is cooked through. (Test the chicken is ready with a meat thermometer if you have one, the internal temperature should read 73°C/165°F when cooked.) To keep the chicken warm, place on the rack-lined baking tray in the oven. Repeat until all the chicken is fried.

Mix together all the ingredients for the honey mustard and serve with the fried chicken, alongside Rice & Peas (see p44) and Pepper Slaw (see p89).

Jerk chicken

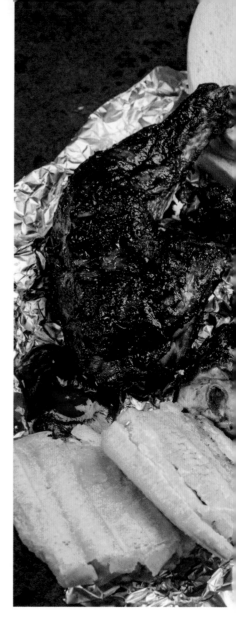

Many older Jamaicans I talk to are bemused about the stratospheric rise of jerk as the poster child of Jamaican food globally. A life without jerk pork or chicken seems a million times more tenable than a life without oxtail, brown stew chicken or saltfish. I can only speak for my family but jerk, while a street-food favourite, was never a home staple, most obviously because you'd be hard pressed to fit a jerk drum, no less a jerk pit, on a London council flat balcony.

That said, jerk has a storied history in Jamaica, deduced to have been brought over from South America by the Amerindian tribes, such as the Taino or Arawaks. The Taino word *"barabicu"*, meant "sacred fire pit" and describes how food was cooked over a fire. (It became *barbacoa*, then eventually barbecue and BBQ.) According to observations at the time, *"Hogs were cut open, the bones taken out, and the flesh... gash'd on the inside into the skin, fill'd with salt and expos'd to the sun, which is called jirking."* (M. Sheller, *Consuming the Caribbean: From Arawaks to Zombies.*) Beyond native hogs, learnings suggest they hunted tropical birds and reptiles, so perhaps we can assume they were "jerked" too. In addition to this, bird pepper (or cayenne), which grew wild in the hills, was often used to flavour and preserve.

Though peculiar to travelling Europeans at the time, this tribal method of cooking was also perfectly suited to the wayfaring needs of the Maroons and escaped African slaves. It was simple, wasted little, preserved meat for some days and, most importantly, it was discreet amidst the canopies of the hilly forested areas. With the abolition of slavery and Jamaica freed from the reins of colonial rule, this method of cooking migrated soon from the hills down to the streets and beach shores across the island – and jerk culture was born.

———

Mix the all-purpose seasoning, salt, pepper, soy sauce, garlic, ginger, jerk seasoning, spring onion and thyme with 1 tablespoon of the BBQ sauce in a large flat-bottomed bowl or casserole dish. Add the chicken (or pork) and, using your hands, turn it in the marinade until coated. Cover and leave to marinate in the fridge for at least 1 hour, better 4 hours, or ideally overnight.

Preheat the oven to 180°C (160°C fan/350°F/Gas 4) and place the grill rack in the top of the oven.

SERVES 4

1½–2 tbsp All-purpose Seasoning (see p239)

1 tsp sea salt

1 tsp freshly ground black pepper

1 tbsp dark soy sauce or browning

1 tbsp minced garlic, or garlic powder (optional)

1 tbsp minced fresh root ginger, or ginger powder

2–3 tbsp Jerk Seasoning (see p238), or shop bought

1 spring onion (scallion), chopped

1 sprig of thyme

2 tbsp BBQ sauce of choice

4 skin-on, bone-in chicken leg quarters, or 700g (1lb 9oz) pork shoulder, ribs or loin roast

1 lime, cut into wedges

Place the marinated chicken or pork on the rack, rubbing any clumps of seasoning over the top and reserving any remaining marinade left in the bowl. Place a roasting tray beneath the chicken or pork to catch any dripping fat or juices from the meat. Roast for 30 minutes, then quickly transfer any juices in the roasting tray to the bowl of marinade, then return the tray to the oven. Spoon the marinade in the bowl liberally over the chicken or pork. Brush the underside of the chicken or the other side of the pork with the marinade.

Turn the oven up to 200°C (180°C fan/400°F/Gas 6). Spoon the remaining BBQ sauce over and cook for a further 30 minutes, until the meat is charred and blackened in places. Serve cut into pieces with Hardo Bread (see p208), Plantain (see p60) and wedges of lime.

BBQ METHOD

To barbecue the chicken or pork, follow the method for marinating, above. Light your barbecue (it should be one with a lid). When ready, add the meat and grill for 50 minutes to 1 hour with the lid closed. Every 10–15 minutes, open the lid and turn the meat, basting with the marinade. After 40 minutes, brush with the BBQ sauce if you like a sweeter jerk and continue cooking for a final 10–20 minutes, until charred in places.

Heggs

The study of Jamaican patois, slang and linguistics in general accounts for thousands of pages of scholarly research: the intricacies of certain stresses and omissions of particular English rules, the relationship with West African tone, and so on. All widely interesting, but none can capture the giggles of me and my cousins every time our Aunty put the letter "H" in front of any word beginning with a vowel. Going to school for a "*h*education", not forgetting our "*h*umbrellas" in case of rain, moving out the way for an oncoming "*h*ambulance", and notably being told we were having "*h*eggs" for breakfast.

For a long period of Jamaican history, it seems chickens were appreciated more for their eggs than for their meat with *"the birds being allowed to grow old and tough in the service of egg-laying".* (B.W. Higman, *Jamaican Food: History, Biology, Culture.*)

Morning sunrises are always partnered with the sound of roosters as keeping a chicken coop is commonplace for many living in rural areas. Rather than the uniform-coloured, uniform-sized eggs I was accustomed to buying in London supermarkets, these hens laid a multi-coloured range of eggs, from the palest nimbus white to off-white and bone to the deepest golden brown, and with a taste hard to revert back from. For those who don't keep their own chickens, it's common to see people carrying open-top trays of eggs on the way home from shopping, and one of my funniest memories was having to rest one of these trays on my lap for a fellow passenger in our shared route taxi, whizzing up an Ochi hill and focussing with intense concentration not to drop them.

I'm not sure if the genesis of this meal was that we pretty much season, flavour and colour every meal we make, or if there's any truth in the idea that older diaspora made it as a visual substitute to ackee in the days before cans were readily available overseas – either way, after eating this it's near impossible to go back to plain scrambled eggs ever again.

In a bowl, place three-quarters of the bell peppers, Scotch bonnet, half of the tomatoes, red onion, olive oil, salt, pepper and all-purpose seasoning, then mix to combine and set aside.

Crack the eggs into a bowl, add the milk, if using, and whisk with a fork until combined.

SERVES 2

1½ bell peppers (colour of choice), deseeded and finely diced
½ Scotch bonnet pepper, deseeded and chopped
3 cherry tomatoes, quartered
½ red onion, finely diced
1 tsp olive oil
pinch of sea salt
pinch of freshly ground black, or white, pepper
½ tsp All-purpose Seasoning (see 239)
3 eggs
2 tbsp milk (optional)
2 tbsp butter or oil
1 spring onion (scallion), thinly sliced

Heat the oil or butter in a frying pan over a medium-low heat, then pour in the eggs. As the edge of the eggs start to cook, gently push them to the middle with a spatula. Distribute any runny egg to the outer edge of the pan and repeat the gentle pushing. When the scrambled eggs are just cooked, move them to one side of the pan. Add the pepper and tomato mixture to the empty half of the pan and saute for 3 minutes, until softened. Gently fold the scrambled eggs into the cooked vegetables.

Serve straightaway topped with the spring onion and reserved bell pepper and tomato. Serve with Hardo Bread (see p208) and Hot Sauce (see p240).

SEAFOOD

The popular adage posits "If trees could talk…", but I often wonder what harrowing tales there'd be if the seas could talk. How history would be re-written if the oceans could narrate all they have witnessed. For me, nothing represents the duality of the Caribbean more than the ocean that surrounds it. Within the same day, the waters emanating the most immense beauty and stillness can erupt into a twisting, devastating deluge. This typical stormy, tropical rage was so awe-inspiring to the Taino tribe, natives of the Caribbean, they believed there was a god of the storms who they called Hurakán (*Juracan* in Spanish), which many believe to be the root of the word hurricane.

"Elders tell the duppy tale of the River Mumma. A female water spirit who guards the source of many Jamaican rivers."

Here, beauty and rage go hand in hand. The most peaceful, tranquil setting can turn into pandemonium at the drop of a hat. This duality is an element of life that everyone who lives in Jamaica and the Caribbean have come to accept, and peril lies for those who upset the balance. Elders tell the duppy tale of the River Mumma. A female water spirit who guards the source of many Jamaican rivers. According to legend, she can sometimes be seen sitting in the river, brushing her hair with a golden comb. She has been known to leave her comb on a rock to entice victims who she then draws into the water. In the days of slavery, sacrifices would be made to the River Mumma in times of drought, or when someone wanted to cross the river that she was guarding. The fish in that location would not be eaten, as these were thought to be her children.

Such is the respect and reverence for the waters and its contents that a folk tale about aquatic-rooted overzealousness exists. In the legend of "The Golden Table", a table of pure gold lies at the bottom of certain rivers, usually at the river head. It rises briefly to the surface from time to time, particularly at midday, affording a glimpse of its golden beauty. The sight of the table mesmerizes whoever sees it, and they become obsessed with the desire to obtain it. Efforts to procure the table always end in disaster and the river eventually claims the lives of those who try to remove the table from the water.

This legend is one of many Jamaican folk tales that likely arose from the European quest to find gold after the Spaniards first arrived in Jamaica. It ties in with the fact that the seas and waterways feed everyone on the island in some shape or form, whether physically, spiritually or financially. On particularly sunny days, many when given the option still use the river or sea to wash and bathe, so any disruption to the water's equilibrium sends ripples that affect everyone and is just as frowned upon as those in folk tales.

Before mass importation, access to meat was limited to what could be farmed on the island, initially by personal farming and then commercially in the latter part of the last century. As such, the eating of meat was limited and, as seen in the Nose-to-Tail chapter (see pp124–51), respect was given to the whole animal. Sources of seafood, however, have always been abundant. In C.V. de Brose Black's *History of Jamaica* the author elaborates on how for the indigenous Indians of Jamaica, seafood as well as turtles, were a very important source of food and that they had various refined modes of catching fish including: *"...fishing hooks made of bone, and fastened to a bark line. For larger fish they used lances as harpoons and they had fishing nets made of cotton and of fibres."*

Given this, by the time the effects of English colonialism had been fully felt on the island, an 1851 anthropological study stated that, *"Abundant as fish is everywhere in the waters in and around Jamaica, yet almost the whole that is consumed by the inhabitants is caught and salted on the banks of Newfoundland (Canada) or on the shores of the west and north of Scotland. Fresh fish is scarce, and dear, though the waters are teeming with fishes."* (J. Ogilvy, *A Description and History of the Island of Jamaica.*)

While documentation on the work of enslaved people usually focusses on plantations and fields, it's less well known that many were assigned to catch fish for consumption on the sugar estates or to be sold in markets for the benefit of their enslavers. As such it became rare for the enslaved to eat it. Dried salted fish, usually cod or pickled herring, consequently rose in popularity as there was no infrastructure at the time to support mass consumption of fresh fish. In the vast heat of the Caribbean, imported salted fish kept for longer with relatively little attention.

As slavery ended, the diet of Jamaica remained rudimentary into the middle of the 20th century. As kitchen appliances, such as cookers and fridges, became more widely available alongside the import of oil, fish consumption grew. An island populated with Amerindian and African descendants mixed with east and south Asian indentured labour, meant that fish dishes combined with herbs and spices were almost an inevitability and since this time, the myriad seafood options that exist across the Caribbean islands are truly impressive.

Somewhere between the port town of Ocho Rios and Runaway Bay on the north coast, a man hawking his seafood wares to my mother, in typically Jamaican braggadocio, professes the extent of his fishing capabilities. In jest, to get him to go away she replies, "Okay, well if you can get [insert slightly ridiculous list of seafood you might ask for if you thought the fisherman was lying] we'll have that." He hops into his boat and vanishes beyond the horizon. We pitch up on the beach completely forgetting about the exchange and before the hour is done a silhouette emerges on the horizon. Back on shore, a roll out of his net reveals pretty much everything my mum had joked about – lobster, snapper, bream, shrimp.

"Seafood gets the party going in Jamaica."

As is such in Jamaica, a verbal agreement can literally be life or death and without hesitation, she of course obliged. There's more though... he ventured into a small beach hut nearby, whipped out a drum, got a fire started and proceeded to season and grill everything he had just caught. That still wasn't it... rice and peas were somehow summoned from somewhere as well as my favourite sweet dumpling festivals. What's more, it couldn't have been anything more than about ten pounds. This story wowed tourists and others, but for our Jamaican family it didn't warrant our excitement.

I came to understand this years later on my usual sunrise foray to the local beach on the other side of Ocho Rios, at the start of the long stretch of road that leads to the White River. Watching the world go by, it was a daily occurrence to see locals barter for a shopping list of seafood with the owners of the rainbow-coloured boats. In the same fashion as my experience more than a decade earlier, the boats readied, and those aboard – sometimes solo, sometimes in pairs or trios – disappeared off into the horizon. An hour or so later, they'd return and would unfold their nets containing myriad fish with glimmering kaleidoscopic scales as others stood around to compare the catches of the day. Very rarely would they fail to snag what was requested. For an arranged price, you could even jump on board to experience the fishing quest. I've heard it's amazing, but I quite like staying on land so I can't say first-hand.

The seafood is so plentiful that excess can end up in the waterways of the cities. On one late-night walk around Kingston, me and a group of Londoners saw a gathering of excited young boys around a gully (city waterway/sewage system) beside the road. Not sure what they were up to, we went to check out the raucous to find that to our amazement they'd caught a trout with an arts and crafts stick and string.

While meat sustains a family, seafood gets the party going in Jamaica. Meat dishes can take days to prep and cook, yet many of the seafood dishes are consumed as quickly as they are made. Flyers and posters for "Fish Friday" adorn lampposts and road signs across the island. At these events, car parks, front yards and shop fronts alike are transformed into joyous occasions of dancing and vibing, centred around fish barbecues. Even after being seasoned, fried or smoked in a drum, you can still taste the remnants of sea salt in the fish, and it truly is something to savour. While the vast array of fresh fish and crustacea available in the Caribbean aren't so readily available in other parts of the world, most major cities have incredible fish markets for those willing to rise early. Fortunately, most of the fish used in the island's popular dishes are readily available at the markets and supermarkets of the UK, US and Europe if you are willing to sacrifice a slight degree of freshness. As reinforced throughout this book, the recipes aren't set in stone, seasonings can be added or subtracted at will and other fish substituted.

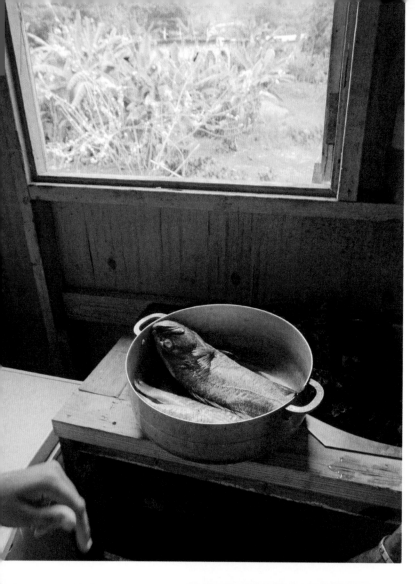

Ackee & saltfish

I have long wondered how and why the combination of a relatively unknown fruit from West Africa and fish primarily imported from North America and Europe, has become the national dish of Jamaica over something indigenous to the island. Yet, looking at the meandering pathway of migration to and from the island, and wider Caribbean, over the last half a millennium it now seems very apt. A fusion and creolization of cultures born thousands of miles apart is exactly what Jamaica is. Ackee and saltfish (never ever saltfish and ackee) is the perfect paradox that represents this. A piece of heritage West Africans brought with them to the island and a European commodity rationed to those same people, used together to create a meal their descendants would enjoy for generations after.

Since the dish's coronation, when the ackee plant is in season during early spring and late autumn, every cookshop on the island is remiss if not selling it. During this time, ackee is so plentiful that I find myself nonchalantly kicking it out of the way; even roadside trees bear the fruit, dropping them like conkers in the autumn. Back in London, I have to pinch myself that these memories are real when I find the price of canned ackee has gone up AGAIN! I pay up with a slight moan and grumble, which the cashier thinks is aimed at them. There is nothing you can replace or bolster ackee with, the canned conglomerations have us in a culinary headlock. It's the can or nothing.

As you can see from this photo of me eating ackee and saltfish taken in my early years, I have been enjoying this dish my most of my life. That said, I still struggle to describe ackee to those who've never tried it before and my explanation does little to expound the wonder of the fruit when steamed with vinegar, doused in peppers, seasoning and tomatoes, then paired with soft flaky salted cod.

In my family, this dish was usually a Sunday affair served as part of a sort of Caribbean-British fry-up fusion with baked beans, Plantain (see p60), Fried Dumplings (see p202) or Hardo Bread (see p208). However, with the growth of Caribbean takeaways in London, it has slowly crept into "whenever I feel like it" – just go easy on the fried dumplings if you have work to do the rest of the day.

SERVES 4

300g (10oz) saltfish (dried
  salted cod)
2 tbsp cooking oil of choice
½ onion, chopped
1 bell pepper (½ red and ½ green),
  deseeded and cut into 1cm
  (½in) dice or sliced
2 garlic cloves, minced
1 tbsp apple cider vinegar
1 tbsp Scotch Bonnet Ketchup
  (see p243), or tomato ketchup
1 tbsp tomato purée (tomato
  paste) (optional)
1 spring onion (scallion), chopped,
  plus extra to serve (optional)
8 cherry tomatoes, halved
1 Scotch bonnet pepper,
  deseeded and finely chopped,
  or 1 tsp paprika
3 sprigs of thyme
1 tsp All-purpose Seasoning
  (see p239)
½ tsp sea salt (optional)
½ tsp freshly ground black
  pepper
540g (19oz) can ackee, drained
1 tbsp chopped dill or parsley,
  to garnish (optional)

Put the saltfish in a bowl, cover with cold water and leave to soak for a minimum of 3 hours, but ideally overnight, until softened. After soaking, drain the fish, discarding the water, and put it into a pan. Cover with fresh water and bring to the boil, then turn the heat down to medium and cook for 30 minutes to reduce the saltiness in the fish. (Alternatively, if you don't have time to soak, cover the fish with water, bring to the boil, then turn the heat down and simmer for 1–1½ hours.)

Drain the fish, leave to cool, then flake into pieces, discarding any skin or bones.

In a medium-large saucepan, heat the oil and sauté the onion, red and green bell peppers and garlic for 3–4 minutes, until softened. Stir in the saltfish, vinegar, ketchup, tomato purée, if using, spring onion and half the tomatoes. Add the Scotch bonnet or paprika, thyme, all-purpose seasoning, salt and pepper and cook, stirring, for 1 minute. Using a fork, gently mash the fish to break up the pieces, then turn the heat to medium-low, cover, and simmer for 3–4 minutes, stirring occasionally, until heated through.

Turn the heat up a notch, then gently fold in the ackee and cook for 3 minutes. Add the remaining tomatoes, then top with the herbs and spring onion, if using, and extra black pepper. Serve with Hard Food (see p56).

Saltfish & cabbage

I like asking people of my grandparents' generation what their favourite dish is. You can see their brains scrolling slowly through a repository of years impossible for anyone young to comprehend. Decades upon decades of memories being dusted off the mental shelf and popped into the VHS player of the mind.

My surrogate grandmother, Aunty Babs, just can't decide on one dish but at a push she excitedly recounts tales of her family's saltfish and steamed cabbage, complete with hand gestures. She tells me it's easy and light and good for lunch, and does not require the overnight soaking that we often see in other saltfish dishes. Now salivating at her story, she tells me to jot down the shopping list and if I buy the ingredients she will cook it for me. An hour later we begin making the meal in her daughter's kitchen in Old Street in East London, where the last plantain and yam vendors hang on under the ever-growing shadows of the skyscrapers.

While we prepare the meal, from chopping the cabbage to boiling the saltfish, unlike other dishes that I'm scolded for changing, Aunty Babs tells me that I have free rein to adjust this one to my taste, just like her brother, Sinclair, had done in the past.

_____

Place the saltfish in a bowl, pour over enough cold water to cover and add the juice of ½ lemon. Place the other half of the lemon into the water and leave the fish to soften for 30 minutes. Drain, discarding the water and lemon, and place the fish in a pan. Cover with fresh water and bring to the boil, then turn the heat down to medium and cook for 30 minutes, or if you prefer a less salty taste, boil for an extra 15 minutes.

Drain the fish in a colander, then run under cold running water to cool it down. Tear the fish into flakes, discarding any skin or bones. Set aside briefly.

Put the light cabbage leaves in a large bowl with the tomatoes, red onions and spring onion and toss until combined. Add the flaked fish.

Mix together the oil, vinegar, ketchup, salt and pepper. Add the dressing to the fish mixture and toss thoroughly with salad forks or clean hands to fully mix everything together. Add the darker cabbage leaves and toss lightly to mix, but not coat as you want to keep the green of the leaves. Top with the radishes and serve with a squeeze of lime.

SERVES 4

375g (12½oz) saltfish (dried salted cod)
1 lemon, halved
500g (1lb 2oz) Savoy cabbage, dark and light leaves separated, thinly sliced
3 tomatoes, quartered
2 red onions, thinly sliced
1 spring onion (scallion), thinly sliced
4 tbsp olive oil
4 tbsp apple cider vinegar
3 tbsp Scotch Bonnet Ketchup (see p243), or tomato ketchup
1–2 tsp sea salt
½ tsp freshly ground black pepper
3 radishes, thinly sliced
1 lime, halved

Fish rundown

If there was a culinary genie in a magic lamp granting me three foodie wishes, I think I'd ask the lineage and origin of Caribbean rundown. Theories of its origins in West Africa seem as plausible as those from Asia, since both have crossed paths with Jamaica and the Caribbean at some point. The slightly nondescript appearance of rundown doesn't give any clues either; it could come from anywhere. The definition of rundown in F.G. Cassidy and R.B. Le Page's *Dictionary of Jamaican English* reads, *"A kind of sauce made by boiling coconut down til it becomes like custard"*, which tells us how it's made, but still reveals no information of its origin.

What's more, rundown, often pronounced *rundung* in Jamaica, has more aliases than any other food I've ever encountered, apart from perhaps Sorrel (see p254). Names such as *dip-and-come-back, dip-and-fall-back, dip-and-shake-off, bread-fruit remedy, dip-dip, elbow-grease, frigasi, kobijong, kuochi waata, oil-down, malongkontong, mulgrave, Pakassa* (see p32), *plaba, plomi, rege, stew-down, swimmer-down* and the list goes on... Additionally, perhaps coincidentally, the Jamaican-ism *rundung* bears a striking resemblance in name and recipe to the Indonesian rendang.

I can only deduce that anywhere and everywhere in the world people have discovered the magic that comes with boiling and simmering coconut milk into a sweet, oozing thick sauce that clings to meat or fish, or a mixture of dense vegetables, and feel a desire to share it wherever they travel. In the Caribbean corner of the world, rundown is traditionally eaten for brunch, although many people (including myself) have decided that being limited to the morning just isn't long enough.

If using saltfish or salted mackerel, follow the initial instructions for soaking and cooking the fish to get rid of any excess saltiness on page 159. Remove the skin and bones and flake the fish into pieces.

Bring the coconut milk to the boil in a wide pan or Dutch pot over a high heat. Stir continuously to prevent the coconut milk sticking to the bottom of the pan; the oil will start to separate from the milk. After bubbling for 3 minutes, turn the heat down to medium.

SERVES 4

400g (14oz) saltfish (dried salted cod), or salted mackerel fillets
800ml (3⅓ cups) coconut milk
2–3 garlic cloves, minced
1 thumb-sized piece of fresh root ginger, peeled and minced
1 onion, thinly sliced
2 spring onions (scallions), chopped
6 pimento seeds (allspice berries)
2–3 sprigs of thyme
1 bell pepper (½ red and ½ green), deseeded and chopped
1 Scotch bonnet pepper, whole
1 tsp freshly ground black pepper
1 tsp All-purpose Seasoning (see p239)
1 tsp apple cider vinegar (optional)

Add the garlic and ginger and stir for 2 minutes before adding the onion, spring onions, pimento and thyme, then cook, stirring, for an another 2–3 minutes.

Gently stir in the saltfish or mackerel, red and green bell peppers and Scotch bonnet. Add the black pepper, all-purpose seasoning and vinegar, if using, and cook for 2 minutes. The coconut milk should have thickened to a custard-like consistency and changed to a yellowish hue with the addition of the fish and seasoning.

Turn the heat down to low, part-cover with the lid and simmer for a final 5 minutes – don't completely cover the pan as you don't want to reintroduce water or steam. Serve with Hard Food (see page 56).

Mackerel &
Bob's baked beans

Jamaica is a land of superlatives: who's the fastest sprinter; who's the best football team; who's the best music artist; and who's the best dancer and so on... In the realm of food, it is no different and the question of the best Jamaican dish is always up for debate. I don't know which one is the best, however, if I were to submit my vote in the primary elections of the *most* Jamaican dish, it may well be any one of a select few dishes featuring the humble mackerel.

Distinguished Anglo-Irish physician, botanist and naturalist, Sir Hans Sloane (of Sloane Square, West London fame), on his documented voyage to Jamaica noted in the 1680s that, *"Salt mackerel are here a great provision, especially for Negroes, who covet them extremely in pepper-pots, or oglios..."* Some 300 years later, mackerel is no less coveted by Jamaicans, purchased en masse in their rectangular metal cans. This one-pot dish is incredibly simple and serves its purpose as a standalone breakfast, lunch or snack, or part of a larger meal. It's partly inspired by my mother's partner's ability to transform a basic can of baked beans into an explosion of taste.

Heat the oil in a frying pan over a medium heat. Add the onion and sauté for 2–3 minutes, stirring occasionally. Next, add the red and green bell peppers, Scotch bonnet and tomatoes and cook for a further 2–3 minutes, until softened.

Add the baked beans and stir, then cook for a few minutes until the sauce starts to bubble a little. Stir in the mackerel. Turn the heat to low, cover with the lid, and simmer for 5 minutes, until heated through. Remove the lid, season with salt and black pepper to taste. Serve with Hardo Bread (see p56) or Fried Dumplings (see p202), or as a side dish.

SERVES 2

1 tsp coconut oil
½ white onion, chopped
1 bell pepper (½ red and ½ green), deseeded and chopped
1 Scotch bonnet pepper, deseeded and chopped
1 handful of cherry tomatoes, chopped
400g (14oz) can baked beans
125g (4½oz) can mackerel fillets in oil, halved lengthways
½ tsp All-purpose Seasoning (see p239)
sea salt and freshly ground black pepper

Chop suey

Many people in Jamaica, tourists especially, are perhaps surprised by the sight and sound of an ethnically Chinese person speaking nonchalantly with a thick patois or Creole accent. The media would have you believe that all residents are black with flowing dreadlocks, but this is far from the case. Since the emancipation of enslaved people in the 1850s, waves of Chinese people, both involuntary and voluntary, have migrated to the Caribbean islands and found vocation in all walks of island life, from music and manufacturing to, of course, the food industry.

Fortunately, classic Chinese ingredients, such as ginger, rice, pork and seafood, were already in the repertoire of the West African descendant populace as well as their Indian indentured compatriots. With this, Chinese food joined the mélange of Jamaican cuisine and meant that a Chinese takeaway was a go-to for many on a Friday night when a two-hour curry cooking session wasn't on the cards. Chinese restaurants are dotted around every Jamaican town and city. You may also notice Chinese dishes on the menu at Jamaican cookshops, both on the island and in diaspora locations.

This recipe (and those opposite) are staples at my local Chinese restaurants in Ochi, just a few minutes' walk away from each other. I've also seen them creep into home-cooked Jamaican dinners.

Soak the cabbage in salted water for 10 minutes, then drain, rinse and set aside.

Heat half the oil in a wok or large frying pan over a high heat, add half the garlic, ginger, celery and prawns and stir-fry for 3–5 minutes, until the prawns turn pink. Add the soy sauce and salt and stir-fry for another minute, then tip into a bowl and set aside.

Wipe the wok or pan clean with kitchen paper and heat the remaining oil over a medium-high heat. Add the green beans, carrots, spring onions and stir-fry for 3 minutes. Add the remaining garlic, thyme and soaked cabbage and stir-fry for another minute, adding more oil if needed. Next, add the bok choi and green and yellow bell peppers and stir-fry for another 3 minutes.

Return the prawn mixture to the wok and heat through briefly. Season with black pepper to taste.

SERVES 2–4

⅓ white cabbage, about 600g
(1lb 5oz) in total, thinly sliced
3 tbsp rapeseed oil
3 garlic cloves, minced,
or ½ tsp garlic powder
1 thumb-sized piece of fresh
root ginger, peeled and
finely chopped
1 rib of celery, finely chopped
400g (14oz) raw, peeled king prawns
1 tbsp soy sauce
½ tsp sea salt
150g (5½oz) green beans, thinly
sliced on the diagonal
2 large carrots, cut into julienne
3 spring onions (scallions),
finely chopped
1 tsp dried thyme
3 bok choi, about 700g (1lb 7oz)
in total, cut into 2cm (¾in) slices
1 bell pepper (½ green and
½ yellow), deseeded and
chopped
freshly ground black pepper

Chow mein

SERVES 4–6

450g (1lb) dried medium egg noodles
2 tbsp light soy sauce
1 tbsp dark soy sauce
2 tbsp oyster sauce
1 tbsp apple cider vinegar
1 tsp light soft brown sugar
2 tbsp rapeseed oil
1 onion, chopped
1 spring onion (scallion), white and green parts
    separated, finely chopped
4 garlic cloves, minced
1 tbsp finely chopped fresh root ginger
100g (3½oz) bok choi, sliced
1 carrot, cut into julienne
1 red bell pepper, deseeded and chopped
400g (14oz) cooked, peeled king prawns
sea salt, to taste

———

Bring a pan of salted water to the boil, add the noodles and cook for 2–3 minutes, until just tender. Drain the noodles, rinse under cold running water, then set aside in a bowl of cold water to stop them sticking together.

In a bowl, mix together both types of soy sauce with the oyster sauce, vinegar, sugar and 2 tablespoons water and set aside.

Heat the oil in a wok or large frying pan over a medium heat. Add the onion, the white part of the spring onion, garlic and ginger and stir-fry for 2–3 minutes.

Next, add the bok choi, carrot and red bell pepper and stir-fry for another 2–3 minutes, until starting to soften.

Drain the noodles, then add them to the wok with the sauce mixture and prawns, then cook for another 2 minutes, until the noodles and prawns have heated through. Serve topped with the reserved green part of the spring onion.

Ginger, shrimp & pea rice

SERVES 4–6

200g (7oz) raw, peeled king prawns
1 tsp dried basil
1 tsp dried oregano
1 tsp dried thyme
1 tbsp rapeseed oil
2 tbsp coconut oil
1 onion, chopped
2 spring onions (scallions), finely chopped
1 thumb-sized piece of fresh root ginger,
    peeled and finely grated
4 garlic cloves, minced
1 rib of celery, finely chopped
350g (12oz) cooked and cooled brown
    long-grain rice
1 tbsp light soft brown sugar
2–3 tbsp soy sauce
30g (1oz) coconut flakes
75g (2½oz) frozen peas
2 tomatoes, chopped
2 tsp black sesame seeds (optional)

———

In a small bowl, place the prawns, followed by the herbs and rapeseed oil. Massage the herb oil into the prawns and leave to marinate in the fridge for 5 minutes, although the longer you leave it the better.

Heat half the coconut oil in a wok or large frying pan over a medium-high heat. Add the seasoned prawns and stir-fry for 3 minutes, until they turn pink, then remove from the pan and set aside.

Add the rest of the coconut oil to the wok or pan, then add the onion and stir-fry for 3–5 minutes. Next, add the spring onions, ginger, garlic and celery while continuing to stir-fry for 2 minutes, until light golden.

Add the cooked brown rice, sugar, soy sauce and coconut flakes and cook, stirring, for 5 minutes to prevent the rice sticking to the bottom of the pan; add a splash of water if needed.

Add the frozen peas, tomatoes and prawns and cook, stirring, for another 3 minutes, until the peas are tender. Remove from the heat and sprinkle the sesame seeds on top, if using.

Steamed salmon

I've been steaming salmon all wrong my Aunty Marcia remarks. She tells me this in the earnestly polite but serious way an elder adopts when they don't agree with something you're doing. You rarely hear the truth directly, but if you happen to eavesdrop a conversation between two elders of equal stature the truth reveals itself with ferocity. Eyebrows are raised in disapproval of changes made to decades' old recipes. Somewhere between naivety and boastfulness, I want to challenge Aunty Marcia but in 20 minutes she produces a dish that ties my idea for a recipe to a thirty-thousand-pound anchor and sends it to Davy Jones' Locker.

Since European and American salmon was first imported to Jamaica over 100 years ago it has been held in high esteem, and perhaps this is the genesis of the remarks about my cooking methods. Where I usually like to submerge fish in liquid and leave it to poach, salmon doesn't need it. This dish is so quick and easy that by the time I'd run to the shop to get some carrots, Aunty Marcia had already finished it and dinner was ready.

———

Heat the oil in a large sauté or frying pan over a medium-low heat. Add the onion and garlic and sauté for 3–5 minutes. Stir in the remaining ingredients, if using, except the butter and salmon.

Turn the heat up to medium and add the butter. Wait for the butter to melt, add 4 tablespoons water and gently stir the contents of the pan. Cover with the lid and cook for 15 minutes, stirring occasionally, until the vegetables have softened.

Place the salmon on top of the vegetables, cover with the lid and cook for another 10–15 minutes, until the salmon is cooked through. Season with salt and pepper to taste and serve straightaway.

SERVES 4

2 tbsp coconut or sunflower oil
1 red onion, sliced into thin rounds
3 garlic cloves, minced
200g (7oz) pumpkin or squash, peeled, deseeded and cut into 4cm (1¾in) chunks (optional)
5 okra, topped and tailed, sliced lengthways (optional)
3–4 sprigs of thyme
2–3 tomatoes, quartered
2 carrots, sliced into 5mm (¼in) rounds
2 spring onions (scallions), chopped
1½ bell peppers (mix of colours), deseeded and chopped
1 chayote, cut into 4cm (1¾in) chunks (optional)
1 Scotch bonnet pepper, sliced (deseeded for less heat)
1 tsp All-purpose Seasoning (see p239)
1 tsp fish seasoning
1 vegetable stock cube, crumbled, or 1 tsp vegetable bouillon powder
1 tbsp butter
4 salmon fillets, about 500g (1lb 2oz) in total
sea salt and freshly ground black pepper

Spiced tuna

It's interesting how many of us assume as children that our experiences are simply the norm, and whatever our family does is what every other family does. Going to school and growing up in a multicultural environment, like London, highlights many similarities between cultures, but also differences. For years, I thought everyone sent 200-kilo blue plastic acquatic barrels stuffed with clothing, dry foods and electronics across the Atlantic, because that's what my family did multiple times a year.

Ever since Caribbean people were dispersed from the islands to new homes in North America, Britain and Europe, like Western Union transfers, these exchanges have been a crucial lifeline to families back home.

I mention this as while staying at a guesthouse with a family in the rural part of St. Andrew, a meal served to me reminded me of those barrels. An incredibly simple pasta dish with canned tuna, the kind of ingredients my family would request. While the vivid array of colourful dishes in Jamaica never fail to excite, I find equal amazement in how incredibly simple meals can effortlessly be made so wholesome. This particular combo of canned fish, pasta and steamed vegetables is versatile in that any shape of pasta or type of canned fish can be used, and similarly any combination of vegetables. With all these elements being relatively common, this is a great delve-in-the-cupboard type of meal.

SERVES 2

½ recipe quantity Steamed Vegetables (see p52), or the following vegetables:
100g (3½oz) white cabbage, thinly sliced
100g (3½oz) small broccoli florets
1 carrot, diced
50g (1¾oz) frozen peas
200g (7oz) dried pasta, such as tagliatelle or pappardelle
1 tbsp coconut or olive oil
½ tsp All-purpose Seasoning (see p239)
½ tsp paprika
½ tsp dried chilli flakes (optional)
200g (7oz) canned tuna in oil
sea salt and freshly ground black pepper

If not using the steamed vegetables, cook your choice of vegetables in a saucepan or Dutch pot for a few minutes until tender, then set aside.

Meanwhile, cook the pasta in a pan of salted boiling water following the instructions on the packet until al dente. Drain and set aside.

Heat the coconut or olive oil in a large sauté pan over a medium heat, add the all-purpose seasoning, paprika and chilli flakes, if using, and stir until combined. Stir in the tuna and any oil and heat through.

Add the cooked pasta and steamed vegetables to the pan and cook for another 2 minutes, until heated through. Season with salt and pepper to taste.

Stuffed crab back

While I enjoy watching the frantic goings on of everyday Jamaican life, I find myself taking advantage of the sun, yard dogs and roosters that all conspire to wake me at the literal crack of dawn. Taking advantage of the morning serenity, a quick trip from Great Pond to Ochi town centre, then a turn onto the road that leads to Oracabessa has a strip of beaches that at this time of the day are free to roam. In the place of sunbathers are fishermen, hanging their nets and docking their boats. By this time, they have already nearly finished their shift for the day, but at a price they'll disappear into the horizon and catch any local aquatic creature you can think of. If the fisherman is in a decent mood, you may also be able to jump on board with him.

In Jamaica, there are many different types of crab, named principally by colour, habitat, shape and size. I wasn't exactly sure what crab I wanted so I gestured a "medium" sort of size with my hands and, like the oceanic equivalent of going to Argos, the man disappeared and 10 minutes later returned with crabs in tow. The objective was to recreate a meal I'd had when visiting the eerily quiet Port Royal, a fishing village that was once a mecca of commerce in Jamaica. Now, a shell of its past colonial prowess, it is populated by coastal fishing shacks, roadside vendors and the occasional person selling cooked food out the front of their house. On one memorable visit, I was presented with a crab back stuffed with buttery, spicy, herby crab meat; it was better than anything I'd ever had at a high-end restaurant. However, if you can't get hold of fresh crab and time is against you, feel free to buy ready-prepared dressed crabs instead.

To prepare the cooked crab, lay it on its back, shell-side down, and twist off the legs and claws and set aside. Using the palm of your hand, press down to release the body from the shell, prising it out in one piece with your fingers. Pull away and discard the feathery gills (dead man's fingers) around the main body. Cut the body in half and prise out the white and brown meat from the shell with a lobster pick or skewer and place in a bowl. Scoop out any brown meat from the shell, after discarding the stomach sac. Using a kitchen mallet or rolling pin, crack the claws and legs and pick out the meat, then place in the bowl with the rest of the meat.

SERVES 2

2 cooked blue crabs or crab of choice, each about 450g (1lb), or 2 dressed crabs, each about 125g (4½oz)

1 lime, halved, plus wedges to serve

1 tbsp apple cider vinegar

1 tbsp oil of choice

½ white onion, finely chopped

2–3 garlic cloves, minced

1 tsp curry powder

1 tsp All-purpose Seasoning (see p239)

1 Scotch bonnet pepper, deseeded and chopped, or 1 tsp dried chilli flakes

2 tbsp finely chopped coriander (cilantro), plus extra to serve

⅓ green bell pepper, deseeded and cut into small dice

1 spring onion (scallion), finely chopped, plus extra to serve (optional)

1 rib of celery, finely chopped

1 tsp freshly ground black pepper

pinch of sea salt

2 tbsp breadcrumbs, or panko crumbs

2 tbsp coconut milk or desiccated coconut

2 tbsp butter

1 tsp chopped chives (optional)

Check the crab meat for any fragments of shell and set aside. Repeat with the second crab. Alternatively, scoop the crab meat out of the dressed crab shells.

Rinse the crab shells, then wash and clean them with the lime halves. Boil the shells in water with the vinegar for 10 minutes, then drain and rinse well.

Heat the oil in a large frying pan over a medium heat. Add the onion and sauté for 2 minutes, then add the garlic and cook for another minute. Next, add the curry powder, all-purpose seasoning and Scotch bonnet or chilli flakes and cook, stirring, for 1 minute.

Add the coriander, green bell pepper, spring onion and celery and continue to cook for 3 minutes. Add the black pepper and salt, then stir in the breadcrumbs and coconut milk or desiccated coconut. Stir until combined, then add the crab meat and butter. Stir again, then turn the heat down to the lowest setting and cook gently for 2 minutes to heat through.

Spoon the crab mixture into the cleaned crab shells, dividing it equally. Serve or place in an oven preheated to 180°C (160°C fan/350°F/Gas 4) for 10 minutes (or you could grill the crab), until slightly crisp on top. Garnish with extra coriander, spring onion and/or chives, if using, and a grinding of black pepper, with wedges of lime for squeezing over.

Christianity, fish & following the music

Christianity in the Caribbean can be traced back to the mid-17th century, when European forces bagged the region in search of financial gain. After the English defeated the Spanish they looked to supplement their lust for gain with slave labour, mostly from western Africa, on Jamaican plantations. As well as enforcing slavery on the island's captive native people and the Africans, the British brought with them several cultural practices, including Christianity, which the Spanish had already initiated, as well as the English language.

Today, there is a much-loved (but questionably fact-checked) statistic that Jamaica has the highest number of churches per square mile in the world. Exact figures aside, Protestant, Orthodox and Catholic churches pepper the small island, and some form of Christian education is the norm for most school children.

Christian teachings depict that Jesus was crucified on a Friday, and it became common practice for people to observe some form of abstinence or fasting on this day. In Jamaica, over the years, the popularity of fasting waned, and instead people abstained from eating "warm-blooded" creatures, such as meat, on Fridays. Subsequently, fish consumption increased and "Fish Friday" was born.

The colourful invitations are everywhere across Jamaica: on shop notice boards; tied to lampposts and road signs; flyers in restaurants; and so on. Advertising music, dance and a basic menu of fish dishes (and actually a few meat dishes, too), these events occur everywhere from restaurants to residential enclaves and most feature a vague closing time of simply "late". Sometimes the occasion is a birthday or a christening, but often it's just a celebration that we made it to another Friday – alive and in one piece.

In a country full of side roads and hillside short cuts, using a phone app for directions to these events mostly proves useless and the ability to decipher and remember a multi-chain string of directions given in rapid patois is a must. I recall my family talking about their younger days of revelling, finding their destination by simply following the music from the blaring sound system, so I followed their tradition. While high-street bars are a nice vibe, nothing beats the lawn parties deep in the residential enclaves, tucked between hills, at the end of driveways and beside neighbourhood dives. Late at night with nothing but orange spotlights illuminating the streets and the sound of crickets, yard dogs and the occasional noise of an approaching and vanishing car, if you listen out for the sound-system base rattling tree leaves and corrugated steel roofs, eventually you'll come across an event.

On one occasion, I followed a trail of music down Ochi's Great Pond Road around midnight only to find the raucous dancehall tunes, cranked up to a solid 11, servicing about three people. Trying to sleep with the music continuing way past 3am, I eventually gave up and retraced my steps to find the entire road jammed with rows of people and parked cars. Here, at 3am, the time London is told by the man to go home, amidst the pulsating bass and synchronized dancers, a mountainous box of rice and peas appeared with a giant spoon to accompany a choice of steamed or escovitch fish – all this for no more than three pounds. Unbeatable.

Steamed fish & okra

Almost everyone in Jamaica takes on the role of cultural ambassador, taking pride in showing you their corner of the island; it's the only place I've been to where a small request during a taxi ride can turn into a half-day detour. On this occasion, a trip from Lee Perry's Black Ark Studios to Orange Street diverts to a small, lively bar neighbouring a fish-based cookshop after my friend enquires on where to find good conch soup. The two shops, while separate, work in tandem to provide sustenance and a cold refreshing beverage. Opinions on the best dish is split. Half the people lazing back on the red plastic chairs, beer in hand, have the remnants of conch and okra in their takeout boxes, while the others are scooping up the last flakes of fish with Bammy (see p248) and water crackers.

On a subsequent trip to Kumasi, a city located in the middle of Ghana, as I watched people pull up plastic chairs lining the street to eat their evening meals, the sight of people tearing a variety of beige solids, using them as cutlery to dunk into okra gravy, while simultaneously picking up fish with their thumb and middle and index fingers, the flashback to Kingston is unreal. These are the same people, but just in a different context, and discussions of collective memory and cultural identity spring to mind. The character of a person from a distinct society and culture maintaining itself over generations through customs and norms, rather than biology: the Africans shipped across the middle passage stripped of physical relics able to keep fragments of themselves alive in their new home.

Like the fish stews of Ghana and the wider West African region, the role of navigating the fish bones in this stew is left to you. Fillets of fish melt into the spiced gravy, formed in the cooking process, and the softened okra and pumpkin all add to the texture. In cross-cultural fashion, the use of knives and forks is completely optional, too.

1kg (2¼lb) fish, such as sea bream, snapper or parrot fish, scaled, gutted and cleaned
1 lime or lemon, halved
1 tsp All-purpose Seasoning (see p239)
½ tsp fish seasoning
½ tsp sea salt
½ tsp freshly ground black pepper
200g (7oz) pumpkin, peeled, deseeded and cut into chunks
3 garlic cloves, minced
2 spring onions (scallions), finely chopped
1 onion, finely chopped
1 carrot, thinly sliced
1 Scotch bonnet pepper, deseeded and chopped
4–5 sprigs of thyme
1 bell pepper (½ red and ½ yellow), deseeded and thinly sliced
5 cherry tomatoes, quartered
2½ tbsp coconut oil, or oil of choice
200ml (¾ cup) coconut milk
200ml (¾ cup) hot water
6–8 okra, topped and tailed, sliced into rounds
1 tbsp butter (optional)
1 handful of water crackers

Using a fish scaler or sharp knife, give the fish a once over to remove any remaining scales that may have been missed. Place the fish in a bowl and rinse with water. Pour away the water, then add the lime or lemon juice and toss the fish in it. Use the squeezed-out citrus halves like a sponge to clean the fish, then rinse again with water. Pat the fish, inside and out, as dry as possible with kitchen paper. Cut 2 shallow slits diagonally across the body of both sides of each fish.

In a bowl, mix the all-purpose seasoning, fish seasoning and salt and pepper, then coat the outside of each fish with some of the seasoning, rubbing it into every crevice, including the slits. Add some of the seasoning to the inside of each fish to ensure it fully permeates the whole fish. Cover and set aside. Save any leftover seasoning for later. If you have time, leave to marinate in the fridge for about 1 hour.

Get 2 regular-sized bowls. Put the pumpkin, garlic, 1 spring onion, onion, carrot, Scotch bonnet and thyme into one. In the second bowl, place the red and yellow bell peppers, second spring onion and the tomatoes.

Heat the oil in a large sauté pan over a medium-high heat until it starts to sizzle, then add everything from the first bowl and sauté for about 5 minutes, stirring frequently. After this, add two-thirds of the contents of the second bowl. Sauté for another 3–5 minutes, stirring regularly, until the vegetables soften. Add any remaining seasoning powder to the pan. If the vegetables start to stick to the bottom of the pan, add another spoonful of oil and stir.

Stir in the coconut milk, then the hot water and continue to stir for a minute. When the liquid starts to bubble, turn the heat down a notch, cover with the lid, and simmer for 7–10 minutes.

Take off the lid and place the fish in the pan so they are submerged in the liquid. If space is tight, it's okay if the fish are snug and not completely flat as the sauce and steam will cook them. Spoon the sauce over the fish. Add the okra, the rest of the contents of the second bowl and the butter, then cover the pan and cook for a further 15–20 minutes, until the fish is cooked.

Once cooked, place the fish in a large, shallow serving dish and spoon the sauce and vegetables over the top. Check the seasoning and top with the water crackers, slightly submerging them into the sauce. Serve with Bammy (see p248), corn and/or rice.

Brown stew fish

Going to a Jamaican function (raves or parties for any reason, be it birthdays, weddings or funerals) in New York is like entering a parallel universe. The same swooning tunes send old timers into a little jig and Cameo's "Candy" has even the most disinterested doing the electric slide. Had my grandad stayed in the Bronx after leaving Jamaica instead of moving to the UK, I've no doubt I'd be doing exactly what I'm doing now, but just across the Atlantic. Had it not been for one of these functions in the aptly named Jamaica area of Queens, I may have never come across this dish as I don't see it offered in British Jamaican cookshops too often and I usually find it hard to forgo good old steamed fish.

Here, the fish is first fried, in the same way as Escovitch Fish (see p182), after which it is submerged in a rich gravy. The method was created over a century ago to combat the perceived blandness of regular steamed fish, so generations of taste testing has been done for us. The gravy is flavoured with all manner of condiments and spices, and some even use annatto powder to give it a distinct red colour. Feel free to adjust the gravy to your umami, sweet or spicy preference.

Pat the cleaned fish, inside and out, as dry as possible with kitchen paper. Cut 2 shallow slits diagonally across the body of both sides of each fish.

In a small bowl, mix together your choice of fish seasoning ingredients, except the Scotch bonnet, then coat the outside of each fish with some of the seasoning, rubbing it into every crevice, including the slits. Next, season the inside of each fish to ensure the seasoning fully permeates the whole fish. If you have time, leave the fish to marinate in the fridge for about 1 hour.

Heat the oil (it should be deep enough to half submerge the fish) in a large, deep, non-stick frying pan over a high heat. When it starts to sizzle, turn the heat down to medium-high and let it cool for 1 minute.

Place one fish in the pan (the oil will spit so take care). After a few seconds, check the fish hasn't stuck to the pan, if it has gently nudge it free with a spatula. If you like your fish spicy, add the Scotch bonnet to the pan. It will darken in colour, but will still do its job. Fry the fish for 6 minutes on each side, until a golden brown. Place on kitchen paper to drain and cool down,

SERVES 2–3

2–3 fish, about 240g (8½oz) each, such as parrot fish, mackerel, kingfish or snapper, scaled, gutted and cleaned with lime or lemon (see method p177)
300ml (1¼ cups) vegetable, sunflower or corn oil, for frying

FOR THE FISH SEASONING:

1 tbsp freshly ground black pepper
1 tbsp sea salt
1 tsp All-purpose Seasoning (see p239) (optional)
1 tsp fish seasoning (optional)
1 tsp garlic powder (optional)
¼ Scotch bonnet pepper, deseeded and finely sliced (optional)

FOR THE GRAVY:

2 tbsp light soft brown sugar
6 pimento seeds (allspice berries), crushed, or ½ tsp ground allspice
4 tbsp Scotch Bonnet Ketchup (see p243), or tomato ketchup
3 garlic cloves, peeled and left whole
3–4 sprigs of thyme, or ½ tsp dried thyme
2 spring onions (scallions), sliced
1 tomato, chopped, or 1 tsp tomato purée (tomato paste)
1 white onion, sliced
½ red bell pepper, deseeded and sliced into thin strips
1 tbsp browning (optional)
1 tbsp soy sauce (optional)
1 tbsp Worcestershire sauce (optional)
1 tsp annatto powder (optional)
½ tsp All-purpose Seasoning (see p239)

while you fry all the fish, adding more oil if needed. Set aside, reserving 100ml (⅓ cup plus 1 tbsp) of the frying oil.

To make the gravy, pour the reserved 100ml (⅓ cup plus 1 tbsp) of the oil back into the frying pan, then turn the heat to medium. Add the sugar, then stir for 2–3 minutes, until dissolved. Add the rest of the gravy ingredients, including your choice of seasonings, and sauté for 30 seconds. Add 400ml (1¾ cups) water and cook for 5–7 minutes.

Place the fish in the pan and ladle the gravy over the top. Turn the heat down to medium-low and simmer for 10–15 minutes, adding a little more water if the sauce looks too dry, until the gravy has reduced and thickened.

Check the seasoning and add extra salt and pepper to taste. If you'd like the red pepper to be softer, cover the pan during cooking.

Hellshire Beach special

In southeast Jamaica, between Kingston and Spanish Town, south of Portmore, lies Hellshire Beach where terraces of brightly coloured painted motifs, usually self-titled by the owners, vie for your attention. Names such as Hopie's, Bev's, Donna's, Mel's, Aunt May's, and more, entice you in with a glitzy array of seafood offerings.

Inside each one, multiple metre-wide, bubbling cauldrons of oil fry dozens of fish and chunks of dough at a time to feed the scores of locals and Jamaican tourists, as many or maybe more than foreign tourists. Many know exactly what they've come for, picking out snapper, kingfish, parrot fish or sea bream to be served steamed, escovitched, or brown stew-style. All the while hawkers insistently move to a beat, travelling from table to table, parasol to parasol, towel to towel, hawking goods, including small aquatic snacks the cookshops may not offer, like pepper shrimp and oysters. All come with a dozen fried Festivals (see p204), Bammy (see p248) or water crackers and a cold brew to create a feast many dream about.

In these literal waterfront restaurants, you can reach out and wash your hands and feet in the sea without even leaving your chair,

adding to the sense of wonder. I try to remember where I've seen this feverish adoration of seafood combined with such an atmosphere before on my travels, and I'm reminded of the crawfish boils and seafood po'boys in New Orleans, Louisiana, between the Mississippi River and Lake Pontchartrain. How coincidental that the two places, the hills of Hellshire and New Orleans, were both the refuge of runaway African slaves at almost the same point in history.

Risking their lives against colonial forces and rival Maroons alike, these fugitives would have only emerged out of the hilly terrain to these coastal shores for want of survival. Today, the descendants of those souls find the same joy they strove for their next of kin in eating the same foods as their predecessors.

That joy is much in evidence at Hellshire Beach every time a plate is served (though now before the bill arrives!). Admittedly, beachfronts around the perimeter of the island sell this fare but Hellshire has its draw, especially at Easter and bank holidays. The feast of seafood has come to represent a certain strand of island happiness, and if you can't make it to Hellshire, then I'll bring Hellshire to you with the following recipes.

Escovitch fish

Escovitch derives from the Spanish word *escabeche*, which in turn is believed to come from the Arabic *iskabej*, meaning "pickled fish", and refers to a process of preservation using an acidic ingredient like vinegar or citrus fruit. This method preserves cooked food for a few days without the need of refrigeration and, in a similar way to jerk, once captured the imagination of those living on a tropically hot island with no refrigeration and limited means of making food last.

While the original way of making escovitch is still used today, its utilization couldn't be further away. Once used as a means of survival, escovitch is now eaten by those looking to enjoy their food at a leisurely pace in the heat, while raving hard to the latest dancehall at a Hellshire Beach party, or bubbling to some old-time reggae at a garden party in Walthamstow, East London.

Both escovitch fish and fried fish are used interchangeably by my family: escovitch referencing the non-coated fried fish, while fried fish refers to the coated version. You can eat it post-fry once cooled, however, the true taste comes from leaving the fish to lie in the vinegar and pepper concoction for at least a few hours. If you have a jar of pickled peppers, then you're in store for some real heat, otherwise it's more than normal to prepare them from scratch before use and they don't take long to prepare.

For me, I'm not too fussed about which fish is used, be it mackerel, kingfish or parrot fish, although in the same way I support a certain red north London football team, I have a preference for snapper, because that's what I was born into.

―――

Using a fish scaler or sharp knife, give the fish a once over to remove any remaining scales that may have been missed. Place the fish in a bowl and rinse with water. Pour away the water, then add the lime or lemon juice and toss the fish in it. Use the squeezed-out citrus halves like a sponge to clean the fish, then rinse again with water. Pat the fish, inside and out, as dry as possible with kitchen paper. Cut 2 shallow slits diagonally across the body of both sides of each fish.

In a small bowl, mix together your choice of fish seasoning ingredients, except the Scotch bonnet, then coat the outside of each fish with some of the seasoning, rubbing it into every crevice, including

SERVES 2–3

2–3 fish, about 240g (8½oz) each, such as parrot fish, mackerel, tilapia, kingfish or snapper, scaled, gutted
1 lime or lemon, halved
300–400ml (1¼–1¾ cups) oil, such as rapeseed or sunflower
¼ Scotch bonnet pepper, deseeded and sliced (optional)

FOR THE FISH SEASONING:

1 tbsp freshly ground black pepper
1 tbsp sea salt
1 tsp All-Purpose Seasoning (see p239) (optional)
1 tsp garlic powder (optional)
1 tsp fish seasoning (optional)
½ Scotch bonnet pepper, deseeded and sliced (optional)

FOR THE QUICK PICKLED PEPPERS (OPTIONAL), OR USE READY-MADE:

1–2 tbsp oil, such as coconut or rapeseed
6–8 pimento seeds (allspice berries), crushed, or ½ tsp ground allspice
5 sprigs of thyme
2 spring onions (scallions), chopped
1½ bell peppers (mix of colours), deseeded and thinly sliced
1 carrot, cut into julienne
½ white onion, chopped and sliced into rounds
⅓ Scotch bonnet pepper, deseeded and sliced into rounds (optional)
5 tbsp white vinegar, or vinegar of choice

Oysters

the slits. Next, season the inside of each fish to ensure the seasoning fully permeates the whole fish. If you have time, leave the fish to marinate, covered, in the fridge for about 1 hour.

Heat the oil (it should be deep enough to half submerge the fish) in a large, deep, non-stick frying pan over a high heat. When it starts to sizzle, turn the heat down to medium-high and let it cool for 1 minute.

Place one fish in the pan (the oil will spit so take care). After a few seconds, check the fish hasn't stuck to the pan, if it has gently nudge it free with a spatula. If you like your fish spicy, add the Scotch bonnet to the pan. It will darken in colour, but will do its job. Fry the fish for 6 minutes on each side, until a deep golden brown. Place on kitchen paper to drain and cool down, while you fry all the fish, adding more oil if needed. Set aside to cool.

Meanwhile, make the quick pickled peppers, if using. Heat the oil (you could also use some leftover spicy oil from cooking the fish) in a sauté pan over a medium heat. Add all the ingredients, except the vinegar, and sauté for 2 minutes. Next, add the vinegar and continue to cook for another 3 minutes, until most of the vinegar has evaporated and been absorbed by the peppers.

If you have time, place the fish in a large, shallow bowl or dish and spoon over the pickled peppers to cover, then leave for 30 minutes, ideally overnight. If serving straightaway, place the fish on a dish and spoon over the pickled peppers. Serve warm or cold with Bammy (see p248) and Festivals (see p204).

Recordings of early Jamaican life by European travellers, dating back to the late 1600s, suggest that oysters, while not necessarily a fundamental part of the diet, were enjoyed nonetheless. As you occasionally still see to this day, oysters latched on to the roots of waterside trees, such as the mangrove. One 1672 account recalls, *"Oyster-trees... were plentiful on the Liguanea side of Kingston Harbour, where the islanders often carry their friends to be merry, and eat oysters, and that they may gather them off the trees themselves."* With slavery, this revelry was prevented and the majority of the population became inland slaves or Maroons with a heavily restricted diet, limited by both access to wealth and time.

Even though the oceans surrounding Jamaica are populated by molluscs of all sorts, for generations oysters in Jamaica were a delicacy mainly for wealthy tourists. International hotels would market all manner of oyster-based dishes, from oyster fritters and oyster sandwiches to oyster omelettes, none of which ever really caught on outside these resorts. While coastal residents may have been privy to oysters, for the majority of the hillside, inland denizens this was not so.

Today, resident Jamaicans, as much as tourists, enjoy a trip to Hellshire Beach and other popular beaches to make up for lost time, necking back pre-shucked oysters at will and dousing them in spicy vinegar, aged like fine wine in the sun.

SERVES 2

6–12 oysters
dash of vinegar from Quick Pickled Peppers (see p182)
2 limes, quartered, to serve (optional)

———

Shuck the oysters and spoon over a little pickled pepper vinegar. Finish with a squeeze of lime to tame the heat, if you like.

Sprats

The popularity of sprats grew out of finding a use for the myriad small fishes plentiful around the island, but not substantial enough to create a meaningful meal in themselves. They were often used as a part of Fish Tea (see p120), although the reduced cost of fish has meant that this is no longer necessary. Nowadays, sprats are mainly eaten as a finger food starter to escovitch or other seafood dish.

SERVES 4

400–500g (14oz–1lb 2oz) sprats or sardines, gutted and cleaned
4 tbsp plain (all-purpose) flour
1 tsp All-purpose Seasoning (see p239)
1 tsp sea salt
1 tsp freshly ground black pepper
oil of choice
1 lemon, quartered, to serve

Preheat the oven to 200°C (180°C fan/ 400°F/ Gas 6) and line a baking tray with baking paper. Pat-dry the fish with kitchen paper.

Combine the flour, all-purpose seasoning, salt and black pepper in a shallow bowl. Dust the fish in the flour mixture until coated.

Spread the fish out on the lined tray, drizzle over a little oil and cook in the oven for 30 minutes, turning once, until golden. (Alternatively, shallow-fry the fish in oil over a medium heat for 5–7 minutes on each side, until crisp and golden. Drain on kitchen paper.) Serve the sprats with Quick Pickled Peppers (see p182), slices of red pepper and wedges of lemon for squeezing over.

Pepper shrimp

While I effused about the radiant red shrimp I'd devoured at Hellshire Beach, a local to where I was staying at Treasure Beach to the south of the island, told me, "ya haven't tried the real until yuh check Middle Quarters uppa Black River." Enough said – two route taxis later and I'm there in a tiny, quiet village.

Cars driving through the village, passing by a roadside seafood stall decelerate and wind their windows down, Jamaican dollars at the ready to make the trade without exiting the car and, in some instances, without even slowing to a halt. I'm getting better at concealing my "foreign" status, but you can't get anything past the vendors who spend their lives watching the world go by from their stalls. They all know what I've come for, so the exchange is simple.

Inside large baby blue, neon green and bright yellow bowls are dozens of clear bags stuffed with dozens of light pink or bright red-coloured shrimp (or prawns), sourced from the nearby Black River. The shrimp flavoured with Scotch bonnet peppers are like a sort of spicy crustacean candy.

This recipe is a slightly jazzed-up version of the roadside pepper shrimp. So far, they've proven a great hit at dinners and the amount of people willing to put up with red digits and slightly garlicky breath at the parties I've taken them to suggest they're okay. In traditional fashion I leave the heads and tails on so each person can decide exactly how much they want to munch.

SERVES 4

500g (1lb 2oz) raw king prawns, cleaned, deveined, heads and tails left on
juice of 1 lime
2 tbsp apple cider vinegar
3 tbsp coconut or vegetable oil

FOR THE SEASONING:

3 sprigs of thyme
2–3 garlic cloves, minced
2 tbsp olive oil
2 spring onions (scallions), finely chopped
1 onion, finely chopped
1 tsp All-purpose Seasoning (see p239)
1 tsp fish seasoning (optional)
1 tsp freshly ground black pepper
1 tsp Jerk Seasoning (see p238), or shop bought
1 tsp paprika
1 tsp sea salt
½ tsp tomato purée (tomato paste)
2 tsp annatto powder or red food colouring (optional)

___

Put the prawns in a bowl and rinse with water, then drain. Add the lime juice and vinegar to the bowl with the prawns, toss until mixed together, then rinse again with water.

Mix together all the seasoning ingredients, except the annatto powder or red food colouring, in a large bowl. Add the prawns and mix with your hands, ideally wear gloves, until combined and coated in the seasoning. Cover the bowl and leave to marinate in the fridge for 30 minutes to 1 hour.

In a large frying pan with a lid, heat the oil over a medium heat. When hot, add the prawns and cook for 5–7 minutes, turning once, until they turn pink.

If you want to go for the reddish look, add the annatto powder or red food colouring when frying the prawns. Cover the pan with the lid intermittently to create steam, which will help to turn everything an even colour of red.

FLOUR
& WATER

"Jesus said to them, 'I am the bread of life; whoever comes to me shall not hunger, and whoever believes in me shall never thirst'."

For all its ethnic diversity, when it comes to religion in Jamaica, Christianity reigns supreme. On a trip home from the School of Visions in Kingston up in the Blue Mountains, a resident told me that if I wished to return the following Sunday, I should make sure I leave before 9am, or not bother at all since everything, including any means of public transport, shuts down during church hours. If it was at all possible for the tranquil settings of rural Jamaica to be even more serene, Sunday morning is that time. Outside the city, the lack of traffic means the sound of hymns, people speaking in tongues, and gospel echo for miles carried by the light breeze, meandering through the forest and bouncing off the mountain side.

Having been made to go to church every Sunday in my "Sunday best" for the first fifteen years of my life, whether it was in the UK, US, Canada or Jamaica, I'm all too familiar with the goings on inside: rhythm and blues renditions of religious songs; spirited dancing; local gossip; the donation collection; and such. Part of this was the Eucharist, the rite of consuming sacramental bread and wine believed to represent the body and blood of Christ. At my grandmother's church in Hackney, East London, which had mostly a white congregation, the "bread" was an object of fear. It was literally a tasteless, rice paper-textured disc, like the shell of a flying saucer sweet if you remember them. The other kids and I would pretend to nibble on them while trying to discreetly hide them in our pockets.

This was in major contrast to my local Baptist church in North London, a predominantly Black Caribbean congregation. Here, the Eucharist was a timely occasion that couldn't come sooner. Instead of the rice paper disc, the minister offered hardo bread, or hard dough bread, a sweet, soft, slightly dense bread widely popular and available pretty much everywhere across Jamaica and the Caribbean. It's obvious that the church offered this bread as the congregation could relate to it. All of this encapsulates modern Jamaica – the English language, Christianity and bread. They are pivotal entities in today's Jamaica, all inextricably linked, and all arrived hand in hand at the shores of the Caribbean.

As English forces took over the island of Jamaica from the Spanish in 1655, they began to import their food norms and among these was wheat for milling into flour and producing bread. Anglo-Irish physician, naturalist and botanist, Sir Hans Sloane, in the early 1700s wrote, *"Wheaten flour is better for many purposes than maize, and much more palatable than cassava, however well prepared"*, and as such wasn't surprised by its growing importation. As far back as the 17th century there were commercial bakeries on the island, although many did not survive until the consumer base grew with the end of slavery. The focus on the likes of sugar cane and molasses took precedence instead, due to the financial rewards for planters. More so, consumption was limited because products made with flour were primarily for the colonists and only occasionally included in the rations given to enslaved people as opposed to native root vegetables.

Records suggest that as early as the 18th century, every Jamaican Creole household had a rudimentary oven, such as a fireplace or brick furnace, and people *"baked as they find occasion"* as mentioned in B.W. Higman's book *Jamaican Food: History, Biology, Culture.* Although without yeast, baking was a limited art at this time.

British officiated schools in the Victorian era instituted bakery into the curriculum, which arguably facilitated its growth in the public consciousness. By the 19th century, home baking was made easier with the introduction of baking powder and self-raising flour, both first imported in 1866, which made bread and pastry *"light and easy of digestion"*. By this time, according to Higman, Jamaica had shifted to a more internally oriented economy, although imported foods still remained important.

"All manner of buns, cakes and breads [...] added to the already vivid hotpot of Jamaican food culture."

The end of slavery left lands across Jamaica ruinous and for a country marred in poverty, wheat, being a cheap crop, soon became a go-to as did the purchase of bread from a growing number of bakeries across the country. The early 1900s, however, saw the British Empire trying to prop up the remnants of the slave trade with indentured labour from south and east Asia. These communities added greatly to the already varied calabash of cultures on the island. The burgeoning Chinese population and, to a lesser extent Lebanese, were able to find success in commerce, including bakeries. They offered all manner of buns, cakes and breads, which added to the already vivid hotpot of Jamaican food culture and sparked a new wave of high-street businesses in the country.

When I was researching my first book, *Belly Full: Caribbean Food in the UK,* many of the oldest businesses I encountered were bakeries. Ironically, what made wheat and its by-products desirable for British envoys to export to Jamaica over a century earlier, were the same things that Caribbean people brought with them to the UK in their mass migration after the Second World War. Thousands of miles away from their tropical produce and food, baked goods and dried seasonings were among the few home comforts that either could survive the transatlantic voyage or be recreated with relative ease.

"Even the most basic of baked goods produce a heavenly aroma that you want to linger around for as long as possible."

With this, Jamaican bakeries sprung up across mid-20th century Britain in cities like London and Birmingham, selling favourites such as hardo bread, spiced buns and plantain tarts. To this day, especially around Christian festivals like Easter, expect the queue to be out the door at the more popular bakeries. Even the most basic of baked goods produce a heavenly aroma that you want to linger around for as long as possible, but imagine that compounded with the fragrance of mixed spices and you may just be able to conceive the joys of baked goods from Jamaica and the other Caribbean islands, from soft and flaky patties to the dazzling coconut gizzada snacks.

When I spoke to Lenny, the affable Jamaican-born owner of Mixed Blessings Caribbean bakery in South London, I asked him why he opened a bakery, rather than a restaurant and he replied, "I didn't want to deal with the people"; such is the personal, spiritual, almost religious, endeavour of baking.

Those growing up in Jamaican households may notice an omission of certain seasonal recipes, such as spiced buns. Quite frankly, this is because I, like most others in my family, never witnessed them being made. Rather, orders to our parents' favourite local bakeries were made and one of us youngins were sent to collect them. For me, this was either a trip to North London's West Green Road to visit the Jamaican-owned Tottenham Town Bakery, or a few miles south on Kingsland Road to Dalston's St. Lucian-owned Rainbow Bakery. Hence, I suggest if you happen to have a bakery of Caribbean heritage in your area to do the same. That said, you'll still find plenty of other traditional recipes in this chapter, and since the genesis of many of these recipes originally emanated from Europe, you should be able to find all the necessary ingredients easily.

I like to see this chapter as one that turns full circle for the Caribbean diaspora, the majority of which live in the US and the UK. What was once impressed on our ancestors has since been adapted and given many of their descendants the ability to sustain and thrive in their new land. As I see it, the ability to turn basic flour and water into bricks and mortar.

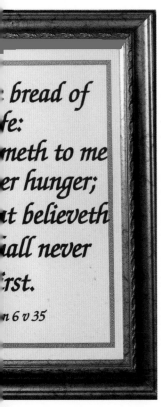

Spiced patties

As you tuck into a flavourful golden patty with its warm spiced filling oozing out with every bite, you just have to accept that the pastry flakes are going to get everywhere: every nook and cranny of your car; nestled in your facial hair; or bonded to your lips; and some flakes you won't even find until later in the day.

This dilemma has plagued Jamaicans for decades, since the shortcrust version, derived perhaps from a combination of the English pasty and Spanish empanada, became popular centuries before.

Nobody likes a cold patty and keeping them hot was a challenge until the mid-20th century. With the emergence of electricity, small shops and veranda stalls had small heat boxes to keep the patties warm, and it wasn't long after this, around the 1940s, that they entered mass production with companies producing the uniform, bright-yellow pastry shell we now know today. Some shops, however, like Mister Patty in Harlesden, London, have remained loyal to the French-style patty with its softer crust, which is more akin to the Cornish pasty, but they are in the minority.

During the same period, for those in their new homes thousands of miles away from the Caribbean, it wasn't always easy to find many of the ingredients needed to make home-cooked traditional dishes. Consequently, bakeries were among the first Caribbean food shops in the UK. A scene in Horace Ové's 1976 film, *Pressure*, on Black British life shows a group of Caribbean teens fiending over patties, illustrating the ravenous desire for them, which to be honest hasn't really changed to this day!

MAKES 12–13

FOR THE PASTRY:

450g (scant 3½ cups) plain
(all-purpose) flour, plus extra
for dusting
2 tsp ground turmeric
1 tsp curry powder
1 tbsp caster (superfine) sugar
1 tsp sea salt
240g (2 sticks plus 1 tbsp)
unsalted butter, frozen
250–300ml (1 cup plus
1 tbsp–1¼ cups) ice-cold water
30g (1oz) vegetable shortening
1 egg, beaten, or 2 tbsp milk,
to glaze (optional)

FOR THE FILLING:

150g (5½oz) saltfish (dried
salted cod), preferably
soaked overnight
200g (7oz) potato, peeled
and diced
80ml (⅓ cup) milk
1–2 garlic cloves, minced
2 tsp freshly ground black pepper
1 spring onion, finely chopped
1 tbsp unsalted butter
1 tsp All-purpose Seasoning
(see p239)
1 tsp ground turmeric
1 tsp cayenne pepper
½ carrot, grated
½ white onion, finely chopped
¼ bell pepper (colour of choice),
deseeded and finely chopped

First prepare the saltfish. Put the saltfish in a bowl, cover with cold water and leave to soak for a minimum of 3 hours, ideally overnight, until softened. (Alternatively, if you don't have time, cover the fish with water, bring to the boil, then turn the heat down and simmer for 1 hour.) Drain the fish and put it into a pan. Cover with fresh water and bring to the boil, then turn the heat down to medium and cook the fish for 30–45 minutes to reduce the saltiness. Drain through a colander and leave to cool, then flake into pieces, discarding any skin or bones.

Meanwhile, make the pastry. Sift the flour, turmeric, curry powder, sugar and salt into a mixing bowl. Grate 120g (1 stick) of the frozen butter into the bowl and rub it into the flour mixture with your fingertips to resemble fine crumbs. Add the water, a small amount at a time (you may not need all of it), and continue until it comes together into a smooth ball of dough; it shouldn't be sticky. Wrap the pastry in cling film and chill for about 30 minutes.

While the pastry is chilling, boil the potato for the filling until tender, then drain. Put all the filling ingredients, including the saltfish and potato, into a food processor and pulse until it resembles lumpy mashed potato. Set aside to cool.

Roll out the pastry on a lightly floured work surface to a rectangle, about 5mm (¼in) thick. Grate the remaining frozen butter and the vegetable shortening over the pastry. Fold the pastry over three times, like folding a letter, then fold it in half. Repeat the rolling and folding, then wrap the pastry and chill for 1 hour.

Preheat the oven to 200°C (180°C fan/400°F/Gas 6) and line a baking tray with baking paper.

Lightly dust the work surface with flour. Roll out the pastry, about 5mm (¼in) thick, then using a 15cm (6in) diameter cutter or plate, cut out as many circles as possible, re-rolling the pastry when needed. Continue until you have about 12–13 circles of pastry.

Spoon 1–1½ tablespoons of the filling into the middle of each pastry circle and flatten slightly with the back of the tablespoon. Wet your finger or a pastry brush with water and lightly dampen the outer edge, then fold the pastry in half over the filling into a semi-circle. Press the edges together with your fingers, then use a fork to crimp the edge and seal in the filling. Repeat to make 12–13 in total. If possible, place each uncooked patty in the fridge while preparing the next one. If not, place straight on the lined baking tray.

Brush the top of each patty with egg or milk, if using, and prick the tops with a fork. Bake for 25–30 minutes, until golden and cooked through. Leave to cool slightly on a wire rack before eating.

Yatties

The yattie – an Ital take on the traditional patty – replaces regular flour with wholemeal and the filling with vegan goodness. Unlike the Spiced Patties (see p194), where flakes of pastry rain down with every bite, the yattie can be soft and bread-like, or sometimes slightly crunchy to the bite, depending on how thick or thin you roll out the pastry.

Being opposed to all things Babylon (colonial or state-run), the Rastafari, descending from enslaved West Africans, created their own passage of speech as a means of instituting and reclaiming some form of identity. In the past, enslaved people in the Caribbean were denied any form of education, other than instructions on how to carry out the work enslaved life might require of them. Additionally, most slave-owners prohibited even a modicum of reading and writing on their grounds and enforced the use of European languages, including Portuguese, Spanish, French and English. This all but eradicated the use of the African language spoken by those taken from their mainland over the generations.

This form of speech – Rasta-isms, Dread Talk or Iyaric, as some term it – make the letter "I" a central figure in the language, referring to the oneness of Jah (God). It is put in place of any reference to "me", so any letters before an "I" may be dropped, as well as the starting letter of certain nouns and pronouns: *I-thiopia* (Ethiopia), *I-quality* (Equality) and so on. When an "I" does not work linguistically, a "Y" is used instead – hence yattie.

In Ital food spots entire *I-enu* (menu: "I" over "me") boards may be written in this slang, signifying a steadfast commitment to Ital (vital minus the "v") food.

MAKES 5–6

FOR THE PASTRY:

250g (1¾ cups plus 2 tbsp)
   wholemeal spelt flour
1 tsp light soft brown sugar
1 tbsp All-purpose Seasoning
   (see p239), or sea salt
120g (1 stick) unsalted vegan
   butter, frozen
120ml (½ cup) ice-cold water
plant-based milk, to glaze

**FOR THE FILLING
(CHOOSE FROM):**

1 recipe quantity Spiced Lentils
   (see p50), left to cool
½ recipe quantity Callaloo
   (see p63), left to cool
½ recipe quantity Creamed
   Coconut Ackee (see p28),
   left to cool

Preheat the oven to 200°C (180°C fan/400°F/Gas 6) and line a baking tray with baking paper.

To make the pastry, sift the flour, sugar and seasoning in a mixing bowl, then stir. Grate the frozen vegan butter into the bowl and rub it into the flour mixture with your fingertips to resemble fine crumbs. Add the water, a small amount at a time (you may not need all of it), and continue until it comes together into a smooth ball of dough; it shouldn't be sticky. Use a little extra flour if the dough is too sticky. Cover the bowl and leave the dough to rest for 10 minutes.

Lightly dust the work surface with flour and roll out the pastry until about 5mm (¼in) thick. Using a 15cm (6in) diameter cutter or plate, cut out as many circles as possible, re-rolling the pastry when needed. Continue until you have about 5–6 circles of pastry.

Spoon 1–1½ tablespoons of the cold filling of your choice into the middle of each pastry circle and flatten slightly with the back of the tablespoon. Wet your finger or a pastry brush with water and lightly dampen the outer edge, then fold the pastry in half over the filling into a semi-circle. Press the edges together with your fingers, then use a fork to crimp the edge and seal in the filling. Repeat to make 5–6 in total. If possible, place each uncooked patty in the fridge while preparing the next one. If not, place straight on the lined baking tray.

Brush the top of each patty with milk and prick the tops with a fork. Bake for 25–30 minutes, until golden and cooked through. Leave to cool slightly on a wire rack before eating.

MAKES 8

FOR THE PASTRY:

250g (1¾ cups plus 2 tbsp) plain (all-purpose) flour, plus extra for dusting

½ tsp ground cinnamon

1 tsp baking powder

1 tbsp coconut oil

75g (5⅓ tbsp) butter, frozen

15g (½oz) raw beetroot, peeled and chopped, or a few drops of red food colouring (optional)

120ml (½ cup) ice-cold water

milk, to glaze (optional)

FOR THE FILLING:

1 tbsp butter

1 ripe plantain, about 200 (7oz) in total, peeled and mashed

1 tsp ground nutmeg

½ tsp ground cinnamon

1 tsp light soft brown sugar

1 tsp vanilla extract

10g–20g (¼–½oz) raw beetroot, peeled and grated, or a few drops of red food colouring (optional)

Plantain tarts

Visiting Cornwall in the southwest of England, I recall hearing about coal miners who in the past would combine a sweet and savoury filling in a single pasty, separating the two with an inner pocket of pastry. I'm not going to suggest a version here, however, I've always wondered why a sweet version of the patty has never really taken off as a snack.

In true conservative Caribbean style, experimentation is usually limited and most bakeries have barely changed their repertoire in the last half a century. The exception to the rule being the plantain tart: ripe plantains cooked down with spices to make an incredibly moreish filling and encased in pastry – yet another use for plantain, the total number of which I have barely scratched the surface.

As plantain tarts aren't meant to mimic the patty, the flaky pastry is optional and consequently, only a cursory folding of the pastry is needed. In fact, I prefer the pastry to be slightly crisp, perhaps in memory of those school tarts that came in a foil casing. The red colour from the beetroot or food colouring is optional, but makes for a fun addition.

To make the pastry, sift the flour, cinnamon and baking powder into a mixing bowl. Add the coconut oil and grate in the frozen butter, then rub in with your fingertips to resemble fine crumbs.

If you want to make the pastry pink, blend the beetroot with a little of the water. Strain, discarding the beetroot excess. (Alternatively, add a few drops of red food colouring to the water.) Add the red coloured or plain water, a small amount at a time (you may not need all of it), and continue mixing until it comes together into a smooth ball of dough; it shouldn't be sticky. Wrap the dough in cling film and chill for 30 minutes.

Meanwhile, make the filling, melt the butter in a saucepan over a low-medium heat. Stir in the plantain, then add the nutmeg, cinnamon, sugar and vanilla. Turn the heat down to low and simmer for 3 minutes, then take the pan off the heat and set aside to cool for about 1 hour. To make the filling pink, stir in the beetroot or add a few drops of food colouring at this point, if using.

Preheat the oven to 190°C (170°C fan/375°F/Gas 5) and line a baking tray with baking paper.

Lightly dust the work surface with flour and roll out the pastry until about 5mm (¼in) thick. Using a 11cm (4¼in) diameter cutter or plate, cut out as many circles as possible, re-rolling the pastry when needed. Continue until you have about 8 circles of pastry.

Spoon 1–1½ tablespoons of the cold filling of your choice into the middle of each pastry circle and flatten slightly with the back of the tablespoon. Wet your finger or a pastry brush with water and lightly dampen the outer edge, then fold the pastry in half over the filling into a semi-circle. Press the edges together with your fingers, then use a fork to crimp the edge and seal in the filling. Repeat to make 8 in total. If possible, place each uncooked patty in the fridge while preparing the next one. If not, place straight on the lined baking tray.

Brush the top of each patty with milk, if using, and prick the tops with a fork. Bake for 25–30 minutes, until golden and cooked through. Leave to cool slightly on a wire rack before eating.

Macaroni cheese

I nearly finished writing this book without adding a recipe for macaroni cheese (or mac 'n' cheese or macaroni and cheese). It's one of those dishes that, like Rice & Peas (see p44), sounds straightforward but on closer inspection the possibilities, combinations and techniques are almost endless.

Since the dish was first noted in Jamaica almost 100 years ago in 1927, it appears many options have been explored. Like Fried Chicken (see p146), there's frequent mention of Jamaican mac 'n' cheese, although what makes it Jamaican is up for discussion. For veteran mac 'n' cheese loyalists, the opinion of what makes a good dish is so deep-rooted in personal nostalgia that it seems almost impossible to satisfy, let alone impress them with a new version.

Another reservation I had was that my preferences change like the wind – sometimes I prefer it "loose" with the macaroni floating in the melted cheese sauce and with a layer of crunch on top, while at other times, I like it dense, almost like the macaroni has been vacuum packed. This recipe is somewhat in the middle: it can be altered depending on the type and quantity of cheese you use as well as how much pasta and the oven temperature it is baked at – the choice is yours.

SERVES 6 (OR 8 AS A SIDE)

200–250g (7–9oz) dried macaroni,
 or similar pasta
50g (3½ tbsp) butter
30g (¼ cup) wholemeal or plain
 (all-purpose) flour
½ tsp sea salt
½ tsp freshly ground black pepper
300ml (1¼ cups) milk
200–250g (7–9oz) cheese, such
 as Cheddar, although pecorino
 works a treat
¾ tsp All-Purpose Seasoning
 (see p239) (optional)

FOR THE TOPPING:

50g (1¾oz) cheese of choice, grated
15g (½oz) breadcrumbs, panko
 or home-made
1 tbsp butter, chopped into pieces
10g (¼oz) desiccated coconut

Preheat the oven 200°–220°C (180°–200°C fan/400°–425°F/Gas 6–7), depending on how crisp you like the top. Meanwhile, cook the pasta for 2 minutes less than instructed on the packet. Drain and tip into a bowl.

To make the sauce, melt the butter in a saucepan or Dutch pot over a medium heat. Mix in the flour, then add the salt and pepper and keep stirring for 2–3 minutes, until a smooth roux. Gradually, add the milk, stirring continuously, to make a smooth sauce. Turn the heat up to medium-high and when the sauce starts to bubble, turn it down to low and simmer, stirring continuously, for 1–2 minutes, until thickened. Add the cheese (the larger amount if you like it cheesy), a handful at a time, and the all-purpose seasoning and stir until melted into the sauce.

Add the sauce to the bowl of pasta and gently turn before decanting into a shallow, rectangular ovenproof dish. Wipe the pan clean.

Next, heat the ingredients for the topping in the same pan and, when hot, stir quickly for about 30 seconds. Scatter the topping over the macaroni cheese and bake for 15–25 minutes, until heated through and depending on how crisp you like the top.

Fried dumplings

Is any meal complete without dumplings? Breakfast, lunch, dinner... there always seems to be a good reason for dumplings to be part of a meal. In our house bemusement ensues when dumplings aren't present. Like most foods in this book, a whole literary discourse could, and probably should, be devoted to dumplings in Jamaica. In her poem "Dutty Tough", the famous Jamaican poet Louise Bennett-Coverley chronicles the rising cost of life staples, as she and her contemporaries shun bread and have to *"Tun dumplin refugee"*.

For centuries, fried dumplings have been the bedrock of the poorest of the poor in Jamaica, since flour was imported to the region by colonial forces and partitioned out to the enslaved. Like song, dance and folk tales, the recipe for dumplings takes up no suitcase space or headroom, and its simplicity means a recipe can easily be replicated from generation to generation the world over. This physical and mental ease of transportation seems to be the reason that these dumplings were known as journey cakes, then Johnny cakes. With this, their presence unassumingly sits at the foundation of Jamaican families and enterprise across the entire diaspora. I term this the ability to turn flour and water into bricks and mortar.

I have no allegiance to any particular method: ingredients and techniques are as varied as there are houses on any given Jamaican street, and I'll happily go door to door trying every single rendition of them.

———

Mix together all the dry ingredients in a mixing bowl. Rub in the butter with your fingertips.

Add the milk and mix into a ball of dough; it shouldn't be sticky. Put the dough in a bowl, cover with a damp kitchen towel and chill for 1 hour, if you have time.

Dust your hands with flour and tear the dough into 50g (1¾oz) portions – you should to able to make 4 dumplings. Roll each one into a small ball, then slightly flatten the top, which allows you to use less oil than you would if deep frying.

To fry the dumplings, heat your chosen amount of oil, depending on whether you want to deep or shallow fry, in a deep pan over a medium heat.

When hot, add the dumplings and fry for 5 minutes on each side, until golden brown all over. Remove with a slotted spoon and drain on kitchen paper.

MAKES ABOUT 4

150g (1 cup plus 2 tbsp) plain (all-purpose) or wholemeal flour, plus extra for dusting
1 tsp baking powder
1 tsp granulated sugar (optional)
½ tsp sea salt
1 tbsp unsalted butter (optional)
120ml (½ cup) milk or water
75–150ml (⅓–⅔ cup) oil of choice, such as rapeseed or sunflower

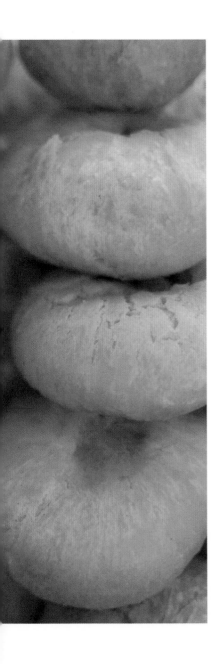

Spinach dumplings

MAKES ABOUT 4

15g (½oz) spinach leaves, tough
    stalks removed
150g (1 cup plus 2 tbsp) spelt or
    wholemeal flour, plus extra for dusting
1 tsp sea salt
1 tsp baking powder
1 tbsp unsalted butter (optional)
75–150ml (⅓–⅔ cup) oil of choice,
    such as rapeseed or sunflower

———

Finely chop the spinach and mix with
4 tablespoons water, or use a blender
or food processor.

Mix together all the dry ingredients in
a mixing bowl. Rub in the butter with your
fingertips. Add the spinach water and mix into
a ball of dough; it shouldn't be sticky. Put the
dough in a bowl, cover with a damp kitchen
towel and chill for 1 hour, if you have time.

Dust your hands with flour and tear the
dough into 50g (1¾oz) portions – you should
to able to make 4 dumplings. Roll each one
into a small ball, then slightly flatten the tops,
which allows you to use less oil than you
would if deep frying.

To fry the dumplings, heat your chosen
amount of oil, depending on whether you
want to deep or shallow fry, in a deep pan
over a medium heat.

When hot, add the dumplings and fry
for 5 minutes on each side, until golden brown
all over. Remove with a slotted spoon and
drain on kitchen paper.

Festivals

My ears prick up to the mention of "festivals"– what is this food named after a joyous occasion? In brief, they are simply elongated Fried Dumplings (see p202) made with cornmeal and a tad more sugar, although this slightly downplays their allure. As a kid, I lived in perpetual excitement in anticipation of when the externally crisp, internally soft, dumplings would make an appearance at mealtimes: sometimes it was on a Sunday breakfast with Ackee & Saltfish (see p158); sometimes in the evening with rice and chicken; or at a function served alongside fried fish. These sweet, golden wonders never seemed out of place, whether they were mopping up a meat gravy or the remnants of baked bean sauce.

Ground corn has long been used in Jamaican cooking, introduced by West Africans, so when the world wars initiated the rationing of wheat in Jamaica and led to the proposed use of corn in the likes of bread, fritters and dumplings, it wasn't far-fetched. Bread made with corn never really caught on, but corn fritters and dumplings have remained popular.

As commercially produced cornmeal became more available, so the making of cornmeal dumplings rose in popularity. It's said that the dumplings were named for the Jamaica Festival of Arts and Culture that marked the annual Independence celebrations starting in the 1970s. While these dumplings are relatively easy to make, few will begrudge you also buying the ready-made store mix that ushered festivals into mass popularity, especially if time is tight.

———

Sift the flour, cornmeal, salt, sugar and baking powder into a mixing bowl and stir until combined. Rub in the butter with your hands until the mixture resembles fine sand. Add the vanilla, then slowly pour in the milk or water, and mix with your hands until it forms a ball of dough; it shouldn't be sticky.

Gently knead the dough on a lightly floured work surface, adding more flour if the dough sticks to your hands. Place it in a bowl, cover with a damp kitchen towel and chill for 30 minutes to 1 hour.

Heat the oil in a large, deep frying pan over a medium-high heat, then turn the heat to medium when it starts to sizzle.

MAKES 8

185g (1⅓ cups) plain (all-purpose)
   flour, plus extra for dusting
4 tbsp fine cornmeal
½ tsp sea salt
3 tbsp light soft brown sugar
1 tsp baking powder
1 tbsp unsalted butter or vegan
   alternative
1 tsp vanilla extract
150ml (⅔ cup) milk of choice,
   or water
200–300ml (¾–1¼ cups)
   vegetable oil

Meanwhile, divide the dough into 8 balls, roughly
50g (1¾oz) each. Take a ball of dough and roll it into
an oblong, about 3cm (1¼in) wide x 8cm (3¼in) long.
Repeat to make 8 dumplings in total.

Fry the dumplings in batches, placing them gently
into the hot oil after shaping. (Note, they will expand in
size so don't overfill the pan.) Fry for 3-4 minutes, until
the underside is golden, then flip and cook the other
side for 3 minutes or so. Using a sharp knife, pierce the
dumplings to make sure they are cooked all the way
through. If not ready, cook for another minute.

Remove the dumplings with a slotted spoon and
drain on kitchen paper. Leave to cool for 10 minutes
before eating.

Syrian flatbread

One of the effects of the convergence of the Caribbean community in the UK and diaspora locales, like New York and Toronto, is that many foods, such as roti and doubles, once more common in the Eastern Caribbean islands have become better known in the West Indies too, including Jamaica, the French Caribbean and other islands with a minuscule Indian populace. Consquently, the flatbreads are now almost expected at every Caribbean takeaway, regardless of providence.

At the Dixon family's pink-fronted, homely restaurant in Port Antonio (not quite Ital but vegan, inspired by their Seventh-day Adventist faith) I stumbled across this flatbread, referred to by punters as wraps, bread and sometimes roti. They are simple, flexible enough to fold, but strong enough to convey food to the mouth, without becoming soggy after filling with the various curries and sauces of the day. The joy is that no two are ever the same – some are round but never a perfect circle, some are perfectly soft, and some are slightly crisp. Arriving first thing as they open, the restaurant ensures the flatbreads are warm and fresh.

This flatbread is no regular flour and water combination but has a yeast base, like the ones from Lebanese takeaways I recall eating late at night in London. As I discovered, this is no coincidence. As the Muslim Ottoman Empire came to a fore in the late 19th century Middle East, many Lebanese and Syrian Christians found themselves under persecution and sought to evacuate. America was an original haven as one of, if not the largest, Christian nations in the world. However, the US was still reeling from the aftermath of its own civil war, so many turned to Britain and its colonial subjects instead, and a large number are also known to have moved to Jamaica. They began to assimilate into Jamaica's complex social structure and introduce elements of their culture to the island. Chief among this was a popular flatbread that became known as Syrian bread.

After the dough has been made, this light and fluffy flatbread requires no special equipment, just a frying pan. I can understand how these have caught on since they go with pretty much anything and everything, from jams to fried chicken, while any of the vegan or meat curries and stews make a welcome filling.

Sift the flour into a mixing bowl, add the yeast, sugar and salt and stir until combined. Mix in the olive oil.

Gradually, add the water (you may not need all of it), and mix with your hands until it forms a ball. Knead the dough for 5–10 minutes, until smooth and elastic. Place in a bowl, cover with a kitchen towel and leave to rise in the fridge overnight. Alternatively, leave at room temperature until doubled in size, about 1 hour.

Lightly dust the work surface with flour. Tip the dough onto the work surface and gently knead to press out the air. Put the dough back into the bowl, cover and leave to prove for 30 minutes, or better still overnight in the fridge.

Divide the dough into 6 balls and lightly flour the work surface. Roll each ball out, one at a time, until about 5mm (¼in) thick. Turn a large bowl upside down and drape one piece of dough over the top, then gently pull until stretched out as much as possible. Repeat with the rest of the dough.

Heat a large, dry frying pan over a medium-high heat. Cook the flatbreads, one at a time, for 45 seconds on each side, until light golden and cooked through. Air bubbles should form in the bread as it cooks. Stack the flatbreads after cooking and cover with a kitchen towel to keep them warm. Serve as an accompaniment to curries and stews, or the choice is yours.

MAKES 6

250g (1¾ cups plus 2 tbsp) plain (all-purpose)flour, plus extra for dusting
2 tsp dried active yeast
1 tsp caster (superfine) sugar
½ tsp sea salt
1 tbsp olive oil
130ml (½ cup) lukewarm water

Hardo bread

My family discovered early on in my life that hard dough (hardo) bread is a life hack to get me to eat anything, and to be very honest it still is. (It lines a bowl of ackee and saltfish I'm eating in a photo of me taken in my early years, see p158.) Fillings as diverse as salami and chocolate spread (not at the same time!) would find their way into the hardo bread sandwiches in my school lunch box. Somehow, even a basic butter and cucumber combination was made tenable served between 2 slices of this Jamaican wonder-loaf. The name is a bit of a paradox, while it is "hard" when compared to the mass-produced bread found in supermarkets, the simple wheat-based recipe produces a soft, dense loaf with a subtle sweetness that is almost cake-like. As a kid I found certain loaves so good I'd happily eat them plain.

There are various stories on the origin of the bread. Some suspect it is an adaptation of the American pullman loaf or the French *pain de mie*, while some claim Chinese origins. However, I can't find adequate evidence to support any of these. All that can be surmised is that for Jamaican people, the regular British loaf of the time wouldn't hold up to being served with Hard Food (see p56) and Dumplings (see p57), let alone deal with curry sauces, meat gravies, and so on. With this, by the early 1900s, hardo bread had become an island favourite.

I think the density of hardo bread can be a bit overwhelming for first timers, so this recipe for a plain white loaf (or wholemeal variation) are quite rudimentary with no secret, or even hard to find ingredients. Hardo bread, like the patty or fried dumpling, has provided a foundation for diaspora bakeries across the UK. The likes of the Old Trafford Bakery in Manchester, Sunrise Bakery on the edge of Birmingham, and a sizeable list of London bakeries have gone from home-based businesses nearly half a century ago to large-scale industrial enterprises. Today, if you live in a town with even a small Afro-Caribbean presence, your local grocers will probably stock hardo bread, and I like to support these family businesses in buying their loaves. That said, do give this recipe a try and you'll be rewarded with the transformative aroma of home-baked hardo.

MAKES 1 LOAF

375g (2¾ cups plus 1½ tbsp) plain
    (all-purpose) flour, or 250g
    (1¾ cups plus 2 tbsp) wholemeal
    flour mixed with 125g (1 cup
    minus 1 tbsp) plain (all-purpose)
    flour, plus extra for dusting
1½ tbsp instant dried yeast
1 tsp sea salt
90ml (⅓ cup) lukewarm water
190ml (¾ cup plus 1 tbsp) warm
    milk or plant-based alternative
3 tbsp light soft brown sugar
60g (4 tbsp) unsalted butter
    or vegan alternative, cut into
    pieces, plus extra for greasing

Sift the flour, yeast and salt into a mixing
bowl and stir to combine.

In a separate bowl or a jug, combine the
water and 180ml (¾ cup) of the milk, then stir
in the sugar. Pour into the flour mix and add
the butter, then mix together with your hands
until it forms a ball of dough.

Tip the dough onto a lightly floured work
surface and knead for 5 minutes, until smooth
and elastic, adding extra flour if needed. Put
the dough into a bowl, cover with a kitchen
towel and leave to rise in a warm place (such
as a very low oven) for about 30 minutes, until
almost doubled in size.

Turn the oven to 220°C (200°C fan/425°F/
Gas 7) and grease a 400g (1lb) loaf tin.

Lightly flour a work surface and knead the
dough for another 5 minutes, forming it into
the shape of the tin. Put the dough into the
loaf tin and bake for 25–30 minutes, until
risen and golden.

After 10 minutes, lightly brush a little
of the remaining milk over the top of the loaf.
Bake for another 15 minutes, then brush again
with milk before baking for a final 5 minutes.
This step is optional, but it does give the bread
a shiny, golden top.

Use a wooden skewer to check the bread
is cooked through; there should be no sticky
residue. Leave to cool in the loaf tin for
10 minutes, then turn out and cool completely
on a wire rack.

Sugar & wheat – armed in arms

If there was ever a good time to speak about sugar it would surely be whenever Jamaican baked goods are mentioned. Where wheat and sugar once competed for share of mind and share of field space, they now work in harmony throughout Jamaica: be it in treats like toto cake, gizzada and bulla cakes, or homely staples like hardo bread, or festive Easter buns and Christmas rum cake. While the two crops are indelibly linked in history, there's no doubt they still remain so in the future of Jamaica as long as nostalgia towards certain treats ceases to change.

No other food in this book has arguably altered the course of the world, politically, ethnically and demographically (and much more), as much as sugar. I can't do the full story complete justice here, but in the crudest way, the combination of the European sweet tooth and the large potential revenue led to an armed race to develop sugar cane plantations. With Europeans (exiled or voluntary) unable to work the fields to maximum efficiency and profit, they set upon the African continent for slave labour.

The large-scale production of originally Mediterranean-sourced sugar essentially turned commercial Jamaica into a monocrop island. Wheat production was minimal in comparison to sugar and was also imported from places like the US and the UK. Sugar plantations engulfed the whole island, as well as countless other islands and regions, and ignited waves of deforestation in the process. British forces, having defeated the Spanish to take control of their resources, brought hundreds of thousands of slaves to the island from West Africa. They were joined by indentured labourers from India, China and other colonial strongholds who worked the fields after the abolition of slavery in 1833. By this time, sugar had already become a substantial part of British exports, meaning the labour on these plantations effectively subsidized the industrial revolution. Although Barbados was thought to be a better locale for sugar production for a variety of reasons, Jamaica became the epicentre of Britain's sugar market.

Enslaved people toiled in rodent-infested fields in the unrelenting Caribbean heat for a documented 45 hours per week, which doesn't include the hours spent on their own provision grounds. They were paid nothing, didn't receive a share of the fruits of their labour, and sugar formed an insignificant part of their rations. If they did get anything, it was often in the form of a new type of sugar-based juice. As noted in B.W. Higman's book *Jamaican Food: History, Biology, Culture*, "*The peasants [favourite beverage] was crude cane sugar and water with the juice of bitter orange.*"

Since the abolishment of slavery and the emancipation, the lands of former sugar plantations have dwindled. Woodlands and overgrowth have taken over many of the fields and the Georgian planter manors that overlooked them. With this, a comparatively minute sugar industry still exists on the island and sugar cane remains a local favourite as bite-sized chunks or cool, refreshing juice.

The large canes, like bamboo, are fed through churning machines, filtering out the bark to produce a sweet, golden juice. Most towns in Jamaica, along with the fresh coconut juice vendors, will have a cane juice vendor vibing and hanging out, effortlessly chopping cane, working the machines, and diluting the juice with a kick of ginger, lime and rum, if desired.

Memories of old man Kano coming to our house in the hills of Brown's Town in St. Ann Parish every morning to sell us fresh sugar cane, meant the juice was a regular part of my life that I miss every time I leave the island. I now have a near one-inch permanent scar on my right thumb trying to emulate the way Mr. Kano effortlessly hacked away the cane bark to reveal the glowing inner.

Date gizzada

While I have my favourite Caribbean bakeries in the UK, North America and in Jamaica, nothing beats the homemade fare of a roaming vendor. Snacks, for me, become less of a treat if I can just go to a shop at any time, while those of a wayward vendor are savoured as I never know when I'll get a chance to eat them again.

The sweetest elderly lady wanders across Port Antonio carrying a light-blue basket full of baked goods, featuring none other than my favourite gizzada. Pronounced "*ghizz-ah-dah*", these open-pastry shells are packed with a sweet, spiced, desiccated coconut filling. Sometimes I see her in Port Antonio town centre, sometimes I see her at Boston Bay awaiting tourists, and each time I rustle in my pocket for some change to buy a couple. Gizzada sellers are not created equal and, unfortunately, I've bought my fair share of stale ones from rogue traders. That first bite should contain equal amounts of soft spiced coconut goodness as well as the crisp snap of fresh pastry. If the filling is inadequate or the pastry has been sitting around for too long it won't pass the taste/texture test.

From the 1500s, people of Portuguese and Spanish descent arrived on the shores of Jamaica and began a lineage of settlers from the Iberian Peninsula. Many were fleeing persecution, including European Jews during the Inquisition. By the 18th century, with numbers roughly totalling 1,000 people, Jamaica is said to have hosted the largest population of Jews in the English Atlantic World outside of London. Today, a single synagogue remains in the heart of Jamaica's capital city Kingston, called *Sha'are Shalom,* and is still serviced by the Island's Jewish population and descendants. It's thought that among the home comforts brought with them to the island was a baked snack called *guisada.* There seems to be no particular culinary reason gizzada's are an astral shape, but I've often wondered whether it could be a reference to the Star of David.

When making gizzada I find it hard to resist eating the filling straight from the pot. The brilliant aroma of coconut, sugar, vanilla, cinnamon, ginger and vanilla immediately fills the house. I like to use dates to reduce the amount of added sugar, and I also find they add to the soft texture, so important to that first bite.

MAKES 7

FOR THE FILLING:

125g (4½oz) pitted dried dates,
    finely chopped
100g (½ cup) light soft brown
    sugar or honey
125g (4½oz) desiccated coconut
1 tsp vanilla extract
1 tsp finely grated fresh
    root ginger
¼ tsp ground allspice
¼ tsp ground cinnamon
¼ tsp finely grated or ground
    nutmeg
2 tsp coconut oil

FOR THE PASTRY:

250g (1¾ cups plus 2 tbsp) plain
    (all-purpose) or wholemeal
    flour, plus extra for dusting
½ tsp sea salt
2 tbsp coconut oil
150ml (⅔ cup) ice-cold water
milk of choice, to glaze

To make the filling, pour 5 tablespoons water into a pan and bring to the boil over a high heat. Reduce the heat to medium-low, add the dates and sugar or honey and cook for 10 minutes, occasionally crushing the dates against the side of the pan with a wooden spoon, until very soft. After a few minutes, stir in the desiccated coconut, vanilla and spices until combined. Continue to cook for 15 minutes, stirring the mixture to prevent it sticking to the bottom of the pan, until a thick paste. Mix in the coconut oil and cook for another 5 minutes. Turn off the heat and set aside to cool.

To make the pastry, sift the flour and salt together in a mixing bowl. Add the coconut oil and rub it in with your fingertips until the mixture resembles fine crumbs. Add the water, a small amount at a time (you may not need all of it), and mix with your hands to form a smooth ball of dough. Wrap the dough in cling film and chill for 30 minutes to 1 hour.

Preheat the oven to 180°C (160°C fan/350°F/Gas 4) and line a baking tray with baking paper.

Lightly dust your hands and a work surface with flour. Roll out the pastry until about 3mm (⅛in) thick. Using a 9–10cm (3½–4in) diameter cutter or a plate, cut out 7 circles, re-rolling the pastry when needed.

To shape the gizzada, take one pastry round and crimp or pinch the edge to make a pastry case with a slight raised border. Repeat to make 7 in total, place on the lined baking tray and brush with milk. Prick the base with a fork, then bake the pastry cases for 10–15 minutes, until crisp and light golden.

Spoon about 3 tablespoons of the filling into each pastry case and spread out to the edges – the cases should be filled to the brim. Bake for 20–30 minutes, until the filling is cooked and the pastry golden. Leave to cool on a wire rack.

Pumpkin & fig duppy pie

For a country primarily populated with the descendants of Africans with a wealth of spiritual beliefs, it makes sense that many believe in the existence of some form of supernatural being, whether religious or not. Chief among the spirits in Jamaica are duppies. These incarnations of the departed or supernatural beings roam the hills and plains of the island, aimlessly or sometimes with a mission of wreaking havoc. While specific tales of the duppy aren't recounted as much, at least in my experience, it's still common for people to explain the cause of a random happening, such as a cup falling over or a door slamming shut, on a visiting duppy.

Much is told about the lives of duppies, however, little is known about their supernatural diets when they aren't on the prowl. Martha Warren Beckwith's *Black Roadways: A Study of Jamaican Folk Life* describes, *"Duppies live in the roots of cottonwood trees and bamboo thickets and feed upon bamboo root, 'fig' leaves, and the gourd-like fruit of a vine called 'duppy pumpkin'."* This pumpkin and fig pie is made to appease any duppy spirit who may be roaming around my kitchen in Peckham, South London. Pies featuring yam and sweet potato are popular in Jamaica and, like pumpkin, when in season, are plentiful and popular on the island – this is my take on one of that ilk.

————

To make the pastry, sift the flour and salt together in a mixing bowl. Add the butter and rub it in with your fingertips until the mixture resembles fine breadcrumbs. Mix in the spices and sugar until combined. Add the water, a small amount at a time (you may not need all of it), and mix with a fork and then your hands until it comes together into ball of dough. Press the dough into a round, about 2.5cm (1in) thick, wrap in cling film and chill for 30 minutes to 1 hour, if time allows.

To make the filling, heat the coconut oil in a frying pan over a medium heat. Gently place the figs, cut-side down, in the pan and cook for 2 minutes, until starting to soften. Remove the figs from the pan with a slotted spoon and set aside briefly. Sprinkle 2 tablespoons of the brown sugar into the pan and place the figs on top, cook for 1–2 minutes until the figs caramelize. Remove from the pan and set aside to cool, skin-side down.

MAKES 1 PIE

FOR THE PASTRY:

250g (1¾ cups plus 2 tbsp) wholemeal flour or plain (all-purpose) flour
½ tsp sea salt
125g (1 stick plus 1 tbsp) chilled unsalted butter, cubed, plus extra for greasing
1 tsp ground cinnamon
¼ tsp ground nutmeg
¼ tsp ground ginger
1 tbsp caster (superfine) sugar
90–100ml (⅓–⅓ cup plus 1 tbsp) ice-cold water

FOR THE FILLING:

1 tbsp coconut oil
4 ripe figs, halved
75g (6 tbsp) light soft brown sugar, plus 2 tbsp for the figs
750g (1lb 10oz) pumpkin, peeled, deseeded, and chopped into 2.5cm (1in) cubes
½ tsp sea salt
75g (6 tbsp) caster (superfine) sugar
1 tsp ground cinnamon
1 tsp ground ginger
½ tsp ground nutmeg
pinch of freshly ground black pepper (optional)
175ml (¾ cup) whole milk or double (heavy) cream
3 eggs

Meanwhile, put the pumpkin into a large saucepan, cover with water and bring to the boil. Turn the heat down slightly, cover with the lid and simmer for about 15 minutes, until tender. (Alternatively, toss the pumpkin in a little coconut oil and roast for 25 minutes in an oven preheated to 190°C (170°C fan/375°F/Gas 5), until tender.

Lightly grease a 23cm (9in) loose-bottomed tart tin with butter.

Roll out the pastry on a lightly floured work surface, about 3mm (⅛in) thick and 30cm (12in) round. Line the tin with the pastry, gently pressing it into the base and up the side, letting it slightly overlap the top of the tin. Using a rolling pin, gently roll it across the top of the tin to remove the excess pastry. Chill for at least 30 minutes.

Preheat the oven, or turn it down, to 180°C (160°C fan/350°F/Gas 4). Line the base of the pastry case with baking paper and weigh down with baking beans. Blind bake for 20 minutes, remove the beans and paper, then prick the base of the pastry in several places with a fork. Return to the oven and bake for a further 10 minutes, until golden and crisp.

Meanwhile, press the pumpkin through a sieve into a large jug – it should look like a smooth paste. Combine the pumpkin with the salt, remaining brown sugar, caster sugar, and spices.

In a separate bowl, beat the milk or cream and eggs until combined, then add to the pumpkin mix. Pour the filling into the pastry case and return to the oven, taking care not to spill any of the mixture.

Bake the pie for 10 minutes, then place the figs, cut-side up, on top. Turn the oven down to 160°C (140°C fan/325°F/Gas 3) and bake for a further 20 minutes, until the filling is set around the edges with a slight wobble in the centre. Remove and leave to cool in the tin. Serve cut into slices.

Dr. Bird cake

The world-famous hummingbird cake has its origins in Jamaica, where it is also known as Dr. Bird Cake, and its popularity comes as no surprise. The interweaving of both pineapple juice and pineapple chunks with spices and banana produces an almost addictive cake, which when bolstered with crunchy pecans and a creamy frosting is even harder to resist.

The cake's history goes back to the 1960s when the Jamaican Tourist Board, looking to foster tourism as a means of creating a new stream of income, utilized fruits of the island, namely banana and pineapple, in a recipe. This recipe distributed to the media sought to spread the word about the island's fresh produce. The spiced banana-pineapple cake was named after the country's national bird, the hummingbird, colloquially known as the doctor bird. Food editors, particularly from the southern states of America, got hold of the recipe and from there it rapidly became part of the annals of American cooking, and then the world. Upon tasting the cake, it's evident why it has attracted so much attention over the years.

———

Preheat the oven to 200°C (180°C fan/400°F/Gas 6) and grease and line the base of a 24cm (9½in) round cake tin. (If making a double-layered cake, use 2 tins and double the quantity of the cake mixture and frosting.)

Put the nuts and pineapple in a blender or food processor and pulse briefly until finely chopped.

Sift all the dry ingredients, up to and including the salt, into a mixing bowl, then stir until combined and set aside.

In a separate bowl, add the bananas, coconut oil or butter, reserved pineapple juice, vanilla, vinegar and egg, if using. Whisk until combined, then add to the dry ingredients with the pecan and pineapple mix. Briefly stir until combined, but do not over-mix the cake batter.

Spoon the mixture into the cake tin and level the top. Bake for 30 minutes, or until a skewer inserted into the middle comes out clean. Leave to cool for 5 minutes, then turn out of the tin onto a rack to cool completely.

Meanwhile, make the frosting. Beat the butter and cream cheese together until light and fluffy. Add the salt and vanilla, then stir in the icing sugar, a little at a time, to make a thick, spreadable icing. Spread the frosting over the top of the cake (or half over each cake if making 2). Sprinkle with the coconut flakes and pecans.

MAKES 1 CAKE

100g (3½oz) pecans
   or walnuts, chopped
100g (3½oz) canned chopped
   pineapple in juice, drained
   and 80ml (⅓ cup) juice
   reserved
250g (1¾ cups plus 2 tbsp)
   wholemeal flour or plain
   (all-purpose) flour
150g (¾ cup) light soft brown sugar
1½ tsp bicarbonate of soda
   (baking soda)
1 tsp baking powder
1 tsp ground cinnamon
½ tsp ground allspice
½ tsp ground nutmeg
¼ tsp sea salt
2 ripe bananas, mashed
50g (1¾oz) coconut oil
   or butter, or oil of choice,
   plus extra for greasing
1 tbsp vanilla extract
2 tbsp apple cider vinegar
1 egg (optional)
25g (1oz) coconut flakes, toasted
1 handful of pecans, roughly
   chopped

FOR THE FROSTING:

200g (1¾ sticks) unsalted butter,
   softened
175g (6oz) full-fat cream cheese
¼ tsp sea salt
1 tsp vanilla extract
250g (2 cups, plus 2 tbsp) icing
   (powdered) sugar, sifted

Plantain loaf

As the mainstream story goes, banana bread originated during the era of America's great depression in the 1930s. It was said to be the result of the emergence of baking powder as an ingredient and consumers looking to economize and jazz-up cheap recipes, along with marketers finding ways to reduce food waste, and likely a nudge from the banana producers, too. Given that the import of bananas into the US at this time was overwhelmingly from the Caribbean, and Jamaica in particular, it was only a matter of time that the people of the region absorbed the recipe into their cuisine and gave it the local treatment.

I hope by now there isn't anyone who needs an introduction to banana bread and, while I'll happily munch on a complimentary slice, I've probably had it a few too many times. Fortunately, anything a banana can do, plantain can do better. The texture of a jet-black, ripe plantain bursting at the seams means it blends into the cake batter with little effort. Compared with banana, plantain gives a richer, denser, more aromatic loaf. Once converted it's hard to go back!

———

Preheat the oven to 180°C (160°C fan/350°F/Gas 4) and grease and line the base of a 400g (1lb) loaf tin with baking paper.

Using an electric hand whisk or stand mixer, beat the butter and sugar until light and fluffy. Beat in the eggs, or soaked flaxseeds, vanilla and milk.

Sift in the flour, salt, bicarbonate of soda, baking powder and fold until combined. Gently fold in the mashed plantain.

Spoon the cake batter into the prepared tin. Bake for 60–70 minutes, until risen and golden on top, and a skewer inserted into the middle comes out clean. Leave the cake to cool for 5 minutes in the tin, then turn out onto a wire rack to cool completely. Serve in slices with thick cream.

MAKES 1 LOAF

125g (1 stick plus 1 tbsp) unsalted butter, softened, plus extra for greasing

200g (1 cup plus 2 tbsp) caster (superfine) sugar

2 eggs lightly beaten, or 10g/¼oz ground flaxseeds mixed with 3 tbsp water and left to stand for 15 minutes

1 tsp vanilla extract

3 tbsp milk

270g (2 cups) plain (all-purpose) flour

½ tsp sea salt

½ tsp bicarbonate of soda (baking soda)

½ tsp baking powder

1 very ripe black plantain, about 200g (7oz) in total, mashed

Spiced carrot cake

Like banana bread, carrot cake is so ingrained in Jamaican cuisine that you just assume it was conceived there; and any story of competing origins is dutifully ignored. A visit to the digital archives of the World Carrot Museum suggests otherwise: carrot puddings in 10th-century Arabic cooking may have provided the foundation of the carrot cakes of 18th-century Europe, where carrots grew with relative ease. The recipes dating back to this time heavily rely on sugar, which of course came from the Caribbean, so inadvertently I reckon Jamaica is owed some recognition here too. The centuries-old British and American recipes for carrot cake aren't dissimilar from the one below. Given that, I just can't imagine life in Jamaica without being given the option of carrot cake or banana bread at a shop counter, at a function, when visiting an Aunty... so here it remains.

Preheat the oven to 180°C (160°C fan/350°F/Gas 4) and grease and line the base of a 400g (1lb) loaf tin with baking paper.

In a mixing bowl, whisk together the butter, vinegar, brown sugar, vanilla and eggs, or soaked flaxseeds. Stir in the carrots and leave to sit for 5 minutes to allow the carrots to release any liquid.

In a separate bowl, sift in the flour, baking powder, bicarbonate of soda, salt, cinnamon and allspice. Gradually fold the dry ingredients into the carrot mixture to make a thick batter.

Spoon the mixture into the prepared tin. Bake for 30–35 minutes, until risen and golden, and a skewer inserted into the middle comes out clean. Leave the cake to cool for 5 minutes in the tin, then turn out onto a wire rack to cool completely.

To make frosting, beat the cream cheese with the butter, icing sugar and lemon juice until a thick, creamy icing, then chill to firm up until ready to use. Spread the frosting over the top of the cake. Decorate with edible flowers, if you like.

MAKES 1 CAKE

125g (1 stick plus 1 tbsp) unsalted butter, softened, plus extra for greasing
1 tbsp apple cider vinegar
150g (¾ cup) light soft brown sugar
1 vanilla pod, or a few drops of vanilla extract
2 eggs, lightly beaten, or 10g/¼oz ground flaxseeds mixed with 3 tbsp water and left to stand for 15 minutes
250g (9oz) carrots, about 3 large, coarsely grated
250g (1¾ cups plus 2 tbsp) plain (all-purpose)flour
1½ tsp baking powder
½ tsp bicarbonate of soda (baking soda)
1 tsp sea salt
1½ tsp ground cinnamon
1 tsp ground allspice
edible flowers, to decorate (optional)

FOR THE FROSTING:

400g (1lb) full-fat cream cheese
50g (3½ tbsp) unsalted butter, softened
75g (½ cup plus 1 tbsp) icing (powdered)sugar, sifted
juice of 1 lemon

A most disappointing rum cake

Most people, Jamaican, Caribbean or other, may not equate rum and raisin cake with disappointment, but that's my immediate split-second emotion. Imagine the feeling as a child when suddenly, unannounced, a colourful tin of your favourite biscuits or sweets makes an appearance in the house. Before opening the lid you've already decided which ones you'll choose, without any consideration for who bought it, or for anyone else in the house. In your mind, you've already unwrapped and popped the bite-sized chocolate treat into your mouth. As you lift the lid reality sets in – there are no chocolates. It's rum and raisin cake. AGAIN! Somehow, you've been duped for the twenty-fifth Christmas in a row. It's hard to sum up in words the disappointment, however, as I'm usually told when recalling this story, "At least it's not a sewing kit!".

This may be sacrilege, but I've never been the biggest fan of rum and raisin cake, especially the deep brown, almost black, dense, rum-heavy, wet sponge-type that is enjoyed in my family, which is traditionally coated in a snow-white layer of icing with an adhesive layer of marzipan beneath. That said, the first time I tried a rum cake that really brought a new appreciation was at Ayanna's, a Caribbean restaurant in East London. I wouldn't dare copy their family recipe, but this is my take on a very different kind of rum cake. Here, the essence of the spices, rum and dried fruit very much remains, but is instead blended into the mix to create a rich, moist sponge cake-like consistency; it's a cake that never lasts for more than a few days in our house.

——

Put all the dried fruit in a bowl, pour over the rum and leave to soak, covered, overnight. If you don't have time to soak the fruit, then bring the rum to the boil, add the fruit and simmer on very low for 15 minutes, then leave to cool. Add the soaked fruit and rum to a blender and pulse until smooth.

Preheat the oven 180°C (160°C fan/350°F/Gas 4) and grease and line the base of a loose-bottomed 22cm (8½in) deep, round cake tin with baking paper.

Sift the flour, ginger, cinnamon, nutmeg, allspice and baking powder into a mixing bowl and stir until combined.

Melt the butter or oil and sugar over a low heat in a saucepan, stirring well to combine. Leave to cool, then

MAKES 1 CAKE

100g (3½oz) pitted dried dates, chopped
80g (2¾oz) raisins
80g (2¾oz) dried cherries
250ml (1 cup plus 1 tbsp) dark rum, plus extra for brushing
315g (2½ cups minus 1 tbsp) plain (all-purpose) flour
1 tbsp ground ginger, or finely grated fresh root ginger
1 tbsp ground cinnamon
¼ tsp ground nutmeg
¼ tsp ground allspice
1½ tsp baking powder
200g (1¾ sticks) unsalted butter or coconut oil, plus extra for greasing
200g (1 cup) light soft brown sugar
juice and finely grated zest of 1 unwaxed lemon
finely grated zest of 1 unwaxed orange
1 tsp vanilla extract
90ml (⅓ cup) milk of choice
2 eggs, beaten, or 10g/¼oz ground flaxseeds mixed with 3 tbsp water and left to stand for 15 minutes

pour into a separate mixing bowl. Mix in the blended fruit, lemon juice, lemon and orange zest, vanilla and milk. Whisk in the eggs, or soaked flaxseeds, until light, glossy and smooth. Fold in the dry ingredients and mix until fully combined. Spoon the cake batter into the prepared tin.

Bake for about 50–55 minutes, until risen and golden, and a skewer inserted into the middle comes out clean. If it's not ready, return the cake to the oven for a few minutes, then test again. Leave to cool in the tin for 15 minutes, then brush the top with extra rum. Turn out onto a wire rack to cool completely.

Toto

Toto, like bulla cakes, grater cakes, mess-around cake and, to a lesser extent, coco bread, hang onto existence in the modern day by a nostalgic string. Many of these baked goods were created over the last couple of hundred years. Novel ways were found to combine sugar and flour with local island produce as well as adapting recipes that had made their way to the island from across the globe.

Older generations of my family gush about walking home from school along gravel roads in the hills of Jamaica passing by their nearest bakery or vendor for such a treat. While high-street bakeries, both in Jamaica and the diaspora, still sell many of them, times are changing, and tastes are shifting away from the dense, sugar-laden treats. More so, the older generations, as they tell me, can no longer wilfully knock back a couple of hundred grams of sugar at a time without any consequences anymore.

Out of the classics, toto (sometimes known as *toetoe*) is perhaps my favourite. To describe toto, think of the finest, softest, warm sprinkle cake from days gone by and imagine it infused with coconut. That, for me, is toto. While it's usual to cut the cake into squares and eat it on its own, I also like to douse mine in custard and pretend I'm having school dinners.

———

Preheat the oven to 190°C (170°C fan/375°F/Gas 5) and grease and line the base of a 20cm (8in) square cake tin with baking paper.

Using an electric hand whisk or stand mixer, beat the butter and sugar until light and fluffy. Whisk in the vanilla and egg, if using.

Sift the flour, baking powder, bicarbonate of soda, nutmeg, ginger, cinnamon and salt into a bowl. Stir in the desiccated coconut until combined.

Fold the dry ingredients into the creamed butter and sugar. Gradually, mix in the coconut milk, you may not need all of it, to make a fairly thick cake batter.

Spoon the mixture into the prepared cake tin and level the top. Bake for 30 minutes, until golden and a skewer inserted into the middle comes out clean.

To glaze the cake, brush the top with milk, then sprinkle with the desiccated coconut. Return the cake to the oven for another 5 minutes, until starting to turn golden. Cut into squares and serve warm or cold.

MAKES 1 CAKE

125g (1 stick plus 1 tbsp) unsalted butter, softened, plus extra for greasing

125g (⅔ cup minus 2 tsp) light soft brown sugar

2 tsp vanilla extract

1 egg (optional)

375g (2¾ cups plus 1½ tbsp) plain (all-purpose) flour

2 tsp baking powder

1 tsp bicarbonate of soda (baking soda) (optional)

1 tsp ground nutmeg

1 tsp ground ginger

1 tsp ground cinnamon

½ tsp sea salt

250g (9oz) desiccated coconut, plus extra to decorate

400ml (13.5fl oz) can coconut milk

1 tbsp milk, to glaze

Peanut or coconut drops

Having grown up with twenty-four-seven transport in inner London, I can't drive. This means my movements in Jamaica are heavily reliant on Hackney carriages and route buses that service the country. At the loading hubs, what initially looks manic is actually controlled chaos with vehicles filled to the brim with passengers before the doors are slammed shut, and they are sent on their way. On the longer distance journeys from parish to parish, the buses (think minivans) usually have a vibe of camaraderie as the drivers' tunes are cranked up and everyone gets comfortable with each other's limbs and adjusts the ventilation to their needs. There's usually someone who manages to have a three-hour conversation, and eavesdropping on a chat can often turn into a debate with the rest of the passengers on board.

At the town stops along the way, passengers who've reached their destination manoeuvre to depart and give way to a replacement. At these pit stops the window frames are filled with drink and snack vendors, who sometimes climb on board to pitch their goods. Transport turbulence means the likelihood of seeing someone wolf down a box of curry on a route bus is quite rare and most opt for the small sweet snacks, including one of my favourite drops, which usually cost no more than a few cents.

The drops are seeds, nuts or dried fruits engulfed in boiling spiced sugar, then spooned into rounds and left to set. The term "drop" seems to come from the action of dropping them, traditionally onto banana leaves, into clumps that flatten during the setting process. The most common flavours being coconut, using small chunks of dried coconut, and peanut using roasted and salted peanuts. Those who enjoy brittle may enjoy drops, although these remind me more of a fusion between fudge and rock, both in taste and the way they effortlessly lodge themselves into your teeth, though that's part of the fun for me.

Line a baking tray with baking paper or foil, or in true Jamaican tradition use a banana leaf.

Pour 250ml (1 cup plus 1 tbsp) water into a heavy-based saucepan and add the cinnamon and ginger, then bring to the boil over a medium heat. After 3 minutes, stir in the peanuts, sugar, vanilla and salt. Let the mixture boil for 40 minutes, stirring occasionally, until the liquid has reduced and the mixture turns syrupy. Remove the cinnamon stick, if using.

At this point, turn the heat down to low and simmer for another 15 minutes, stirring occasionally – the mixture should have reduced to a thick syrup with the peanuts clinging together.

Now it's time to move quickly: remove the pan from the heat and, using a tablespoon, quickly scoop heaped spoonfuls of the peanut-syrup mixture onto the prepared tray or banana leaf, spacing them apart so they don't stick together. If the mixture sticks to the spoon, use another spoon to scrape it off. (Be careful not to use your hands and resist the temptation to taste it immediately as it will be extremely hot.) Continue to quickly scoop and drop while the mixture is still hot; you can use the back of the spoon to flatten the heaps slightly, but this is optional.

Leave the peanut drops to cool for about 30 minutes before eating. Store in an airtight container.

MAKES 8–9

banana leaf (optional)
1 cinnamon stick, or ½ tsp ground cinnamon
4 tsp finely grated fresh root ginger
300g (10oz) roasted salted peanuts
300g (1½ cups) light soft brown sugar
1 tsp vanilla extract
¼ tsp sea salt

NOTE *To make coconut drops, replace the roasted peanuts with 300g (10oz) dried chunks of coconut, diced.*

Tie-a-leaf

In every corner of the world where banana trees grow, different cultures not only honour the fruit, but have come to appreciate the tough, durable prowess of the leaves, commandeering them for all manner of culinary techniques and meals.

Given the diversity of peoples in the Caribbean, the far-reaching use of the banana leaf perhaps explains why it has so many different names. For instance, the name of this recipe, *tie-a-leaf*, is also known as *dukanoo*, which appears to derive directly from the Ghanaian Ashanti word, *dokono*, a steamed cornbread parcel. Another Ghanaian speciality, *kenkey*, traditionally used banana leaves, and it is possible the Barbados-named *conkie* also derives from the same word. The intermingling of various languages and patois slang means that over the years names such as *tie-a-leaf* and *blue drawers* emerged, referencing the use of string to hold the banana leaf parcel in place.

The melting pot of the Caribbean means that the providence of this recipe is hard to pin down and, as such, it is an incredibly fluid one. Regardless, the ethos of the parcel filling remains the same: coarse flour, like cornmeal and/or any form of starch (yams for substance, sweet potato for sweetness), mashed together, then wrapped in a parcel and steamed. The consistency of the filling is also contested – some people prefer theirs to be like a boiled dumpling, while others like the end result to be closer to a pudding, both of which depend on how you make the batter. If your mixture doesn't set after steaming, it means the batter was too wet, or the parcel wasn't secure enough to keep the water out, or both.

The use of banana leaves to wrap the parcels is of course optional, the likes of foil providing an adequate alternative. However, the aroma of the banana leaf can't be replicated. The process of making these parcels, fanning the banana leaves over a flame, then wrapping and tying them feels therapeutic, and of all the dishes I've cooked this almost mentally transports me back centuries to the woodland hills of Jamaica.

MAKES ABOUT 10

250g (9oz) fine cornmeal
140g (¾ cup minus 2 tsp) light
    soft brown sugar
75g (½ cup plus 1 tbsp) wholemeal
    flour or flour of choice
1 tsp baking powder
1 tsp ground cinnamon
1 tsp ground nutmeg
½ tsp sea salt
2 green bananas, about 250g (9oz)
    in total, peeled and grated
1 sweet potato, about 200g (7oz)
    in total, peeled and grated
50g (1¾oz) desiccated coconut,
    or grated fresh coconut
270ml (1 cup plus 1 tbsp) coconut
    milk
1 tsp vanilla extract

FOR THE PARCELS:

about 10 banana leaves, with leaf
    vein cut out and saved, or foil
kitchen string (optional if using
    banana leaf)

If using banana leaves to wrap the parcels, you need
to soften them first. Using tongs, pass the leaves, one at
a time, over a low-medium flame on a gas hob, turning
and exposing all parts to make them pliable. Cut the
leaves (or foil) into ten 15cm (6in) squares and set aside.

Mix all the dry ingredients, up to and including the
salt, in a large mixing bowl. Add the bananas, sweet
potato and desiccated or fresh coconut and mix together
with a wooden spoon. Add the coconut milk and vanilla
and mix until combined. (Alternatively, if you like
a smoother filling, blend the bananas and sweet potato
with the coconut milk and vanilla, then mix into the
dry ingredients.)

Scoop 2 tablespoons of the cornmeal mixture into
the middle of one square of banana leaf/foil. Fold in the
sides, then the bottom and top to enclose the filling.
Use the saved vein of the banana leaf, or kitchen string,
to secure the parcel tightly. (If using foil, there is no
need to use string.) Repeat to make 10 parcels in total.
You want to make sure there are no gaps in the parcels
or water will get in and make the filling soggy.

Steam or boil the parcels in a large saucepan for
1 hour, until the filling is cooked, then remove with
a spatula or slotted spoon and leave to rest on a kitchen
towel for 10 minutes. Tilt your banana leaf parcels
to remove any errant water.

The parcels can be eaten hot straightaway or left to
cool and chilled until ready to serve – they'll keep in the
fridge for up to 1 week. To reheat, place in boiling water
for 10 minutes.

FERMENT
& PRESERVE

"...to understand preservation is to understand survival in the Caribbean."

The multicultural legion of millions who devour spice-marinated jerk chicken en masse every year at London's famous Notting Hill Carnival, couldn't be further away from its tumultuous genesis. For me, to understand preservation is to understand survival in the Caribbean.

Colonial settlers as far back as the mid-1600s noted the importance of preservation to the Jamaican people, particularly as a way to extend the life of fresh foods from the land and sea, such as salted beef and pork, saltfish and mackerel as well as spirits and wine, most notably Madeira. During this period, when English forces defeated the Spanish for control of Jamaica, rather than facilitate a transition period the Spanish released their enslaved African population. After British rule came into effect, with the continued brutality others sought to escape slavery by trekking into the dense woodlands of the mountains. African tribes, like the Kromanti, who came from a natural environment in West Africa very similar to that of Jamaica, also rebelled against slavery and ran away to the mountains of St. Ann, Clarendon and St. Elizabeth. This melting pot of Africans and indigenous Amerindians became known as the Maroons, whose culture still thrives to this day in Maroon towns across the island.

In the mountainous peaks, the non-Maroon runaways as well as the Maroons, like their native Amerindian predecessors, lived a precarious existence. To avoid detection, they leaned heavily on culinary techniques pioneered by Amerindian tribes like the Taino. The most well-known of these was *charqui* or what is now known as "jerking", the process of cooking meat slowly in a covered shallow pit over a low heat. To extend the life of the meat (and reduce the frequency of needing to relight the fire), it was preserved in a broad concoction of herbs and spices, including pimento seeds and Scotch bonnet peppers. So the same food that sustains millions of revellers bopping to towering sound-systems at Carnival each year, is ironically likely to be the same food that powered numerous slave upheavals, from Nanny Maroon's 1728 First Maroon War and the Christmas Uprising in 1831, to the Great Jamaican Slave Revolt of 1831–32, featuring rebel and national hero Samuel Sharpe. As opposition to slavery grew towards the end of the century, the Maroons were granted greater rights and the need for tribes to hide in the mountains waned. With the eventual end of the transatlantic slave trade in the early 1800s, Jamaica moved away from its plantation-based economy and focussed on manufacturing and mining.

When the Maroons spread out to all corners of the island so too did their gastronomic expertise that likely appealed to those of limited financial resources. Alongside their preserving skills, many of these tribes people showed impressive culinary prowess in curating brilliant flavours, the legacy of which lasts today.

It should be noted that fridges and freezers are a relatively new phenomenon. Many of the Rastafari I stayed with who live off-grid, in addition to people who live deep in the countryside without electricity, continue to prosper without such amenities: either way, in the modern era, jerk cooking and other methods of conserving remain a fundamental part of the Caribbean kitchen.

In Caribbean culture we use "aunty" as a term of reference to elder women who are close to our families, like the friends of parents and so forth. Naturally, in all corners of London where my family had friends, I would tell people my aunty and cousins lived there before I properly knew what aunty meant – eventually, leading me to believe that I could potentially be related to any Black person I saw on the street. At my primary school in North London, where I was one of only a handful of Black people, this ultimately led to ridicule as other kids wondered how on earth I had so many aunties and enquired if I had them everywhere, from Poland to Japan.

> **"Everything we celebrate about Caribbean cuisine – it's easy, simple and tastes amazing – is undoubtedly bolstered by the wide range of pre-made, big-flavour extras, like peppers, slaws, sauces and seasonings."**

Trips to these various aunties were usually frequent and as lunch or dinner time approached one of two things were certain: hot sauce and pickled peppers. These were an unquestionable staple, and the absence of either could cause much distress and disappointment. Everything we celebrate about Caribbean cuisine – it's easy, simple and tastes amazing – is undoubtedly bolstered by the wide range of pre-made, big-flavour extras, like peppers, slaws, sauces and seasonings. These liven up the most basic of vegetable and rice dishes, add a new dimension to fish, and when used to marinate meat can send the taste buds into overdrive. There was a joke in secondary school that we'd even splash our Caribbean hot pepper sauce over school lunches.

As memes and jokes about the perils of under-seasoned meat appear on social media, the power of even the most basic seasoning is deep-rooted in our Caribbean psyche. Lore tells us, for instance, that if you feel inexplicably hot, you may have a duppy (restless spirit) near you, which can be chased away by eating salt – for some reason they absolutely hate salt. In *The Wizard of Oz*, the Wicked Witch of the West is defeated by simple water, but no such liquid works against the island duppy of Ol' Higue, a witch who sheds her skin and, so the story goes, flies around at night in the form of an owl preying on children. Unfortunately, for the witch, the habit of shedding her skin leaves her vulnerable, and if you happen to find it a dab of salt and pepper will prevent her putting the skin back on without burning her. Without her skin, Ol' Higue can be slayed.

"Herein lies a clue to the one true secret ingredient in the recipes in this book that everyone, regardless of creed or kind, can harness, and that is time."

We've come a long way from just salt and pepper; the Ol' Higue's of the 21st century would probably need a whole spice rack to defeat them. The Rastafari, Maroons, native Amerindians, indentured Indians, West Africans and the plethora of diverse identities that make up Jamaica, have all added to the assortment of seasonings and condiments that make today's dinner table what it is. They all naturally tapped into the notion of preservation and fermentation as a means of survival, be that from a bacterial foe or a human one, and it just so happens that in the process their creations taste completely brilliant.

Herein lies a clue to the one true secret "ingredient" in the recipes in this book that everyone, regardless of creed or kind, can harness, and that is time. Time to let your chicken or pork sit in its marinade for an extra day. Time to let your ginger bug ferment for another week to get an extra level of buzz in your ginger beer, or even an extra month for that additional potency in your hot sauce.

STERILIZING JARS

Many of the recipes in this chapter call for a sterilized jar or bottle. To do this, wash the jar in hot, soapy water and when still wet place upside-down in an oven preheated to 180°C (160°C fan/350°F/Gas 4) for 10–15 minutes, until dry. Alternatively, sterilize your jar in a pan of boiling water for 10 minutes. Leave to dry upside down on a clean kitchen towel. When ready, ladle or pour your hot preserve into the still-warm jar, almost to the top and then screw on the lid tightly (it's always a good idea to use new lids), then leave to cool.

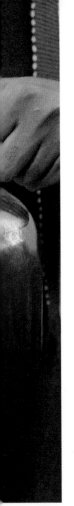

Pickled peppers

I'm going to be honest, testing this recipe was the first time I'd made my own jar of pickled peppers. Writing it down, just turning thirty, it occurred to me that I don't recall seeing any family member make pickled peppers either – they've just always been there in the cabinet or on the kitchen table, a fixture and as much a part of the furniture as the plastic-wrapped settees, artificial flowers and glass cabinets full of rarely used china.

Pickled peppers (or as we call them "peppers") to the uninitiated are incredibly deceptive: humble peppers, carrots and other vegetables submerged in a clear liquid surely can't be *that* hot? I've seen many people caught in this snare. Unlike the instant remedies to calm the heat of chilli-based hot sauces, like milk and yogurt, there's no such cure for the unique inferno of peppers. What's left of the pepper's sweet crunch after being slowly fermented in the jar is followed like a laggard by a vinegary, peppery, one-two punch that for some reason many people, myself included, can't get enough of.

The relevance of pickled peppers in Jamaica and the wider Caribbean is mostly tied to Escovitch Fish (see p182), when it's used to preserve fried fish for days at a time. However, it's not uncommon for people to dress rice on the side of a meal with a ladleful of peppers and the accompanying liquid. Jars of peppers are most potent when the transparent liquid changes to amber and the bright colours of the peppers fade; this is how you would age a jar if you were a peppers' sommelier. Here, I chopped the vegetables the same size and shape I recall from years of visits, but you can slice them as you desire, just make sure they're not too fine.

———

First sterilize a 1 litre (1 quart) jar (see p231).

In a saucepan, heat both types of vinegar, if using, with the salt and sugar over a medium-low heat for 3–5 minutes, stirring occasionally, until the sugar has dissolved, taking care not to let the mixture boil. (If you see any bubbles remove the pan from the heat.) When the vinegar is warm, turn off the heat, but keep the pan on the hot ring.

The jar packing process should be fun and is completely up to your own discretion. I layer in the following order, using some of each: pimento, carrots, onion, Scotch bonnets, then chayote, garlic, thyme and lastly bell peppers. After each layer, take a spatula

MAKES 1 LITRE (1 QUART)

200ml (¾ cup) white distilled vinegar
200ml (¾ cup) apple cider vinegar (or 400ml/1¾ cups of one type of vinegar)
1 tsp sea salt
1 tbsp granulated sugar
1 tbsp pimento seeds (allspice berries)
3 carrots, thinly sliced
1 white onion, thinly sliced
5 Scotch bonnet peppers (colour of choice), deseeded, if preferred, thinly sliced (use habanero chillies if you can't find Scotch bonnets)
1 chayote, about 200g (7oz) in total, thinly sliced
1 garlic clove, sliced
1 sprig of thyme, leaves picked
1½ bell peppers (colour of choice), deseeded and thinly sliced

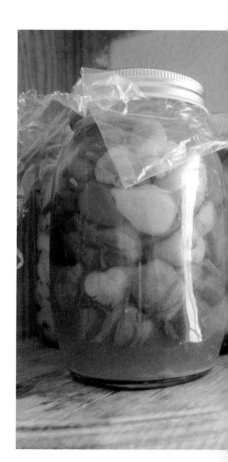

or any utensil that fits, and press the contents to pack them down tightly and maximize the space. Continue to layer until the jar is almost full, leaving enough room to allow for the vinegar.

Pour the lukewarm vinegar into the jar until the contents are submerged. Leave to cool for 10 minutes before putting on the lid. Make sure the lid is on tight, then slowly tilt the jar upside down a few times to ensure a good distribution of the liquid.

Leave in a cool, dark place for at least 48 hours – I usually wait 1 week – before eating. To extend the shelf life, place a piece of cling film over the top of the jar before putting on the lid. The pickle will keep for up to 6 months. Once opened, store in the fridge.

Solomon gundy

Preserved fish, both sun-dried and smoked, was a favourite in slave genesis regions, such as Gambia. Historians suggest fish maintained its importance in the coastal communities of the Caribbean, where, after preservation, it kept for months, despite the blazing heat; unlike meat, which lasted only a short time even when preserved.

The Jamaican solomon gundy, a preserved fish dish based on herring and spices (likely derived from *salmagundy,* an English interpretation of the French dish *salmigondis*), is somewhat different from the centuries-old European descriptions. Perhaps then, European travellers to the Caribbean noted these West African-derived preserved concoctions and brought them under the umbrella of *salmagundy*, utilizing them for the multiple, month-long middle passage voyages.

Nowadays, solomon gundy most commonly appears in Jamaica as a snack and is served in all sorts of places, from the raucous domino and ludo tables in bars to the front lawns of neighbourhood yards, where it is usually spread over sliced cucumber, crackers or small pieces of bread. It has a pepper-based heat to it that can be adjusted at will, as can the desired sweetness which, once curated to your taste buds, will make for a snack suitable for any time of the day.

———

First sterilize a 350–500ml (12–16oz) jar (see p231).

If you don't like your herring overly salty, place the fillets in a bowl, cover with water and leave to soak for 30 minutes to 1 hour. Drain, then remove any bones, but don't fret too much about removing every single one as they are edible, and chopping will make them tiny. Pat the herrings dry with kitchen paper.

If you don't mind the saltiness, break the herrings into chunks and remove as many bones as possible.

Chop the herrings into 5mm-1cm (¼–½in) dice and put them into a bowl. Next, add the onion, Scotch bonnet, spring onions and red or yellow bell pepper, if using.

In a saucepan, add the vinegar, sugar and pimento and cook over a very low heat for about 3 minutes, stirring occasionally, until the sugar has dissolved.

Stir the oil into the herring mixture, then add the black pepper and the vinegar solution. Spoon into the sterilized jar and put on the lid. Eat straightaway, or store in the fridge for up to 1 month.

MAKES 350–500ML (12–16FL OZ)

250g (9oz) smoked herring fillets
1 red onion, finely diced
1 Scotch bonnet pepper, thinly sliced
2 spring onions (scallions), cut into 5mm (¼in) rounds
½ red or yellow bell pepper, deseeded and cut into 1cm (½in) dice (optional)
2 tbsp vinegar of choice
2 tsp light soft brown sugar
6 pimento seeds (allspice berries)
2 tbsp oil of choice, such as sunflower or coconut
pinch of freshly ground black pepper

Jerk seasoning

Beyond the debate about whether you can make "real" jerk at home is the use of dry rub seasoning versus wet, like the one here. For meats, other than pork or chicken, especially lamb and goat, I suspect the dry rub may be the better option, but in all my travels I've only seen jerk prepped one way and that's with a wet rub. Hanging out with Jamaican jerk dons of London, such as Lenny at People's Choice in Hackney, East London, Louie at Smokey Jerkey in Southeast London's New Cross, and Jen and Bill, husband and wife duo, at JB's just down the road in Peckham (to name just a few), wet is the method of choice.

Hefty chicken thighs are submerged in buckets of brown, multi-textured seasoning, speckled with bits of red and green, where each element with some focus can be picked out by its scent. The thighs are accommodated in their new seasoning abode for a time, with the wet mixture seeping into every nook and cranny of the meat. After this, the meat is applied to intense heat.

I rarely make the same jerk seasoning twice, mostly due to running out of different things, but I like to think that's more in keeping with the Taino Amerindian genesis of "*jirking*" a millennium ago. I imagine they didn't have a set list of tablespoons and weights, but rather a generalist roster of herbs and spices that they would source and forage for. Do adjust this version to your own taste – the bragging rights of saying you make your own jerk seasoning can't be beat.

———

First sterilize a 250ml (8oz) jar (see p231).

Add all the ingredients to a bowl and mix thoroughly, or you can use a blender or mini food processor and blend until smooth.

Spoon the seasoning into the jar and put on the lid. Store in the fridge for up to 1 month.

MAKES ABOUT 250ML (8FL OZ)

- 120ml (½ cup) olive oil or coconut oil
- 120ml (½ cup) soy sauce or browning
- 4 tbsp light soft brown sugar
- 3 tbsp pimento seeds (allspice berries), crushed, or 1 tbsp ground allspice
- 3 spring onions (scallions), finely chopped
- 2 tbsp apple cider vinegar
- 2 tbsp chopped fresh thyme, or 1 tbsp dried thyme
- juice of 2 limes, or 1 lemon
- 1–2 Scotch bonnet peppers, deseeded and thinly sliced (or leave seeds in for extra heat)
- 1½ tbsp freshly ground black pepper
- 1½ tbsp minced fresh root ginger, or ground ginger
- 1½ tbsp minced garlic or garlic powder
- 1 tbsp ground cinnamon
- 1 tsp sea salt
- ½ tsp ground nutmeg

All-purpose seasoning

I find friends who are new to Caribbean cooking are often confused by the names allspice and all-purpose seasoning, which they often use interchangeably. This seems ironic as mislabelling seems to have been a common theme in colonial-era Jamaican history. Allspice was named by the English as far back as 1623, when they concluded these native berries tasted like, and had the aroma of, a combination of cinnamon, nutmeg and cloves. When King Philip IV of Spain was introduced to allspice berries, due to their near identical appearance to black peppercorns, he named them *la pimienta de Jamaica* (Jamaican pepper), or colloquially as pimento. As Spain still ruled over Jamaica at this time, the name was forced into use, hence the confusion between pimento and allspice. This would have been less confusing to the outside world had the Spanish forces not also given the name pimento to chillies.

The Jamaican origin of seasoning food with dry spices goes back to the indigenous peoples, who would use an array of spices, such as cinnamon, nutmeg, ginger, black pepper, cloves and dried pimento berries to preserve and flavour meats before they were cooked. The story behind each of these spices is interesting in itself with some being native to the island and others introduced by human movement to and from the Caribbean, most notably Africa and Asia, over the centuries. As a result, spices became used at almost every meal, then somewhere down the line some thoughtful people decided to combine all the staple spices into one mixture and all-purpose seasoning was born.

I always say time is the best secret ingredient when it comes to Caribbean cooking, but the second best is probably all-purpose seasoning. The spices when combined create a compound umami. All-purpose seasoning is found at nearly all diaspora grocery shops and many supermarkets so it's understandable if you just want to buy a pack, however, the joy of creating your own blend is not to be missed.

MAKES ABOUT 200G (7OZ)

3 tbsp garlic powder
3 tbsp onion powder
3 tbsp paprika
1 tbsp cayenne pepper
1 tbsp freshly ground black pepper
1 tbsp pimento seeds (allspice berries), crushed, or 1 tsp ground allspice
1 tbsp sea salt flakes
1 tsp granulated brown sugar
1 tsp ground cumin
1 tsp ground nutmeg

Add all the ingredients to a bowl and mix with a spoon. Pour into an airtight container or jar with a lid and shake until combined. The seasoning will keep in a cool, dry place for up to 6 months.

Scotch bonnet
hot sauces

I remember coming across an article on hereditary taste influences that had me thinking back to dinner as a kid. From as early as I can remember without instruction or guidance, though perhaps maybe through osmosis, I've been liberally dousing hot sauce over dinner, whether it be curry goat with rice and peas or fish and chips.

Carbonized remains of foodstuffs, including hot peppers, have been discovered across the Caribbean dating as far back as the 1400s, which suggests the people of Jamaica have strived to not only preserve but cook their food for centuries at the minimum. Given that records of rival tribes combining peppers with water dates back to almost 7000 BC, I'd hazard a guess that this practice in Jamaica precedes its European "discovery" by some years.

For a good year or two, me and my friends would eschew the commercially made tomato ketchup on the counter of our school's local chicken shops and would sneakily pack bottles of hot sauce into our school bags for the after-school occasion (making sure it was back in place immediately after returning home). This, of course, was maddening to the non-hot-sauce-background kids who could barely handle a drop of the stuff. Some of us were team Grace, others were team Encona, and in true adversarial Caribbean style endless debates ensued. These two brands formed both my tolerance and education of hot sauce as a kid, however, this all changed when a relative returned from Barbados one year.

The usual fiery-orange sauce was replaced with what I thought was a tamer yellow sauce, deceptively named Delish. On the colour-scale of danger, yellow is usually low, while red is high – well that's what a famous fried chicken restaurant has led us to believe. Dousing it over my dinner one evening resulted in my lips feeling like they'd been dragged over sandpaper and all sources of dairy, from yogurt to milk, were needed to quell the heat.

This sauce literally woke me up to the range of flavours and products that derive from fresh chillies, including Jamaica's renowned Scotch bonnet pepper (so named due to its perceived resemblance to the Scot's famed tam-o'-shanter hats worn by British colonial travellers).

I suggest you try the following recipes as a starting point, then explore the deeper depths of fiery pleasure. Experiment with the amount of peppers you use, the amount of seeds you keep, the fruits you add, and so on. The only rule is PLEASE wear rubber gloves when chopping hot peppers, or wash your hands really well!

Quick hot sauce

MAKES ABOUT 500ML (16FL OZ)

150ml (⅔ cup) apple cider vinegar
2.5cm (1in) piece of fresh root ginger, peeled
    and chopped, or 1 tsp ground ginger
1 red bell pepper, deseeded and chopped
6–8 red Scotch bonnet peppers, deseeded
    and chopped, if preferred
1 carrot, chopped
6 pimento seeds (allspice berries), crushed,
    or ½ tsp ground allspice
1 lime (optional)
1 tbsp coconut oil
½ white onion, chopped
2–3 garlic cloves, minced
1–2 spring onions (scallions), chopped

FOR THE DRY INGREDIENTS:

4–5 sprigs of thyme, or 1 tsp dried thyme
2–3 tbsp light soft brown sugar
2 tsp sea salt
1 tsp paprika
½ tsp ground nutmeg

——

First sterilize a 500ml (16oz) bottle (see p231).
    Add the vinegar, ginger, red bell pepper,
Scotch bonnets, carrot, pimento and lime,
if using, to a blender or food processor with
120ml (½ cup) water and blend until smooth.
    Heat the coconut oil in a large saucepan
or Dutch pot over a medium heat and fry
the onion for 2–3 minutes, until softened.
Add the garlic and spring onions and sauté
for another minute, until softened. Tip into
the blender or processor and blend again
until smooth.
    Pour the blended ingredients into the pan.
Stir in the dry ingredients and turn the heat
to medium-high. Bring the sauce to the boil
and let it bubble for 3 minutes before turning
the heat down to low, then simmer for another
20 minutes, until reduced and thickened.
(An optional step is to blend the mixture again.)
    Pour the sauce through a funnel into the
bottle and put on the lid. Leave to cool. It will
keep in the fridge for up to 1 month.

Mango & pineapple hot sauce

MAKES ABOUT 500ML (16FL OZ)

150ml (⅔ cup) apple cider vinegar
2.5cm (1in) piece of fresh root ginger, peeled
    and chopped, or 1 tsp ground ginger
1 yellow or orange bell pepper, deseeded
    and chopped
6–8 yellow Scotch bonnet peppers, halved
1 tbsp coconut oil
½ white onion, chopped
2–3 garlic cloves, minced
2 spring onions (scallions), chopped
150g (5½oz) pineapple, chopped
100g (3½oz) mango, chopped
1 lime (optional)

FOR THE DRY INGREDIENTS:

6 pimento seeds (allspice berries), crushed,
    or ½ tsp ground allspice
1 tbsp light soft brown sugar
4–5 sprigs of thyme, or 1 tsp dried thyme
2 tsp sea salt
1 tsp paprika
½ tsp ground nutmeg

——

First sterilize a 500ml (16oz) bottle (see p231).
    Add the vinegar, ginger, yellow or orange
bell pepper and Scotch bonnets to a blender
or food processor with 120ml (½ cup) water
and blend until smooth.
    Heat the coconut oil in a large saucepan
or Dutch pot over a medium heat and fry the
onion for 2–3 minutes, until softened. Add
the garlic, spring onions, pineapple and mango
and sauté for another minute, until softened.
Blend again until smooth. Tip into the blender
or processor and blend again until smooth.
    Pour the blended ingredients into the pan.
Stir in the dry ingredients and turn the heat
to medium-high. Bring the sauce to the boil
and let it bubble for 3 minutes before turning
down the heat to low, then simmer for another
20 minutes, until reduced and thickened.
(An optional step is to blend the mixture again.)
    Pour the sauce through a funnel into the
bottle and put on the lid. Leave to cool. It will
keep in the fridge for up to 1 month.

Fermented hot sauce

MAKES ABOUT 1 LITRE (1 QUART)

6–8 red Scotch bonnet peppers, deseeded
    and chopped, if preferred
1 carrot, chopped
1 red bell pepper, deseeded and chopped
½ red onion, chopped
2.5cm (1in) piece of fresh root ginger,
    peeled and chopped
3 garlic cloves, sliced

FOR THE DRY INGREDIENTS:

6 pimento seeds (allspice berries), crushed,
    or ½ tsp ground allspice
5 sprigs of thyme, or 1 tsp dried thyme
3 tbsp light soft brown sugar
2 spring onions (scallions), chopped
½ tsp ground nutmeg
½ tsp freshly ground black pepper
2 tsp sea salt

———

First sterilize a 1 litre (1 quart) bottle
(see p231).

In a bowl, mix all the dry ingredients,
except the salt. Pour 500ml (2 cups plus
2 tbsp) water in a jug and stir in the salt
until it has dissolved, then set aside.

In your jar, layer the Scotch bonnets,
vegetables, ginger and garlic, adding some of
the dry seasoning between each layer. Repeat
until everything is used up. If needed, use the
back of a spoon to squash down the ingredients
so they are tightly packed. Pour the salt-water
mix into the jar until everything is submerged
and the liquid is just below the neck of the
jar. Put the lid on and leave somewhere cool
and dark for at least 1 week and up to 1 month,
until the vegetables have softened and the
liquid turns yellow.

Strain the liquid from the jar into a jug
and save. Add the fermented ingredients to
a blender with the saved liquid (use as much
as preferred, depending on how thick you like
your hot sauce), then blend until smooth.

Pour the sauce through a funnel into
the bottle and put on the lid. It will keep
in the fridge for up to 1 month.

Scotch bonnet ketchup

MAKES ABOUT 1 LITRE (1 QUART)

2 x 400g (14oz) cans plum tomatoes, or 800g (1¾lb)
    tomatoes, chopped
120ml (½ cup) apple cider vinegar
80g (6½ tbsp) light soft brown sugar or honey
2–4 red Scotch bonnet peppers, deseeded
    and chopped
1 red bell pepper, deseeded and chopped
1 tbsp tomato purée (tomato paste)
1 tsp ground cinnamon
1 tsp freshly ground black pepper
1 tsp sea salt
½ tsp dried thyme
½ tsp ground nutmeg
2 tbsp coconut oil
1 red onion, finely chopped
2 garlic cloves, finely chopped

———

First sterilize a 1 litre (1 quart) bottle
(see p231).

Add all ingredients, except the oil, onion
and garlic, to a blender or food processor and
blend until smooth, then set aside. (If you
do not have a blender, very finely chop all the
vegetables and combine with the spices,
vinegar and sugar.)

Heat the oil in a large saucepan or Dutch
pot over a medium heat. Add the onion and
fry for 2 minutes, then add the garlic and cook
for another minute. Add the blended mixture
and stir.

Turn the heat up to medium-high and
let the mixture bubble for 2–3 minutes, then
turn the heat down to low and simmer for
45 minutes to 1 hour, until reduced and
thickened. Stir every 15 minutes or so. (If you
haven't blended the ingredients, use a fork
or potato masher to mash them as much as
possible while you stir.) Remove from the heat
and leave to cool for 5 minutes, then blend
again until smooth.

Pour the sauce through a funnel into the
bottle and put on the lid. Leave to cool. It will
keep in the fridge for up to 1 month.

Jams

Up until I was introduced to the following jams, I was subjected to years of bland supermarket ones, so flavourless – apart from perhaps strawberry. With this aversion, I ignored the guava jam in the cupboard as a kid, thinking it would also disappoint in comparison to the almighty strawberry. Of course, faith was restored the first time it was spread onto a slice of Hardo Bread (see p208) and ushered into my mouth by an aunty.

Considering the turbulent history of sugar production in the Caribbean and given the amount of sugar needed to make preserves, they were once seen as a delicacy and only served at high-end restaurants and resorts.

With the growth of commercial industry and imports, these preserves soon became available to the masses. Guava jam (or jelly) has remained an island favourite, but a new rival that features one of the island's staples is hot pepper jam, made with Scotch bonnets, as well as mango and pineapple chilli jam. The sweetness is in perfect harmony with the delayed hit of heat to tantalize rather than traumatize the palate. These make for an exciting change from the regular jam line-up.

Scotch bonnet jam

MAKES ABOUT 500G (18OZ)

250ml (1 cup plus 1 tbsp) apple cider vinegar, or red wine vinegar
500g (2½ cups) jam sugar, or granulated sugar mixed with 2 tbsp powdered classic pectin
5 red Scotch bonnet peppers, stalks removed and deseeded, if preferred
½ red bell pepper, deseeded and chopped
2.5cm (1in) piece of fresh root ginger, peeled and chopped
2 garlic cloves, minced
juice of 1 lime

———

First sterilize a 500ml (16oz) jar (see p231).

Add the vinegar and sugar to a large, heavy-based saucepan or Dutch pot and stir over a medium heat for 10 minutes, until the sugar has dissolved.

Blend the Scotch bonnets with the red bell pepper, ginger, garlic and lime juice until almost smooth. Add the mixture to the pan or pot and stir. Turn the heat up to medium-high and boil for 3–5 minutes.

Follow the cooking, bottling and storage instructions for the Mango & Pineapple Chilli Jam, see opposite.

Mango & pineapple chilli jam

MAKES ABOUT 500G (18OZ)

250ml (1 cup plus 1 tbsp) apple cider vinegar, or red wine vinegar
500g (2½ cups) jam sugar, or granulated sugar mixed with 2 tbsp powdered classic pectin
50g (1¾oz) mango, chopped
100g (3½oz) pineapple, chopped
5 yellow Scotch bonnet peppers, stalks removed and deseeded, if preferred
½ yellow bell pepper, deseeded and chopped
2.5cm (1in) piece of fresh root ginger, peeled and chopped
2 garlic cloves, minced
juice of 1 lime

——

First sterilize a 500ml (16oz) jar (see p231).

Add the vinegar and sugar to a large, heavy-based saucepan or Dutch pot and stir over a medium heat for 10 minutes, until the sugar has dissolved.

Blend the mango and pineapple with the Scotch bonnets, yellow bell pepper, ginger, garlic and lime juice until almost smooth. Add the mixture to the pan and stir. Turn the heat up to medium-high and boil for 3–5 minutes.

Turn the heat down to medium-low and continue to boil for 20 minutes, or until it forms a jam-like consistency; it should read about 105°C (220°F) on a sugar thermometer. If you don't have a thermometer, spoon a little jam onto a cold saucer. Leave it for 30 seconds, then push with your finger; if the jam wrinkles and doesn't flood to fill the gap, it is ready. If not, return the pan to the heat and boil for another 2 minutes, then test again. Repeat until ready.

Skim any foam from the surface of the jam, then pour through a funnel into the jar. Put on a new lid and secure tightly, then cool. The jam will keep for up to 6 months in a cool, dry place. Once opened, store in the fridge.

NOTE *To seal the jars after filling, as recommended in the US, use a boiling-water canner following the manufacturer's instructions for 10 minutes.*

Guava jam

MAKES ABOUT 500G (18OZ)

650g (1lb 7oz) guava (pink inside preferable), chopped
2.5cm (1in) piece of fresh root ginger, peeled and minced
juice of ½ lime (optional)
½ tsp ground cinnamon (optional)
¼ tsp ground nutmeg (optional)
400g (2 cups) jam sugar, or granulated sugar mixed with 2 tbsp powdered classic pectin

——

First sterilize a 500ml (16oz) jar (see p231).

Put the guava into a large, heavy-based saucepan or Dutch pot. Pour in enough water to cover the guava and bring to the boil over a medium-high heat. Boil for about 30 minutes, until soft. Strain, discarding the water, then leave the guava to cool.

Using your hands, or the back of a spoon, mash the guava, pressing the pulp through a sieve into a bowl. Discard the seeds and fibrous parts left in the sieve.

Put the guava pulp into the pan or pot and bring to the boil over a medium heat. Add the lime juice, cinnamon and nutmeg, if using, and stir. Next, add the sugar and stir until it has dissolved, about 10 minutes. Turn the heat up to high and boil for 2–3 minutes, then turn it down to low and simmer for a final 30 minutes, or until it forms a jam-like consistency; it should read about 105°C (220°F) on a sugar thermometer. If you don't have a thermometer, spoon a little jam onto a cold saucer. Leave it for 30 seconds, then push with your finger; if the jam wrinkles and doesn't flood to fill the gap, it is ready. If not, return the pan to the heat and boil for another 2 minutes, then test again. Repeat until ready.

Skim any foam from the surface of the jam, then pour through a funnel into the jar. Put on a new lid and secure tightly, then cool. The jam will keep for up to 6 months in a cool, dry place. Once opened, store in the fridge.

Sea moss

Was the Jamaican legend of "The Golden Table" based on a real golden table? Perhaps it was jetsam from a Spanish hoard? The myth tells us of the coveted object, *"It rises briefly to the surface from time to time, particularly at midday, affording a glimpse of its golden beauty. The sight of the table mesmerizes whoever sees it, and they become obsessed with the desire to obtain it."* (jamaicanfolktales.weebly.com).

For me, this golden beauty can be no other than sea moss. Radiant in its natural form, often bobbing up to the water's surface, and now the obsession of many. The various health benefits and uses of sea moss are touted frequently: as a face scrub, hair massage, supplement or for its use in cooking. My particular joy is the sensual transformation that its mucilaginous property gives to Smoothies (see p96) as well as soups and Bush Tea (see p256).

The preparation of sea moss is incredibly meditative, and it is among the recipes in this book that I'd invite you to see less as a recipe and more as just one of those things you enjoy making regularly. It keeps for about a fortnight, although it's so good mine never seems to last that long.

———

First sterilize 2 x 500ml (16oz) jars (see p231).

Put the sea moss into a large mixing bowl (the moss expands greatly), then cover with cold water and rinse and clean thoroughly. Hold the moss and tilt the bowl over the sink to drain the water and any initial debris.

Cover the sea moss with fresh water until completely submerged. Squeeze the juice of the lemon or lime into the bowl, then add the squeezed citrus halves. Cover and leave for a minimum of 4 hours, but ideally overnight, until the sea moss expands and becomes almost luminous. Again, drain the water and any excess debris. If necessary, use your hands to remove stubborn bits of sand and debris, then strain.

There are now two methods – Raw and Boiled, see opposite – to follow, which produce slightly different end results in terms of taste and texture, but both can be used in the same way. Those who follow a raw food diet may prefer the uncooked version.

MAKES 2 X 500ML (16OZ) JARS

100g (3½oz) dried sea moss
1 lemon or lime, halved

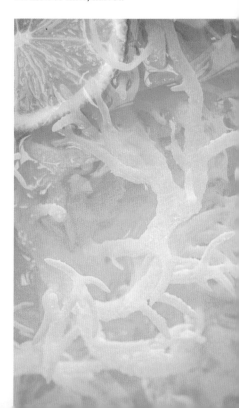

RAW METHOD

Put the cleaned sea moss into a blender: it is up to you and your personal gelatinous preference regarding how much water you add – more water means a looser solution, while less water gives a firmer end result. Add the water to the blender, bit by bit, and pulse until the sea moss dissolves and is smooth. Decant into the glass jars and put on the lids. Use straightaway or store in the fridge for up to 2 weeks.

BOILED METHOD

Put the cleaned sea moss into a saucepan and cover with fresh water. Bring to the boil, then turn the heat down to medium-low and simmer for 25 minutes, until a slightly luminous yellow. Strain, leave to cool for 10 minutes, then blend in a blender with your desired quantity of water until smooth. This method requires slightly less water in the blending process and gives a deeper-coloured gel than the raw method. Decant into the glass jars and put on the lids. Use straightaway or store in the fridge for up to 2 weeks.

Bammy

I often wonder what renowned reggae artist, Augustus Pablo, was referring to when he named one of my favourite songs, the melodica instrumental tune "Cassava Piece". With his birthplace being the capital of Jamaica, it's possible it may have been a nod to the quintessential use of cassava root on the island.

Bammy – grated and squeezed cassava, shaped into cakes and cooked – is described as analogous to a coarse oatmeal cake, although that doesn't do it justice. Those of West African heritage can imagine it, perhaps, as being similar to a flatbread made with *gari*. Like ackee, bammy is hard to describe to those who haven't tried it, and similarly makes little culinary sense if served by itself yet, once submerged in the flowing juices of fish, its wonders are revealed. That said, its origins were as a standalone snack some centuries ago with the indigenous Arawak peoples of the island (who called themselves Caçabí) as well as the Tupí, Carib and Guarani tribes people and West Africans. They favoured bammy as the method of preparation as it meant it could be kept for many months or even years.

From the hills of the countryside to the coast and urban cities, market higglers, street vendors and high-street shops alike pedal bammy, which are still made in much the same arduous fashion as they were way back then. The feeling of making bammy, like that of making Tie-a-leaf (see p226), is one that seemingly transports you back to times past.

The unassuming, plain-looking bammy belies the truly painstaking hard work that goes into making it. I have included an old-style recipe should you have the time to go through the process and potentially envisage the travails of the people who forge hundreds each day, with or without some form of mechanized press. There are levels to making bammy, using cassava or cassava flour – and fortunately, if you live in a metropolis, like London, you can easily find pre-made bammy discs that only require soaking and frying, which I sneakily would probably recommend if time is tight.

**MAKES 3 MEDIUM BAMMY
(OR 2 LARGE)**

500–600g (1lb 2oz–1lb 5oz)
    cassava, peeled, or 300g
    (2¼ cups) cassava flour,
    or ready-made bammy
1 tsp sea salt
2 tbsp coconut oil, or oil of choice
200ml (¾ cup) coconut milk
    (optional)

Fresh cassava bammy

If using fresh cassava, slice it lengthways and cut out and discard the tough spine that runs through the middle. Cut the cassava into chunks, then grate into a large bowl.

Tip the grated cassava into the middle of a piece of cheesecloth and gather up the sides, or use a press, and squeeze out as much liquid as possible applying as much force as needed. Discard the liquid.

Place the cassava into a bowl and leave to sit for 10 minutes. Add the salt and mix in with your hands. Using your hands, form the cassava into 3 tight, compact balls. Roll out each ball into a round, about 1cm (½in) thick; you can use a 9–10cm (3½–4in) cutter or plate to form them into a perfect circle. (The bammy can now be kept for 1–2 months in the freezer, alternatively cook following the instructions below.)

Heat the coconut oil in a small-medium frying pan over a medium heat. When hot, place one bammy disc in the pan and fry for 5–6 minutes on each side, until light golden. Be careful not to tamper with the bammy too soon or it may fall apart. Remove from the heat with a spatula and drain on kitchen paper while you cook the remaining bammy.

NOTE *If you like, pour the coconut milk into a shallow bowl, then soak the fried bammy for 5 minutes. Remove the bammy with a slotted spoon, then fry for a second time until golden brown on both sides.*

Cassava flour bammy

If using cassava flour, combine the flour and salt in a large mixing bowl. Slowly pour in 200ml (¾ cup) water until it comes together into a ball of smooth dough; it shouldn't be sticky. Divide the dough into 3 balls. Roll out each ball into a round, about 1cm (½in) thick; you can use a 9–10cm (3½–4in) cutter or plate to form them into a perfect circle.

Follow the cooking instructions for the Fresh Cassava Bammy, left.

Ready-made cassava bammy

Soak the bammy in the coconut milk for 10 minutes, then remove with a spatula.

Heat the coconut oil in a small-medium frying pan over a medium heat. When hot, place one bammy disc in the pan and fry for 8–10 minutes on each side, until light golden. Remove from the heat with a spatula and drain on kitchen paper while you cook the remaining bammy.

Ginger beer

Ginger beer is one of those drinks that has become so warped by commercially made versions that few people know what the real stuff tastes like. Similar to a host of other famous fizzy drinks, ginger beer has been reduced to mainly being a mixer for alcohol and displaced from its original botanical roots (excuse the pun). Early colonial travellers praised Jamaican ginger (as opposed to Indian ginger, for example) for its taste, while most marketing campaigns focused on its health benefits.

An 1834 advert by Owen & Gerdes Chemists and Druggists in Liverpool's Tarleton Street, proclaims Jamaican ginger beer as being helpful in assisting *"indigestion, flatulence, spasms, gout, and for restorying the tone of a debilitated stomach"*. There were also many recipes for it reproduced in a number of 1800s medical and remedy journals. Nearly two centuries on, several scientific journals have confirmed and compounded the health benefits of ginger consumption, including, "Ginger Beer: An Overview of Health Benefits and Recent Developments" published by C. Nutakor, E.A. Justice, A. Parise and N.K. Osman in 2020.

While ginger's use for the benefit of health has a deep-rooted history across the world, the creation of a ginger drink incorporating large quantities of mass-produced sugar appears to be a product of European colonialism and the coinciding industrial revolution, which allowed tens of thousands of bottles to be produced at a time and shipped around the New World.

When people taste these recipes on the following pages, which feel more in keeping with the recipes found in centuries-old journals, there always seems to be an initial shock – the taste of fresh ginger fermented to form a natural fizz – and it's almost impossible to go back to the fabricated carbonation and manufactured syrupy-sweetness of mass-produced ginger beer.

Many journals in the past refer to both aerated and fermented versions of ginger beer, the latter taking longer to make, so if you're strapped for time and trying to knock some real ginger beer out before a rave or the Notting Hill Carnival, like my old friends at the food collective The Groundnut would do, go for the quick version, on the next page.

"Quick" ginger beer

MAKES ABOUT 1 LITRE (1 QUART)

150g (5½oz) fresh root ginger, preferably organic,
  grated
1 tsp cloves
1 cinnamon stick, or ½ tsp ground cinnamon
juice of 2 limes
100g (½ cup) granulated sugar

————

First sterilize a 1 litre (1 quart) bottle
(see p231).

Pour 1 litre (4 cups plus 3 tbsp) water
into a heavy-based saucepan or Dutch pot
over a medium heat. Add the ginger, cloves,
cinnamon and lime juice, then stir. When
the water starts to bubble, turn the heat
down and simmer for 15 minutes. Take the
pan off the heat, stir in the sugar until it has
dissolved, then leave the liquid to cool to
room temperature.

Pour the liquid through a sieve or piece
of cheesecloth into a jug. Discard the spices,
then pour the ginger beer through a funnel
into the bottle, seal with a lid and chill for
at least 1 hour before drinking. Serve with a
shot of rum.

Fermented ginger beer

MAKES ABOUT 1 LITRE (1 QUART)

30g (1oz) fresh root ginger, preferably
    organic, grated
1 tsp cloves
1 cinnamon stick
juice of 1 lime
100g (½ cup) granulated sugar
50–60ml (3½–4 tbsp) Ginger Bug, strained
    (see right)

——

First sterilize a 1 litre (1 quart) bottle
(see p231).

Heat 1 litre (4 cups plus 3 tbsp) water
in a heavy-based saucepan or Dutch pot
over a medium heat. Add the ginger, cloves,
cinnamon and lime juice, then stir. When the
water starts to bubble, turn the heat down
and simmer for 15 minutes. Take the pan off
the heat, stir in the sugar until dissolved, then
leave the liquid to cool to room temperature.

Pour the liquid through a sieve or piece
of cheesecloth into a jug. Discard the spices.
Add the ginger bug and stir well, then pour
the ginger beer through a funnel into the
sterilized bottle, seal with a lid and chill for
2–3 days before drinking. It will keep for
at least 1 week in the fridge. Serve with a shot
of rum.

Ginger bug

TO START THE GINGER BUG:

5 tbsp grated fresh root ginger, preferably organic
5 tbsp granulated sugar
500ml (2 cups plus 2 tbsp) filtered water

——

First sterilize a 600ml (24oz) jar (see p231).

Put 1 tablespoon of the ginger and
1 tablespoon of the sugar into the jar, add the
water and stir until the sugar has dissolved.
Cover the top of the jar with a clean cloth and
secure with an elastic band.

Leave the jar at room temperature for
5 days, adding another 1 tablespoon ginger
and 1 tablespoon sugar each day and stirring
well. After 3–5 days, the contents of the jar
should start to bubble. After 5 days, it should
be more bubbly and ready to use. If not using
straightaway, store the ginger bug in the
fridge and bring back to room temperature
before use.

NOTE *If you can't get to your ginger bug for
a few days, then store it in the fridge. To bring
it back to life, remove from the fridge and leave
it to come to room temperature for half a day
before resuming the feeding schedule with more
ginger and sugar until bubbly again.*

*After using, replenish the ginger bug with the
same amount of water, ginger and sugar to keep
it going for future use.*

Sorrel

In the same way that you know Christmas is around the corner when advent calendars start appearing in shops and jolly commercials sneak their way into advert breaks, such is the case at home when a nondescript bottle of deep-red liquid appears in the fridge. Without having to question, it's a given that this drink is sorrel.

While sorrel blooms in late November to early December in the Caribbean, which is how it has become associated with Christmas, in its dried form it's widely available all year round, which I'm not complaining about. Though many people outside of the Caribbean aren't familiar with the name sorrel, apart from the herb perhaps, many are more familiar with the flower than they realize as sorrel is also known as hibiscus.

Wherever the hibiscus plant grows in the world, it seems to be highly lauded and even exalted. In the African-rooted Brazilian religion of Candomblé, sorrel is prepared as an offering to the African deity, Shango. Across Africa, where the plant originates, it has been consumed over millennia in all manner of ways. More so, such is the affinity for it that it has been given its own localized names: *bissap* in Senegambia; *de bellini* in Mali and Burkina Faso; *sobolo* in Ghana; and *karkade* in North African locales. Outside of Africa, there exists *gudhal* or *arhul ka phool* in India and *gumamela* in Indonesia, among hundreds more monikers I'm sure. My favourite, found in Spanish-speaking nations of the Americas, is *agua de Jamaica* or "water (drink) of Jamaica".

To some, the slightly bitter taste of sorrel may be an acquired one, but to get the best out of it you must finely tune the drink to your liking: you can adjust the heat with ginger; the acidity with citrus fruits; the strength by increasing the amount of hibiscus flowers; and the sweetness with added sugar – if all else fails up the amount of rum you chase it with. You don't need to go overboard with the dried flowers, just a tablespoon of red petals will turn a litre of water a deep magenta colour.

—

First sterilize a 1 litre (1 quart) bottle (see p231).

Rinse and clean the hibiscus flowers in a sieve under cold running water. Put the hibiscus in a saucepan with 1 litre (4 cups plus 3 tbsp) water and the rest of the ingredients and bring to the boil. Turn the heat down to

MAKES 1 LITRE (1 QUART)

100g (3½oz) dried hibiscus flowers
200g (1 cup) light soft brown sugar
6 pimento seeds (allspice berries), crushed, or ½ tsp ground allspice
5–8cm (2–3¼in) piece of fresh root ginger, chopped
2 cinnamon sticks
peel of 1 orange
1 lime, chopped
½ tsp cloves (optional)

TO SERVE

ice
slices of lime
strips of orange peel
white rum (optional)

low and simmer for 40 minutes, until syrupy and deep red. Leave to cool and infuse overnight in the fridge.

Strain the liquid through a cheesecloth-lined sieve into a jug and discard the solids. Pour into the bottle and seal with a lid. It will keep for up to 1 month in the fridge or can be frozen, or serve straightaway with ice, a slice of lime, a strip of orange peel and white rum, if you like.

Bush tea

On one of my first morning's volunteering at Durga's Den farm in Orange Hill, north of Ocho Rios, Lise, one-half of the proprietor couple, asks what I'd like to drink with my breakfast – tea or coffee? Upon answering tea, she reels off several enticing options, including my choice of lemongrass. "Okay, well the lemongrass is down there," she says, pointing to the driveway some 100 metres away. I know what lemongrass looks like when it's wrapped in plastic on a supermarket shelf, or at least I thought I did. In the wild rough, shoulder-to-shoulder with dozens of green bushes I was suddenly lost, and dare I say a bit embarrassed. I didn't want to go back empty handed for fear of my newly minted Jamaican passport being revoked so I persevered, rubbing leaves from a shortlist of bushes, sniffing the aroma on my fingertips. I was pretty sure of one of the bushes so I picked a small handful, returned to the kitchen and handed the leaves to Lise, hiding my uncertainty, as she put them in a pot with absolutely zero fanfare.

After this mini-identity crisis, I have a much-renewed admiration for the bush doctors, as we call them – people who roam the nature of Jamaica foraging for plants, from root to leaf, to keep the tradition of bush tea alive. Bush doctors, akin to perhaps Traditional Chinese Medicine or Ayurvedic practitioners, use specific natural products to treat human ailments.

In Jamaica, this not only highlights the rich history of culinary plant tradition, but illuminates religious, philosophical and medicinal practices, specifically influenced by the diverse West African tribes. These include the Akan, Igbo and Yoruba, along with many religions borne out of these tribes, namely Obeah, Vodou, Santeria and Candomblé.

Many colonial physicians who worked in Jamaica in the early 19th century declared the virtues of African remedies, with one in 1826 praising the plant aloe vera, preferring it over *"those feeble adulterated preparations that are sent to us from Europe".* (M.C. Alleyne and A. Payne-Jackson, *Jamaican Folk Medicine: A Source of Healing.*)

Outside the islands in places with a sizeable Caribbean community, you can be sure to find someone somewhere selling roots for bush tea. You can be mid-haircut or in the queue at a local Caribbean takeout and someone will appear with a box or coat lined with herbs and dried roots. For the converted, it's like preaching to the choir as bags of guinea hen weed, cerasee and soursop leaf are snatched up.

I can't speak of any scientific health benefits of these drinks, but instead have gone for taste and the availability of ingredients in European shops. These teas should act as a cursory introduction to bush teas if you don't run into a healer dealer.

Hibiscus & ginger tea

SERVES 1

1 tbsp dried hibiscus flowers
2.5cm (1in) piece of fresh root ginger, sliced
½ tsp cloves (optional)
1 tbsp honey or light soft brown sugar

———

Bring 300ml (1¼ cups) water to the boil in a small saucepan.

Put the hibiscus, ginger and cloves, if using, in a tea infuser basket, if you have one, or put straight into the pan of boiling water. Turn the heat down to low and simmer for 5–10 minutes to infuse before drinking (strain if necessary). Sweeten with honey or sugar and serve hot.

Fever tree tea

SERVES 1

2.5cm (1in) piece of fresh root ginger, peeled
  and chopped
2 tbsp dried lemongrass, or 8 sticks of fresh
  lemongrass
½ tsp cloves (optional)
1 cinnamon stick
juice of 1 lemon or lime
1 tbsp honey or light soft brown sugar

Bring 300ml (1¼ cups) water to the boil in
a small saucepan.

Put the, ginger, dried lemongrass and
cloves, if using, in a tea infuser basket, if you
have one. (Alternatively, wrap the ginger and
cloves inside the lemongrass stalks, then tie
in place.) Put into the pan of boiling water
with the cinnamon stick and lemon or lime
juice. Turn the heat down to low and simmer
for 5–10 minutes to infuse before drinking
(strain if necessary). Sweeten with honey
or sugar and serve hot.

Moringa

Tea

SERVES 1

2.5cm (1in) piece of fresh root
    ginger, chopped
2.5cm (1in) piece of fresh
    turmeric, chopped
1 tbsp moringa powder
1 tbsp honey or light soft brown
    sugar (optional)

———

Pour 300ml (1¼ cups) water into a small saucepan, add the ginger and turmeric and bring to the boil. Simmer for 10 minutes, then remove from the heat.

Stir in the moringa powder until mixed in. Cover with the lid and simmer for 10 minutes.

When ready, pour into a cup (you can pour the tea through a tea strainer into your cup to get rid of any moringa powder residue, if preferred), then add honey or sugar to taste.

One of my favourite days while travelling across the UK writing my first book was hanging out with Earl Brown, known across the southwest London locale of Brixton as Bushman. His eatery, Bushman Kitchen, located under the steps of the area's renowned recreation centre, is no bigger than the arm span of two interlinked adults. The flavours emerging from the kitchen give no indication of its diminutive size. These flavours are bolstered by the fact that Bushman wakes every day in the early hours of the morning to source fresh produce from the local Brixton Market.

Bushman is of my grandfather's generation and when I quiz him about the source of his endless energy while he banters with locals, he invites me to a corner of his shop where he reveals a bottle of moringa bitters. I'd heard of moringa, but never tried it and so he pours me a glass while he and his son eagerly await my reaction. If you've seen those viral videos where parents feed their children slices of lemon you'll have some idea of my reaction, which triggered instant laughs from the duo. After this, he pulls out a small plastic bag from his pocket full of what he tells me are moringa seeds. The seeds have a dry, white, pithy outer layer that conceals a sizeable spherical soft seed, edible in one bite.

Moringa oleifera is a slim tree averaging about 6 metres (20ft) tall. Almost every part of it, from the roots and leaves to the seeds, has been eaten in Jamaica for centuries, after coming from the Indian subcontinent where it was a staple of Ayurvedic medicine. In an 1890 American medical science journal, *The Monthly Cyclopædia of Practical Medicine*, the physician-author noted, *"Among the popular remedies in use among the peasantry of Jamaica, the first that struck me of being worth testing carefully was moring-root."*

Unless you're lucky to find moringa leaves in the freezer of a food shop, it's most likely that you'll come across the seeds or the green powder in health food shops – I use the powder in these recipes for convenience.

Shots

2.5cm (1in) piece of fresh root ginger, chopped
1 tbsp moringa powder
300ml (1¼ cups) apple cider vinegar
juice and zest of ½ lemon or lime or orange
honey or light soft brown sugar, to taste (optional)

FOR THE FLAVOURINGS:

1 garlic clove, peeled
½ tsp cardamom pods, split (optional)
½ tsp cayenne pepper
½ tsp fennel seeds (optional)
½ tsp fenugreek seeds (optional)
½ tsp freshly ground black pepper
½ tsp ground cinnamon

First sterilize a 300ml (12oz) jar (see p231).

Put your choice of flavourings into the jar, add the ginger and moringa and pour over the vinegar and citrus juice. Put the lid on and shake the jar until combined. Chill overnight, or for up to 3 weeks. If keeping for longer than a few days, shake the jar every day.

When ready to drink, strain a serving into a shot glass and add honey or sugar to taste – if you're feeling brave you can drink without. Enjoy a shot every morning!

Night nurse

Migrant Caribbean families like mine often believe in catch-all remedies; certain things are hailed, like magic, for curing anything and everything. I can't get away from the notion that this is rooted in West African medicinal practices, but has mutated over the years with colonial intervention and the products that came with it to the Caribbean shores: broken arm? Vicks VapoRub; rash? Tiger Balm; anything oral? Bonjela; anything internal? Pepto Bismol – should you mention any ailment to your parent or an elder, like a phone call to an IT department, you're asked if you've tried any of these first.

In winter, the sound of a toddler sniffling sets off parental alarm and the nightcap of Horlicks or Ovaltine is replaced with an intense hot-lemon drink, which any normal child screws their face up to after drinking. That child was definitely me, and for a long time I detested being forced to knock back this bitter, citrusy concoction.

Given that my grandad frequently hounds both me and my mum for not drinking hot drinks every day, and since fortunately my taste buds have changed a bit over the years, I've turned to this as a winter go-to, which is as easy to make as my childhood favourite fruit cordials.

MAKES ABOUT 400–500ML (14–16FL OZ)

8 lemons, preferably unwaxed, or regular lemons washed with bicarbonate of soda (baking soda)
250g (1¼ cups) granulated sugar
slices of fresh root ginger, to serve (optional)

———

First sterilize a 500ml (16oz) jar (see p231).

Squeeze the lemons into a bowl over a sieve to catch any errant flesh and pips – you need about 300ml (1¼ cups) juice.

In a small pan, combine the sugar with the lemon juice and warm over a medium heat, stirring for 8–10 minutes, until the sugar has dissolved.

Turn the heat up to high and boil for 2–3 minutes, then turn the heat down to low and simmer for 20 minutes, until a light syrup. Take off the heat and leave to sit for 20 minutes. Pour the syrup into the jar and put on the lid and leave to cool completely. Store in the fridge for up to 3 months.

To serve, for 1–2 people, heat 300ml (1¼ cups) water in a pan, with optional slices of ginger and 4 tablespoons of the sugar/lemon syrup. Bring to the boil, then turn the heat down to low and simmer for 10 minutes. Pour into a mug and serve warm.

NOTE *For an extra lemony taste, before juicing grate the zest of 3–4 unwaxed lemons into the pan after the sugar has dissolved. Turn the heat up to high and boil for 2–3 minutes, then turn the heat down to low and simmer for 20 minutes. Take the pan off the heat and leave to sit for 20 minutes. Strain the liquid before use.*

Hot chocolate drops

While Jamaica is known internationally for its Blue Mountain coffee and has a history of herbal tea consumption, less is known about its role in another famed beverage, hot chocolate, sometimes known as "cocoa tea". The story, as told, is that Anglo-Irish physician, botanist and traveller, Sir Hans Sloane, spent some time in Jamaica in the early 1700s, where the local people gave him a cocoa drink that they used for medicinal purposes. Apparently, he found it *"nauseous"* and mixed it with hot milk to make it more palatable. When he returned to England, Sloane introduced the idea of the milk and cocoa mix, and for many years it was sold as a medicine before becoming a popular drink. Other Europeans also compete for the title of "inventing hot chocolate".

Given the long history of cocoa cultivation in West Africa and that indigenous South American tribes, such as the Maya, are documented to have consumed a form of hot water mixed with cocoa, it seems that revisionist history may have been at play here. However, as Sloane patented his mix of chocolate liquid, he essentially wrote the history, so to speak. The patent was sold to a man named John Cadbury, who owned a confectionery company, and so the commercial product went mainstream. Given that sugar was used to make the chocolate even more palatable, and that Jamaica provided most of Britain's sugar, it seems that Jamaica is inextricably linked to the history of the drink.

While powder is usually the go-to form for making hot chocolate, a read of *Culture and Customs of Jamaica* by P. and M. Mordecai, reveals, *"as well as coffee and tea, there would be Country chocolate made from handballs of cocoa, boiled in water or milk, with cinnamon and brown sugar added"*.

Having stayed at guesthouses where these balls were served, I can attest that their deep, rich, chocolatey taste far exceeds anything possible with powder.

MAKES 12 BALLS

250g (9oz) chocolate (plain or milk), chopped
3 tbsp coconut milk, or double (heavy) cream or plant-based alternative, chilled
about 1 tbsp rum (optional)
10g (1 tbsp) raisins, finely chopped (optional)
1 tsp vanilla extract (optional)
2 tbsp good-quality cocoa powder
200ml (¾ cup) milk of choice, to serve

FOR THE SPICES:

1 tsp ground cinnamon (optional)
¼ tsp cayenne pepper (optional)
¼ tsp chilli powder (optional)
¼ tsp ground allspice (optional)
¼ tsp ground nutmeg (optional)

Put the chocolate into a heatproof bowl.

Heat the coconut milk or cream in a small saucepan over a medium-high heat. Before it reaches boiling point, remove from the heat and pour it over the chocolate. Leave the chocolate to melt for 1–2 minutes, stirring occasionally. Stir in your choice of spices and the rum, raisins and vanilla, if using, until combined. Cover the bowl and chill for about 30 minutes, until set.

Line a baking tray with baking paper and place the cocoa powder in a small bowl.

Remove the chocolate mixture from the fridge. Using a spoon, scoop out 2 tablespoons and quickly form into a ball with your hands. Dunk the ball into the cocoa powder and roll it around until coated. Place on the lined baking tray and repeat until the chocolate mixture is used up. Cover and chill to firm up, then store in the fridge for up to 2 weeks, or freeze the balls for up to 3 months, until ready to use.

To serve, heat the milk in a saucepan (or microwave for 2 minutes), then pour into a mug, about 80 per cent full, then drop a chocolate ball into the mug. Using a teaspoon, push the ball to the bottom, using light force to break it up and let it melt into the milk.

Nine-nights, rum & ting

You may have noted the lack of elaborate rum cocktails in this book. At the small bars I visit on the edge of markets, on beach fronts, and up in the hills, frequented by slot-machine and domino players, you'll rarely see anyone order the type of drink that British Caribbean high-street restaurants may try and persuade you otherwise. More so, you won't see any umbrella-decorated concoctions unless you're in a tourist location on the island.

Another reason for the lack of any specific rum recipes in this book is that it's often liberally added to all manner of drinks: sorrel, smoothies, cane juice and hot chocolate can be transformed with a dash of rum. Additionally, it's often poured, without measure, into cakes and bakes for taste and preservation.

One thing I've learnt about rum is that until you venture to the Caribbean (or go to a special function when the "real ting" gets whipped out) is that you've never really tried *real* rum. I was introduced to a certain rooster-brand of rum at a very young age by a family member, who shall remain nameless, so I've always had an idea when the "inner-dragon" was summoned after drinking proper overproof stuff. Such is my family's feverish demand for rum, I often keep my sojourns to the Caribbean a secret to ensure I don't have to buy a new suitcase to fulfil all the requests.

Rum has precedents around the world from Cyprus to Malaysia, but the Caribbean's part in its development remains unparalleled. It was there in the 17th century that the enslaved people of Nevis, Barbados and beyond discovered that molasses, a by-product of sugar refinery, could be fermented into alcohol. This is likely to have come from the West African's history of fermentation before arriving on the island. After yeast fermentation, the distillation of this sugary by-product concentrated the alcohol, removing impurities that caused sickness, hence rum as we know it today. As Jamaica was the largest producer of sugar its prowess in rum production grew exponentially.

Rum rocketed in popularity in North America to the level that US powers raised duty fees on it, and so the commercial rum market was born. Most plantations that otherwise may have focussed on ground provisions, such as cotton or bananas, directed their resources, including slave labour, to the production of sugar. However, the enslaved barely received rations of the things they produced.

In the late 1700s, grog shops – the bodegas or off-licences of their day – that sold to sailors, pirates and travellers were prohibited from selling rum to enslaved people as the legislators believed the formation of conspiracies and revolts was aided by the effects of the intoxicating liquor. Regardless of legislation and punishment, the enslaved found ways to access the things that they were prohibited from consuming, including meat and rum.

Rum, being one of the first widely available alcoholic drinks in Jamaica, became part of the fabric of Caribbean culture. To see the respect and reverence towards rum we can look at the Afro-Jamaican religion, Kumina, said to originate in Congo, which sees the sprinkling of the alcoholic drink on the ground during drum-based festivities as a libation for the spirits. More so, in Jamaican funerals of those descending from the Ghanaian Ga tribe, rum is placed by the feet of the deceased after days of merriment.

While the frequency of these distinctly African-heritage ceremonies has decreased, the importance of rum at wakes remains to this day, particularly in the spirit-based tradition known as Nine-nights, so named in the belief that on the ninth night after death the spirit of the deceased returns to its home to be "*entertained before being consigned to the world of duppie*".

From birth to death and every step in between, rum has been a deep-rooted part of island culture, so my family's fierce desire for *real* rum makes sense.

Bibliography

BOOKS

1. Alleyne, M.C.; Payne-Jackson, A. *Jamaican Folk Medicine: A Source of Healing* (University of the West Indies Press, 2012)
2. Barringer, T.; Modest, W. *Victorian Jamaica* (Duke University Press, 2018)
3. Beckwith, M. W. *Black Roadways: A Study of Jamaican Folk Life* (University of North Carolina Press, 1929)
4. Beckwith, M.W. *Jamaica Anansi Stories* (G.E. Stechert & Co., 1924)
5. Bennett-Coverley, L.; Nettleford, R. *Jamaica Labrish: Jamaica Dialect Poems* (Sangster's Book Stores Jamaica, 1965)
6. Black, C.V. de B. *History of Jamaica* (Collins Clear-Type Press, 1973)
7. Blome R.; Lynch T. *A Description of the Island of Jamaica* (Hansebooks, 2017)
8. Brathwaite, K. *Development of Creole Society in Jamaica, 1770–1820* (Ian Randle, 2005)
9. Breverton, T. *The Tudor Cookbook: From Gilded Peacock to Calves' Feet Pie* (Amberley Publishing, 2019)
10. Brown-Glaude, W. *Higglers in Kingston: Women's Informal Work in Jamaica* (Vanderbilt University Press, 2011)
11. Brown, Y. S. *Dead Woman Pickney: A Memoir of Childhood in Jamaica* (Wilfrid Laurier University Press, 2010)
12. Carney, J.; Rosomoff, R.N. *In the Shadow of Slavery: Africa's Botanical Legacy in the Atlantic World* (University of California Press, 2011)
13. Casid J.H. *Sowing Empire: Landscape and Colonization* (University of Minnesota Press, 2004)
14. Cassidy, F.G. *Jamaica Talk: Three Hundred Years of the English Language in Jamaica* (Macmillan Education, 1982)
15. Cassidy, F.G.; Le Page R.B. *Dictionary of Jamaican English* (University of the West Indies Press, 2002)
16. Dance, D.C. *Folklore from Contemporary Jamaicans* (University of Tennessee Press, 1985)
17. Deutsch J. *They Eat That? A Cultural Encyclopedia of Weird and Exotic Food from Around the World* (ABC-CLIO, 2012)
18. Edmonds, E.B. *Rastafari: from Outcasts to Cultural Bearers* (Oxford University Press, 2003)
19. Forde, M.; Paton, D. *Obeah and Other Powers: The Politics of Caribbean Religion and Healing* (Duke University Press, 2012)
20. Gardner, W.J. *History of Jamaica: From its Discovery by Christopher Columbus to the Year 1872* (Taylor & Francis, 2005)
21. Greene, J.P.; Knight, J. *The Natural, Moral, and Political History of Jamaica, and the Territories Thereon Depending: From the First Discovery of the Island by Christopher Columbus to the Year 1746* (University of Virginia Press, 2021)
22. Grenis, A.T.; Tainter, D.R. *Spices and Seasonings: Food Technology Handbook* (Wiley, 2001)
23. Higman, B.W. *Jamaican Food: History, Biology, Culture.* (University of the West Indies Press, 2008)
24. Higman B.W. *Slave Population and Economy in Jamaica 1807–1834* (Cambridge University Press, 1976)
25. Higman, B.W.; Aarons G.A.; Karklins K.; and Reitz E.J. *Montpelier, Jamaica: a Plantation Community in Slavery and Freedom, 1739-1912* (University of the West Indies Press, 1998)
26. Higman, B.W.; Hudson, B.J. *Jamaican Place Names* (University of the West Indies Press, 2009)
27. Holton, W. *Liberty is Sweet: The Hidden History of the American Revolution* (Simon & Schuster, 2021)
28. Hooper, F.A. *Bee-keeping Jamaica* (Franklin Classics, 2018)
29. James, M. *A Brief History of Seven Killings* (Oneworld, 2015)
30. Keegan, W.F.; Carlson, L.A.; Curet L.A. *Talking Taino: Caribbean Natural History from a Native Perspective* (University of Alabama Press, 2008)
31. La Fleur, J.D. *Fusion Foodways of Africa's Gold Coast in the Atlantic Era* (Brill, 2012)
32. Long, E. *The History of Jamaica* (T. Lowndes, 1774)
33. Mair L.M. *A Historical Study of Women in Jamaica, 1655–1844* (University of the West Indies Press, 2007)
34. Martin S.C. *The SAGE Encyclopedia of Alcohol: Social, Cultural, and Historical Perspectives* (SAGE Publications, 2015)
35. Mirvis, S. *The Jews of Eighteenth-Century Jamaica: A Testamentary History of a Diaspora in Transition* (Yale University Press, 2020)
36. Mishra, V. *The Literature of the Indian Diaspora: Theorizing the Diasporic Imaginary* (Routledge Research in Postcolonial Literature, 2007)
37. Mordecai, M.; Mordecai, P. *Culture and Customs of Jamaica* (Greenwood Press, 2000)
38. Morriss, R. *The Foundations of British Maritime Ascendancy: Resources, Logistics and the State, 1755–1815* (Cambridge University Press, 2010)
39. Moseley, J. *The Mystery of Herbs and Spices* (Xlibris, 2006)
40. Ogilvy J.*A Description and History of the Island of Jamaica 1851* (ebook)
41. Om Books Editorial, *365 Folk Tales* (OM Books International, 2008)
42. Opie, F.D. *Zora Neale Hurston on Florida Food: Recipes, Remedies & Simple Pleasures* (The History Press, 2015)
43. *Oxford English Dictionary* (2 ed.) (Clarendon Press, 1989)
44. Palmatier, R.A. *Food: A Dictionary of Literal and Nonliteral Terms* (Greenwood Press, 2000)
45. *The Penguin Book of Caribbean Verse in English* (Penguin Adult, 2005)
46. Phillips, R. *Belly Full: Caribbean Food in the UK* (Tezeta Press, 2017)
47. Shapiro, H-Y.; Grivetti, L.E. *Chocolate: History, Culture, and Heritage* (Wiley-Interscience, 2009)
48. Sheller, M. *Consuming the Caribbean: From Arawaks to Zombies* (Routledge, 2003)
49. Stankovic M.S. *Medicinal Plants and Natural Product Research* (MDPI AG, 2020)
50. Temple F. *Tiger Soup: An Anansi Story from Jamaica* (Orchard Books, 1994)

51. Tucker, R.P. *Insatiable Appetite: The United States and the Ecological Degradation of the Tropical World* (University of California Press, 2000)

52. Vasconcellos, C.A. *Slavery, Childhood, and Abolition in Jamaica, 1788-1838* (University of Georgia Press, 2015)

53. Walker, C. *Jamaica Ladies: Female Slaveholders and the Creation of Britain's Atlantic Empire* (Omohundro Institute and University of North Carolina, 2020)

54. Yentsch, A.E. *A Chesapeake Family and Their Slaves: A Study in Historical Archaeology* (Cambridge University Press, 1994)

JOURNALS/RESEARCH/ONLINE

55. Abdulqader, G.; Barsanti L.; Tredici M.R. *Harvest of Arthrospira Platensis from Lake Kossorom (Chad) and Its Household Usage among the Kanembu* (Journal of Applied Phycology, 2000)

56. Aoyagi A.; Shurtleff, W. *History of Soy Flour, Flakes and Grits (510 CE To 2013)*: Extensively Annotated Bibliography and Sourcebook (Soyinfo Center, 2013)

57. Assmann, J.; Czaplicka J. "Collective Memory and Cultural Identity" (*New German Critique*, No.65, 1995)

58. Breadfruit Institute. "Breadfruit History" (National Tropical Botanical Garden, US)

59. Burnard T.; Panza L.; Williamson J. "Living Costs, Real Incomes and Inequality in Colonial Jamaica." (*Explorations in Economic History*, Elsevier, Vol.71, 2019)

60. Davorbailey, *The Origins and Growth of the Jamaican Higgler* (2014)

61. Drayna D. *Human taste genetics* (Annu Rev Genomics Hum Genet, 2005; 6:217-235. doi: 10.1146/annurev. genom.6.080604.162340)

62. Forbes J. *The Monthly Cyclopædia of Practical Medicine* v1-21, v22, No.1–5, Aug. 1887–Apr. 1908. (F.A. Davis Company, 1889)

63. Gore J. *Gore's Directory of Liverpool and Its Environs for the Year 1834* (Oxford University, 2007)

64. Howard, R.A. "Captain Bligh and the Breadfruit." (*Scientific American* 188, No.3, 1953)

65. "JMEA expresses concerns after release of import-export figures" (*Jamaica Observer*, January 15, 2020)

66. Karkos P.D.; Leong S.C; Karkos C.D; Sivaji N.; Assimakopoulos D.A. "Spirulina in clinical practice:" (*Evid Based Complement Alternat Med.* 2011; 531053. doi:10.1093/ecam/nen058)

67. Katzin, M.F. "The Business of Higglering in Jamaica." (*Social and Economic Studies* 9, No.3, 1960)

68. McFarlane, D. "The Future of the Banana Industry in The West Indies: "An Assessment of Supply Prospects for 1965 and 1975." (*Social and Economic Studies* 13, No.1, 1964): 38–93

69. Moreton, J.B. "West India Customs and Manners: Containing Strictures on the Soil, Cultivation, Produce, Trade, Officers, and Inhabitants: with the Method of Establishing, and Conducting a Sugar Plantation. To which is Added, the Practice of Training New Slaves" (1793)

70. "New Remedies" (*The American Journal of the Medical Sciences*, Wm. Wood & Company, 1881)

71. Nin, L.W. "Language of the Voiceless: Traces of Taino Language, Food, and Culture in the Americas from 1492 to the Present" (Masters thesis, Harvard Extension School, 2020)

72. Nutakor, C.; Essiedu J.A.; Adadi P.; Kanwugu O.N. "Ginger Beer: An Overview of Health Benefits and Recent Developments" (*Fermentation* 6, No.4: 102, 2020)

73. Patterson, O. *Slavery and Slave Revolts: A Sociohistorical Analysis of the First Maroon War, 1655–1740* (1970-01-01; Social and Economic Studies)

74. Price, R. and S. "Rundown" (*NWIG: New West Indian Guide / Nieuwe West-Indische Gids* Vol.67, No.1/2, 1993)

75. "Rasta Spirit Knows No Boundaries" (*Daily Gleaner*, June 22, 1960)

76. Roberston J. "A 1748 'Petition of Negro Slaves' and the Local Politics of Slavery in Jamaica" (*The William and Mary Quarterly* 67, No.2, 2010)

77. Royal Botanic Gardens (*Kew Bulletin*, H.M. Stationery Office, 1894)

78. Sloane H. Sir. "A Voyage to the islands Madera, Barbados, Nieves, S. Christopher's and Jamaica" v.1, 1707 (Royal Collection Trust)

79. Smith, R.W. "The Legal Status of Jamaican Slaves Before the Anti-Slavery Movement" (*Journal of Negro History*, 1945)

80. Sweeney, S.J. "Market Marronage: Fugitive Women and the Internal Marketing System in Jamaica, 1781–1834" (*The William and Mary Quarterly* 76, No.2, 2019)

81. *The Journal of the Jamaica Agricultural Society*, 1924, Vol.26, Issues 12–27

82. *The Monthly Cyclopædia of Practical Medicine*, V1-21, V22, No.1–5, Aug. 1887–Apr. 1908. (F.A. Davis Company, 1908)

83. Warrington I. "Turmeric: Botany & Production Practices" *Horticultural Reviews*. Vol.46 (Wiley, 2018)

WEBSITES

84. doi.org/10.2307/488538
85. jamaicanfolktales.weebly.com
86. jstor.org/stable/41849499
87. ntbg.org/breadfruit
88. southernliving.com/desserts/cakes/hummingbird-cake-history
89. www.foodtimeline.org
90. www.jstor.org/stable/27853773
91. old.jamaica-gleaner.com/pages/history/story0056.htm
92. old.jamaica-gleaner.com/gleaner/20090801/life/life2.html
93. historytoday.com/archive/historians-cookbook/jerk-authentic-taste-jamaican-liberty
94. jstor.org/stable/2639565
95. tinyurl.com/y3oe3wln
96. scholar.library.miami.edu/slaves/Maroons/individual_essays/leanna
97. samsharpeproject.org/sam-sharpe
98. jamaica-history.weebly.com/beekeepers.html
99. bbc.co.uk/news/uk-43808007
100. jamaica-star.com/article/news/20180923/kingston-communities-under-state-emergency

Index

Acknowledgments

AUTHOR'S ACKNOWLEDGMENTS

Although this book was written in the space of a few months, everything that led up to it encompassed much of my life. None of this book could have been possible without my lovely mother, Sandi Phillips, who sadly passed away shortly before the book was published. I hope I did her recipes proud.

Of course, huge thanks to everyone in my family who spurred my interest in Caribbean food, especially the cooks: Grandma Mavis, Aunty Babs, Granny Nanny Ervie, Aunty Diana, Aunty Sandra, Aunty Madge, Aunty Ruth, Aunty Ciselyn, Aunty Phyliss, Aunty Veronica, Aunty Leslie, cousins Bianca, Sophia and Fabienne. In Jamaica, a special thanks to my extended family Ms Chyna, Ms Rose and Ms Daphne.

Thanks also for the support over the years from my Dad, Uncle Ian, Uncle Tony, Uncle Howard and Uncle Michael, Uncle Murvin. In Jamaica, I'd like to thank Rastaman Rev, Chucky and Prince Nyah.

For friends, basically everyone who's ever known me, though special thanks always for support, physically, financially and mentally, go to Chantal Hamilton, Chloe Schwartz, Ejike Onuchukwu, Esme Toler, Harry Mitchell, Hugo Bax, Jack Gove, Joby Weston, Josh Bernie, Kindima Bah, Konrad Kay, Micky Down, Naz Ramadan, Otis Clarke, Saleem Dar and Tom Lazenby.

Oshane Warren, aka Chef Vita, Chef Kriss Kofi and every chef/owner in *Belly Full* who inspired and spurred this journey.

Lastly, thanks to the Bodleian Library and Lady Margaret Hall, University of Oxford, for the continued help and support even though it took me years to pay back library fines and battels.

Jack Mandora, mi nuh choose none!

PUBLISHER'S ACKNOWLEDGMENTS

DK would like to thank Grace Wynter for providing a sensitivity read, Katie Hardwicke for proofreading, and Angie Hipkin for indexing. The publisher would also like to thank Jessica McIntosh for assistance food styling, Danny Millar and Danny Walker for photography assistance, and Adam Brackenbury for repro work.

CREDITS

DK and Riaz Phillips would like to thank OM Books International for the right to inlcude an extract from *365 Folk Tales* on page 43.

All photography by Riaz Phillips except recipe images on pages 26, 31t, 33, 35, 36, 39, 40, 49, 54-55, 65, 69, 77, 80-81, 82, 85l, 87, 88, 93, 94, 98, 116, 119, 130-131, 133, 139, 144-145, 146-147, 148-149tl, 151, 163, 164, 168-169, 173, 178-179, 180, 186-187, 194, 198, 200-201, 212-213t, 215, 217, 220-221, 236, 241, 244, 246, 247, 251, 255, 257 by Caitlin Isola.

(Key: a-above; b-below/bottom; c-centre; f-far; l-left; r-right; t-top)

Editors	Nicola Graimes, Lucy Philpott
Senior Americanization Editor	Megan Douglass
Designers	Evi O. & Susan Le | Evi-O.Studio
	Amy Cox
Senior Acquisitions Editor	Stephanie Milner
Senior Designer	Barbara Zuniga
Design Manager	Marianne Markham
Production Editor	David Almond
Senior Producer	Stephanie McConnell
Jacket Coordinator	Jasmin Lennie
Art Director	Maxine Pedliham
Publishing Director	Katie Cowan
Photographer	Caitlin Isola
Prop Stylist	Nyasha Haukozi-Jones
Food Stylist	Alex James Gray

First American Edition, 2022
Published in the United States by DK publishing
1450 Broadway, Suite 801, New York, NY 10018

Text copyright © Riaz Phillips 2022
Images copyright © Caitlin Isola 2022
Copyright © 2022 Dorling Kindersley Limited
DK, a Division of Penguin Random House LLC
22 23 24 25 26 10 9 8 7 6 5 4 3 2 1
002–327471–Jul/2022

A catalog record for this book
is available from the Library of Congress.
ISBN 978-0-7440-5682-2

DK books are available at special discounts when purchased
in bulk for sales promotions, premiums, fund-raising, or
educational use. For details, contact: DK Publishing Special
Markets, 1450 Broadway, Suite 801, New York, NY 10018
SpecialSales@dk.com

Printed and bound in China

For the curious
www.dk.com

This book was made with Forest Stewardship Council™
certified paper – one small step in DK's
commitment to a sustainable future.
For more information go to www.dk.com/our-green-pledge

About the Author

Riaz Phillips is an award-winning writer, video maker and photographer. Born and raised in London and now based in Berlin, Riaz self-published and released his first book *Belly Full: Caribbean Food in the UK* in 2017, for which he was marked as one of the Observer Food Monthly 50 "Things we Love" annual list, and awarded a Young British Foodie (YBF) Award.

When not moonlighting in kitchens or bars, his freelance writing can be found in the *Evening Standard*, *Vice*, Eater and Resy among other publications and blogs. His YouTube channel of short films and mini-docs, focussed on food and travel, has garnered millions of views.

In 2020, he edited the *Community Comfort* cookbook, a collection of over 100 global recipes from cooks of immigrant backgrounds raising funds for the families of Covid-19 victims in their own community. Through his works Riaz has been featured on Masterchef, the BBC News, ITV News, Channel 4 News and Channel 5 News.

Follow his food journey @riazphillips on most platforms.